The Good
and the True

MICHAEL MORRIS

CLARENDON PRESS · OXFORD
1992

Oxford University Press, Walton Street, Oxford OX2 6DP

Oxford New York Toronto
Delhi Bombay Calcutta Madras Karachi
Petaling Jaya Singapore Hong Kong Tokyo
Nairobi Dar es Salaam Cape Town
Melbourne Auckland

and associated companies in
Berlin Ibadan

Oxford is a trade mark of Oxford University Press

Published in the United States
by Oxford University Press, New York

British Library Cataloguing in Publication Data
Data available

Library of Congress Cataloging-in-Publication Data
Morris, Micheal (Michael Rowland)
The good and the true/Michael Morris.
p. cm.—(Oxford philosophical monographs)
Includes bibliographical references and index.
1. Metaphysics. 2. Scientism. 3. Content (Psychology)
4. Ethics. 5. Language and languages—Philosophy. I. Title.
II. Series.
BD111.M67 1992   110—dc20   92–462
ISBN 0–19–823944–0

Set by Pentacor PLC, High Wycombe, Bucks.
Printed in Great Britain by
Biddles Ltd, Guildford & King's Lynn

For Judith, Elizabeth, and David

Preface

A number of people have helped with this book, sometimes in the form of criticism of things I have said or written, sometimes in sympathy, sometimes in apparently insignificant conversational remarks which have stuck in my mind. I would like to record my gratitude to these people in particular: Andy Clark, David Charles, Leo Cheung, Rickie Dammann, Julian Dodd, Ben Gibbs, Bernard Harrison, Michael Ireland, Aaron Sloman, Barry Smith, Stephen Williams, and Tim Williamson. There have also been many students who have refused to believe me; I am very grateful to them too.

A cruder and uglier first attempt at the book was submitted as a doctoral thesis. Michael Woods patiently supervised it, and Jane Heal and Paul Snowdon conscientiously examined it. In a sense their help was in the line of duty, but the help they gave was beyond what duty called for.

I have learnt from all these people. I hope they will not be too displeased with what they have unwittingly helped to produce. The book itself argues that the responsibility for it is mine.

Contents

Part III. An Evaluative Theory of Content

Notational Convention

I have used one device of notational convenience. At certain points I use a quoted schematic letter to refer to whatever replaces that letter in an instance of the relevant schema: thus " '*p*' " will sometimes be used to refer to whatever replaces '*p*'. In similar style, I use quotation to represent substitutional quantification, as in,

For some '*a*', *Fa*.

I also use quotation in the now standard way, using " '*a*' ", for example, to refer to the first letter of the alphabet. I take it as obvious that English quotation allows this degree of flexibility; we know how to write a name of the first letter of the alphabet, and we also understand without difficulty such formulations as this:

'*p*' is true if and only if *p*.

(No one is really likely to take this as a remark about a letter of the alphabet.) It should always be clear how quotation is being used in a particular context, but the first few occurrences of the non-standard use are flagged in the footnotes, and referred back to this explanation.

Introduction

This book offers a general metaphysical picture, a theory of content, and a transcendental argument for a form of moral realism. It might seem that it would have been more sensible to have tackled only one of these, but it is one of the book's contentions that you need all three together.

The idea of the book lies in noticing a similarity between two kinds of attitude. The first has never been better expressed than by Hume, in this famous passage:

Thus the distinct boundaries and offices of *reason* and of *taste* are easily ascertained. The former conveys the knowledge of truth and falsehood: the latter gives the sentiment of beauty and deformity, vice and virtue. The one discovers objects as they really stand in nature, without addition or diminution: the other has a productive faculty, and gilding or staining all natural objects with colours, borrowed from internal sentiment, raises in a manner a new creation.[1]

There is much to object to in this. Talk of a 'productive faculty' and a 'new creation' suggests a subjectivism about value that Hume himself could not sustain. Similarly, one might wonder what conception of objects it is that can reveal them 'as they really stand in nature, without addition or diminution'—at least if it is to be contrasted with some other conception. And one might think that truth and falsity are easily bestowed on judgements of value, in the light of the schema 'It is true that *p* if and only if *p*'.

But, despite these obvious objections, we are almost all in the grip of exactly the picture which Hume expresses here. We are almost all inclined to think that value is somehow secondary, somehow not fundamental to the nature of things. We may just hear the distant sound of a trumpet playing a different tune:

The good is the source not only of the intelligibility of what can be understood, but also of its being and essence.[2]

But the sound is so faint, the music so foreign, and it is so easy to set it aside as just another Platonic aberration, that the call does not move us. We remain fixed to our seats, facing the way Hume faces.

[1] D. Hume, *An Enquiry Concerning the Principles of Morals* (1751), ed. L. Selby-Bigge, 3rd edn., rev. P. Nidditch (Oxford: Clarendon Press, 1975), 294.

[2] Plato, *Republic*, 509B 6–8. The translation (mine) is a little bland in underplaying the metaphysical significance of the Greek word translated as both 'intelligibility' and 'understood'.

The other kind of attitude relates to an apparently quite different area of philosophy. The area is often known as 'the theory of content', as if all those concerned with the issues were joint participants in a common scientific research project.

That impression is itself a manifestation of the attitude I have in mind. The topic, in fact, is *having things in mind*. It is the philosophy of thought and desire and of the notion of what is thought or desired. The attitude that tends to hold us in its grip is one which assumes that, if there is to be an account of these things, it will have to be a 'naturalistic' theory: that is, one couched in terms suitable for describing the facts of natural science.

This attitude is too prevalent, and too variously manifested, for there to be a single perfect expression of it. It is assumed that psychologists—at least, sufficiently technically minded ones—are authoritative about the nature of perception. It is assumed that the difference between belief and desire lies in the different ways in which they contribute to the causation of behaviour. It is assumed that, if we understood the workings of the brain properly, we would understand more about the nature of the mind. Above all, it is assumed that a 'naturalistic' theory of the mind is *desirable*: if someone announces that she proposes to offer a naturalistic theory of content, no further motivation is felt to be required.

These assumptions, too, are often questioned. Concessions are made; positions are more cautiously formulated. But, for all that, we remain in the grip of the central thought: mental facts are facts about phenomena in the natural world, the world described by natural science.

Those are the two attitudes. Here are two links between them. The first link is Hume himself. The *Treatise* justifies itself as being an exercise of 'the science of MAN':[3] that is, philosophy is regarded as replaceable by, or assimilable to, natural science.[4] And the first *Enquiry* ends with the most famous passage of all:

When we run over libraries, persuaded of these principles, what havoc must we make? If we take in our hand any volume; of divinity or school metaphysics, for instance; let us ask, *Does it contain any abstract reasoning*

---

[3] D. Hume, *A Treatise of Human Nature* (1739), ed. L. Selby-Bigge, 3rd edn., rev. P. Nidditch (Oxford: Clarendon Press, 1978), p. xv.

[4] For the classic modern expression of this view, see W. V. Quine, 'Epistemology Naturalized', in his *Ontological Relativity and other Essays* (New York: Columbia University Press, 1969), 69–90.

concerning quantity or number? No. *Does it contain any experimental reasoning concerning matter of fact and existence?* No. Commit it then to the flames: for it can contain nothing but sophistry and illusion.[5]

We are faced with a stark three-way alternation: mathematics *or* science *or* sophistry and illusion. (And that paragraph of Hume's?) Perhaps the reason we think *value* is secondary is like Hume's: just that it does not form part of what science can describe.

The second link between the attitudes runs the other way. Everyone acknowledges that it is no easy matter to produce a 'naturalistic' theory of content. It is natural to wonder whether the reason it is difficult might be just that it is impossible. Several philosophers have remarked that there is something 'normative' about content—something to do with being right or wrong—which seems to resist scientific analysis.[6] It takes no great imagination to wonder whether it is something to do with *value* which creates the problem. And then perhaps our unargued insistence that a theory of content must be 'naturalistic' is just a manifestation of a fear that otherwise truth itself will end up being shuffled aside as secondary, and the scientific world-view will collapse.

Once these two links have been made, it is hard not to be just slightly suspicious of the Humean attitudes which seem so natural to us. But nothing can be made of these suspicions without some alternative conception to the Humean one. Piecemeal criticism is not enough: the 'naturalistic' cast of mind is too deeply set; it will always be resilient to grapeshot. It seemed to me that an alternative conception needed to be fairly thoroughly worked out. This book is an attempt to do just that. The aim is to put valves on Plato's trumpet, so that its music can be heard by a modern ear.

The idea is just to see if a theory of content—that is, an *analysis* or *reduction* of content—can be given which is explicitly evaluative. But even to contemplate that requires that we rethink our conception of a philosophical theory (or analysis, or reduction). If we retain our conception of what is 'intuitively' problematic and

[5] D. Hume, *An Enquiry Concerning Human Understanding* (1748), ed. L. Selby-Bigge, 3rd edn., rev. P. Nidditch (Oxford: Clarendon Press, 1975), 165.
[6] e.g. S. Kripke, *Wittgenstein on Rules and Private Language* (Oxford: Blackwell, 1962), 37; H. Putnam, 'Reflexive Reflections', *Erkenntnis*, 22 (1985), 143–53; J. McDowell, 'Functionalism and Anomalous Monism', in E. LePore and B. McLaughlin (eds.), *Actions and Events: Perspectives on the Philosophy of Donald Davidson* (Oxford: Blackwell, 1985), 387–98.

what is 'intuitively' unproblematic, and attempt simply to analyse or reduce the 'intuitively' problematic to the 'intuitively' unproblematic, there must be at least a risk that we will end up demanding a 'naturalistic' theory of content once again. So the whole idea of providing a philosophical analysis or reduction needs to be re-examined.

On the other hand, a theory of content must at some point engage with the detail of what we are doing with words when we say what someone believes. For content is just what we ascribe when we report people's attitudes. So it seems that, if we are to provide a theory of content which does what is wanted, we need to move all the way from a very general metaphysical picture at one end, to the intricacies of the function of words in contexts of propositional attitude at the other.

That exactly describes the course of this book. In Part I I present a conception of the kind of philosophical explanation we are concerned with. That conception requires a certain view of the relation between reality and our concepts of it, which I call *conceptualism*.[7] Conceptualism, as I define it, is a neo-Kantian view which embraces these two tenets:

(A) There can be interesting metaphysical explanations (in a certain semi-technical sense of 'metaphysical').

(B) The nature of the objects, properties, and facts which correspond to our concepts is not fixed independently of the nature of the concepts which correspond to them.

(B) is defended against the charge that it is idealist, and it is argued that it is required by (A). The task is then to develop a conception of what philosophical theories must do, if they are to be illuminating without being mere fantasy. We need some constraint which two expressions must meet if they are to count as describing the same object, property, or fact.

It is argued in Chapter 4 that scientism—roughly, the view that there are only *scientific* facts—cannot provide any suitable constraint, and so must be rejected as the basis of any philosophical theory. Three morals are drawn from its demise: philosophical explanation (in fact, all explanation) must be subject to a priori constraints; our conception of philosophical explanation should

---

[7] Roughly following D. Wiggins, *Sameness and Substance* (Oxford: Blackwell, 1980), chs. 4, 5.

not be foundationalist; and there can be no causal reduction of reference or aboutness. In Chapter 5 a constraint on philosophical theories is proposed, based on the idea that the nature of an object, property, or fact is determined by what it would be to have knowledge of it. I argue that this is not verificationist, in any standard sense.

Part II argues for a series of constraints on a theory of *content* in particular. These are mostly related ultimately to the special role given to content by tenet (*B*) of conceptualism. It is argued, for instance, that a theory of content must generate something like an analysis of knowledge, and that it must be extensionalist at base. There then follow two longer chapters in which questions at the heart of much current discussion are tackled. Chapter 7 argues for a form of 'externalism' about content: the view that the truth condition of a thought is essential to its identity. This seems to be required by conceptualism, and it appears that alternatives to it are scarcely coherent. It follows from externalism and the rejection in Part I of any causal theory of aboutness that there can be no causal, or more generally natural-scientific, theory of content.

In Chapter 8 I say, uncontroversially, that a theory of content must cohere with an adequate account of the way in which reports of belief explain behaviour. Then the idea that talk of belief and desire constitutes a kind of 'folk psychology' is attacked, and it is argued further that beliefs are not causes of the behaviour they explain. More specifically, it is claimed that the best causal theory of behaviour is the one implicit in Descartes. If it is asked what *does* cause the behaviour, the answer is that the relevant kind of behaviour is not caused at all (though, of course, it is not random).

In Part III I offer the outline of a theory of content which meets the conditions imposed in Part II. The triggering thought is just that it should be clear from the nature of content why no natural-scientific reduction can be given. It is suggested, following the lead I mentioned before in linking the two Humean attitudes, that the reason is that content is inextricably involved with value. So an explicitly evaluative theory of content is proposed.

The heart of the theory lies in the simple thought that truth is, quite literally, a value. This will not do as it stands as the basis of a theory of content, since the notion of truth seems to presuppose that of content. So I posit a truth-*like* value, which I call the value T, which applies to behaviour. The skeleton of the theory which is proposed in Chapter 9 can be stated as follows: having a belief or a concept is a matter of being *liable* to behave in ways which are *intrinsically assessable* with respect to the value T. The italics mark explanatory debts, which are paid off in the following three chapters.

Chapter 10 provides an account of the notion of *intrinsic assessability*. It also offers an analysis of knowledge which parallels precisely an account of what makes the display on a calculator, for example, a display of the sum of the entered numbers. The notion of intrinsic assessability (and that of knowledge too) turns out to involve the idea of a subject who is responsible for the correctness or incorrectness of what she does. That notion in turn is briefly defined.

The aim in Chapter 11 is to characterize the value T. It is argued first that we need an evaluative theory of desire, as a complement to the proposed evaluative theory of belief. This means that we need to explain desire in terms of some suitable value, just as the theory explains belief in terms of the value T. The value T is then defined by contrast with the kind of value which we need to appeal to in order to explain desire, which I call *orectic* value. It is argued that nothing can be properly assessable in terms of a truth-like value unless it is also properly assessable in terms of an orectic value, and vice versa. (I call this the holism of assessability.) This is then used to argue against evolutionary theories of content: there are no orectic values in evolution. (There is nothing good or bad about the survival of genes.) Finally, it is claimed that orectic values are more or less moral values. Given the holism of assessability, the Humean divide between a primary truth-directed faculty, and a secondary moral and aesthetic faculty seems unsustainable.

In Chapter 12 I present an account of the kind of explanation of behaviour provided by reports of belief, which does not represent the explanation as causal. Briefly, the idea is that the content of belief is visible in behaviour. I try to make this plausible by means of some everyday examples which remind us what the relevant kind of behaviour actually looks like. The chapter ends with a swift recapitulation of the conception of the place of the mind in the world which the evaluative theory provides.

Throughout Chapters 9, 10, 11, and 12, details of and perspectives upon, a conception of the world which is radically opposed to Hume's gradually emerge, in response to particular objections to particular stages of the presentation of the theory. The aim in these sections is to meet head-on the Humean qualms that are bound to be felt about a conception of the world in which value is so central. The conception is not presented here complete—how could it be? But I hope at least that enough has been done to indicate how it would respond to any further rebellion from our recurrently Humean intuitions.

As these chapters progress, the opposition to the evaluative theory appears more and more sharply as a form of scientism. The evaluative theory of content requires the abandonment of the view that the facts of natural science are metaphysically fundamental. This scientistic view emerges at different places, and in different forms. I try to counter it whenever, and however, it appears.

Someone might misinterpret this as showing that the evaluative theory of content is hostile to natural science. It is not. It is hostile just to a certain *metaphysical* view, which ends up giving natural science ultimate authority over everything. It is not a thesis of any natural science that science has such authority; so denying that thesis threatens no natural science.

Chapter 13 just offers a treatment of the intensionality of belief reports. It is designed to suit the evaluative theory of content, but the same points could be adapted to suit other theories. I try to show how we can make sense of variable or flexible opacity, according to which circumstances determine how fine grained the relevant individuation of thoughts is. The idea is to do this without appealing to anything more than is required to understand words as they are used *outside* contexts of propositional attitude. It appears, however, that, if we are to make sense of this, we need to abandon the conception of language which has been dominant in the analytical tradition.

It may be apparent from this summary that the book is not uniformly cautious in its claims. I have tried not to sit on fences. Indeed, whenever a fence has come into view, I have felt under an obligation to jump it. My concern has been to try to make sure that we end up with an alternative to the Humean view whose outline is sharply focused, and whose commitments are clear. In the same spirit I have tried to offer explicit definitions and precise formulations of the more important proposals. I hope that falsehoods, naïveties, and infelicities will be quickly exposed. What we all should want, after all, is the truth.

PART I

Metaphysics and Content

1

Philosophical Theories and Metaphysical Schemes

1.1. Theories of Content and Metaphysical Presuppositions

My aim is to provide a philosophical theory of content. 'Content' here means *conceptual* content, the content of propositional attitudes: what is believed when someone has a belief, for example. I take a *concept* to be a component of what is believed in just the same sense of 'component' as that in which a word or phrase is a component of a sentence.

If we are to provide a philosophical theory of content, we need to be clear about what philosophical theories in general should do, and about the general metaphysical stance which that presumes. This would be desirable for a philosophical theory of any subject-matter, to make it clear whether a proposed theory actually does what it needs to do. But it seems essential for a philosophical theory of *content*.

The reason is this. A conception of what philosophical theories should do will presuppose some very general metaphysical stance. A general metaphysical stance will be a view of the nature of the things our thoughts are about, and of the relation between those things and our thoughts. And a theory of content will inevitably be committed to some view of the relation between thoughts and things.

We cannot, therefore, uncritically adopt some metaphysical stance and insist that our theory of content should conform to that. A general metaphysical view and a theory of content must be mutually supporting, and each should be questioned in the light of the other. The point needs labouring in view of recent work on content: it is often just assumed that we need or want a 'naturalistic' theory of content, without any serious questioning of the general metaphysics of 'naturalism'. It should come as no surprise if, as I think is generally the case, the fundamental objections to the resulting theories trace back to the adoption of the contentious metaphysics of 'naturalism'.

It follows from what I have said that a conception of philosophical explanation and a theory of content cannot be wholly independent of one another. Nevertheless, there are considerations of different levels of generality, which can be appealed to separately.

In Part I I will put forward a general metaphysical view and a conception of philosophical explanation, appealing to very general considerations to support me. In Part II I will draw out from that general view some specific constraints on theories of content, which I will try to support, where appropriate, by appeal to more specific considerations.

1.2. Some Basic Terminology

The kinds of thing we may be doing in providing philosophical explanations are no doubt very various. But when we are offering a philosophical *theory* (or *analysis*, or *reduction*) of something, we are concerned with explanations of a certain kind. We are then concerned to give an account of what it is *in virtue of which* some set of truths is true. That is, in offering philosophical theories, we are concerned with explanations which conform to this schema:

(T) It is true that p, because q.

That this is a distinctively philosophical kind of explanation can be seen intuitively by considering the intuitive difference between these two questions:

(1) Why is she mowing the lawn?
(2) Why is it true that she is mowing the lawn?

(1), but not (2), could be answered by saying: because she thinks the grass is too long. (2), but not (1), could be correctly, if uninformatively, answered by saying: because, as a matter of fact, she *is* mowing the lawn.

Explanations which conform to schema (T) I call *metaphysical explanations*. This is a terminological stipulation, though I think it is in tune with much current usage of the term 'metaphysical'.

We can also relate explanations of this form to a range of other familiar philosophical terms.

I assume that when 'true' is used as a predicate it applies to conceptual content (something believed, for example), or to things which have conceptual content. Taking *thoughts* to be the things which are believed, thoughts are the things which can be true or false, and a truth is a true thought.

If we are offering an explanation of the form of (T), we are explaining what makes some thought true. If we use a different replacement for '*p*', which is not conceptually equivalent to the first, we will be explaining the truth of a different thought. If we are to preserve the identity of the subject-matter, alternative replacements for '*p*' in (T) must be conceptually equivalent. We might say: the condition for identity of subject-matter, in *this* context, is identity of thought or conceptual content.

That in virtue of which a thought is true is a *fact*. We can, of course, always characterize that in virtue of which the thought that *p* is true by describing it as the fact that *p* (as in the uninformative but correct answer to (2)). Alternative characterizations of that in virtue of which the same thought is true—if there can be any—will have to describe the same fact. We might say: the condition on substitution within the '*q*' position of (T), for any given replacement for '*p*', will be *factual* equivalence.

I take it that a *property* or *relation* is what is common to that in virtue of which all true thoughts expressible by means of the same predicate are true, and that an *object* is what is common to that in virtue of which all true thoughts expressible by means of the same singular term are true.

If we take an expression to be *significant* if it can be used to say something true, it will then follow that there is a property or relation corresponding to every significant predicate, and an object corresponding to every significant singular term. This is obviously quite a generous conception of objects and properties, but I think this generosity is harmless. Those who regard the notions of object and property as somehow honorific, and therefore want to be more parsimonious in applying them, can take what I have said as providing merely *necessary* conditions for being an object or a property, to which some more restrictive condition can be added.

It will also follow from what I have said that objects, properties, and relations are components of facts in just the same sense as that in which singular terms and predicates are components of sentences, and in which concepts are components of thoughts.

I think these characterizations of the notions of object, property, and fact are in line with common philosophical usage; but, again, they may be regarded as terminological stipulations.

We are generally not interested in piecemeal explanations of the form of (T), explaining the truth of different thoughts one by one. We are generally interested in giving metaphysical explanations of truths of general sorts. A general sort may be defined by the fact that the relevant truths are expressed by means of the same predicate or operator, or by means of predicates or operators within the same (interestingly unified) class; but it may be defined in some other way.

We are also not much interested in uninformative metaphysical explanations, like the answer offered to question (2) above. And we may want our metaphysical explanations to meet some further condition of explanatory priority, if they are to count as *explanations*.

I shall say that we have a philosophical *reduction* when two conditions are met:

(i) Our explanation of a general sort of truths provides a common feature corresponding to the commonality which defines the general sort;

(ii) Our favoured further condition of explanatory priority—whatever that may be—is met.

This provides a fairly generous (indeed anti-etymological) conception of reduction, since there is no presupposition of minimalism in the mention of explanatory priority. But, again, this should be regarded as a terminological stipulation, only roughly in line with established usage.

Finally, I shall call a conception of what is needed for a reduction to be adequate a *general metaphysical theory* or *scheme*. This requires several things of a general metaphysical scheme.

First, it will presuppose some conception of when two sentences count as expressing the same thought: this is the condition for metaphysical explanations being explanations of the same subject-matter. Secondly, it will involve a conception of what is required for two expressions to refer to or describe the same object, property, or fact. Thirdly, it will involve some conception of what condition of explanatory priority (if any) a reduction should be expected to meet.

This characterization brings out clearly the interdependence between general metaphysics and philosophical theories of content. Some general metaphysical scheme, in the sense I have defined, will be presupposed by any philosophical theory of any subject-matter. But the first two of the three features I have just mentioned are clearly within the province of a theory of content. Together they amount to a conception of the 'in-virtue-of' relation of metaphysical explanation, which, from another point of view, is just the relation which holds between thoughts and the things they are about.

So much for terminological preliminaries. I shall now lay out three fundamental alternatives on the question of metaphysical explanation. The rest of Part I will be devoted to supporting one of them.

1.3. Conceptualism, Platonism, and the No-Theory View

I think there are three fundamental approaches to metaphysical issues. These three approaches may not exhaust the options, but I think they are the most significant. I call them *conceptualism*, *Platonism*, and the *no-theory view*. The term 'conceptualism' is borrowed from Wiggins.[1] I think the position I attach that label to is very like Wiggins's view, but I shall not feel constrained to defer to him for its proper statement. 'Platonism' is used here in very much the sense it has in discussions of Wittgenstein's views on meaning.[2] There are significant connections with Plato, but we should not expect every feature of Plato's metaphysics to be relevant.

My definition of conceptualism defines the other two approaches too. As I define the term, conceptualism is the confluence of two fundamental tenets:

(*A*) There can be interesting metaphysical explanations.

---

[1] D. Wiggins, *Sameness and Substance*, chs. 4, 5, and 'On Singling out an Object Determinately', in P. Pettit and J. McDowell (eds.), *Subject, Thought, and Context* (Oxford: Clarendon Press, 1986), 169–70.

[2] See, e.g., D. Pears, *The False Prison*, ii (Oxford: Clarendon Press, 1988), ch. 17.

(*B*) The nature of the objects, properties, and facts to which our concepts correspond is not fixed independently of the nature of the concepts which correspond to them.

(*B*) may also be put in another way: there would not have been *those* objects, properties, and facts, if they had not corresponded to *those* concepts. It follows that the nature of the world we think about is at least partially determined by the concepts involved in the thoughts we have about it. It should be noted, however, that (*B*) is quite compatible with its converse: there would not have been *those* concepts if they had not corresponded to *those* objects, properties, and facts. If we accepted that converse, we could say: the nature of the thoughts we have about the world is at least partially determined by the nature of the world we think about. That is, thoughts and world would be mutually determining. (For more on this, see 7.1.)

Platonism denies (*B*), holding that the nature of the objects, properties, and facts to which our concepts correspond precisely *is* fixed independently of the concepts which correspond to them.

The no-theory view denies (*A*), for non-Platonistic reasons.

In the rest of Part I I shall be developing and defending a version of conceptualism. But it might help to have some idea of the motivation for it now. I take it that (*A*) needs no special defence to anyone who is concerned to provide a philosophical theory of anything, provided that the notion of an *interesting* metaphysical explanation is reasonably plausibly understood. But why should anyone believe (*B*)?

One motivation is provided by this remark of Wittgenstein's, although it was made in another connection: 'It would seem to be a sort of accident, if it turned out that a situation would fit a thing that could already exist entirely on its own.'[3] Similarly, it would seem to be a sort of accident if a concept turned out to be a concept *of* something, if it was not essential to the thing that such a concept was a concept of it. Alternatively, if the world is to be capable of being thought about at all, it must be essential to the world that it is such as to be thought about. Or one might put it like this: the notion of a world is just the notion of something to be thought about. The idea here is close to the spirit of traditional rationalism;

---

[3] L. Wittgenstein, *Tractatus logico-philosophicus*, trans. D. Pears and B. McGuinness (London: Routledge and Kegan Paul, 1961), 2.0121.

one might bring out the connection by restating it like this: it is essential to the world that the world can be made sense of. And that way of putting it suggests a kind of link with (*A*) which I will be exploiting later. (It also gives a hint of what it is about Humean empiricism which can seem utterly terrifying.)

That may not be enough to make everyone blithely content with (*B*). The rest of Part I will provide further encouragement, but some worries can be dealt with immediately. Unease is likely to be felt at the claim that the three basic approaches to metaphysics can be characterized in terms of their views on (*A*) and (*B*). Some of that disquiet can be removed by more-or-less terminological observations.

First, 'metaphysical explanations' in (*A*) has the sense defined in the last section: they are explanations of that in-virtue-of which truths are true. Secondly, the notion of correspondence used in (*B*) involves no commitment to a classical correspondence theory of truth. It is used here just to express aspects of the 'in virtue of' relation of metaphysical explanations: just as thoughts are true in virtue of facts, components of thoughts (concepts) correspond to components of facts (objects and properties). A classical correspondence theory of truth is just a particular (Platonistic) way of viewing that 'in virtue of' relation.

Most importantly, (*B*) is likely to be read as advocating an absurd idealism. It might seem to imply that things cannot exist without anyone thinking of them, or that, if they exist without being thought of, they somehow exist with no nature. The common-sense absurdity of such claims is expressed by this kind of simple appeal: surely the mountains of Skye were there, craggy and volcanic, long before there were any sentient beings at all.

The reading of (*B*) which has this absurd consequence is avoided by insisting on a certain understanding of the notion of a concept. Crucially, concepts must be thought of as existing *timelessly*—that is, *atemporally*. That needs some explanation, first by redescribing what is meant by 'concept' here, and then by explaining what it is for concepts, so understood, to exist timelessly. To explain what (*B*) means, with 'concept' understood in the sense intended, I shall use double quotation marks to refer to concepts—so one might speak of the concept "red", for example.

For the case of objects, (*B*) claims that the nature of an object, *a*, is not fixed independently of the concept "*a*", where the concept "*a*" is what would be common to anyone at all who believed that . . . *a* . . . , for some filling of the blanks,[4] '*a*' being a singular term.[5] For the case of properties, (*B*) claims that the nature of the property, *F*-ness, is not fixed independently of the concept "*F*", where the concept "*F*" is what would be common to anyone who believed that . . . *F* . . . , for some filling of the blanks, '*F*' being a predicate. The crucial point is that we are speaking of *the* concept "*a*", or *the* concept "*F*", rather than *someone's* concept of this or that. This is what is needed for the timeless existence of concepts to be even remotely plausible.

The timeless existence of concepts, so described, can now itself be explained as follows. The existence of a concept is a matter of there being something which it would be to possess that concept. And there being something which it would be to possess the concept "*e*" (where '*e*' is any kind of expression) is just a matter of there being something which it would be, for example, to believe that . . . *e* . . . , for some filling of the blanks. (I am assuming throughout this explanation that having a belief involving a concept is a necessary and sufficient condition for possessing that concept. If someone thought that one could possess a concept without having a *belief* involving that concept, provided that one had some other kind of attitude involving that concept, they could still give essentially the same account.)

Given that, we can say that for the concept "*e*" to exist timelessly is just for it to be timelessly true that there is something which it would be to believe that . . . *e* . . . , for some filling of the blanks. To put it another way: the existence of a concept is a matter of there being some condition which would have to be met by anyone for her to count as having a belief involving that concept. And that there is such a condition in the case of any given concept is timelessly true.

Some people might be worried about the timeless existence of concepts because they hold that the existence of concepts depends upon the social and political (or more generally historical) circumstances which enable people to possess them, which is obviously a temporal business. This is essentially the same

[4] The quantifier here, and in related phrases in this paragraph and the next, has narrow scope.

[5] This use of single quotation marks refers to whatever replaces the quoted letter in an instance of the schema, in line with the Notational Convention.

misunderstanding of the intended sense of 'concept' as that which led to the idealistic reading of (*B*). It can perfectly well be timelessly true that certain historical circumstances would have to obtain for anyone to possess some given concept. Indeed, it is hard to make sense of the claim that certain historical circumstances are *required* for the possession of a concept unless concepts exist timelessly in the way I have explained: what holds for all possible worlds can hardly be restricted to specific times.

There are two important consequences for the understanding of (*B*) which follow from the timeless existence of concepts. The first is that (*B*) cannot be taken as claiming that concepts determine the nature of reality in any *empirical* sense of 'determine'. It is, therefore, quite inappropriate to represent (*B*) as saying that concepts 'construct' reality in any sense, for example.[6] And (*B*) does not endorse any such view as that our concepts 'carve up' the world in a certain way.

The second significant consequence of the timeless existence of concepts is that both conceptualism and Platonism are thereby committed to a certain view of subjunctive conditionals. Conceptualism is committed to something like this: if there had not been *those* concepts, there would not have been *those* objects, properties, and facts. Platonism is committed to this: there *would* have been those objects, properties, and facts, even if there had not been those concepts. If concepts exist timelessly, the antecedents of these conditionals are surely impossible. Conceptualism and Platonism, as I have characterized them, are therefore committed to the view that subjunctive conditionals with impossible antecedents can be non-vacuously true. This is at odds with some modern theories of subjunctive conditionals. I shall return to the point in 5.2.

Even if insisting that the concepts spoken of in (*B*) exist timelessly stops conceptualism looking like an absurd idealism, there is still a feature of the characterization I have provided of the view which might make someone hesitate before accepting that the three approaches I have outlined are of fundamental importance. Why is conceptualism portrayed as involving *two* theses? What have (*A*) and (*B*) to do with one another?

The answer is that arguments against Platonism generally depend upon accepting (*A*). What makes Platonism so hard to accept is

---

[6] Wiggins shows himself keen to distance his conceptualism from such an interpretation at *Sameness and Substance*, 141.

what also rules out interesting metaphysical explanations, in a natural sense of 'interesting'. This will emerge in the course of the next chapter. If acceptance of (*A*) drives one to accepting (*B*), a position comprising (*A*) and (*B*) together is not just an arbitrary amalgam: it has a certain natural unity.

This does not automatically prevent the no-theory view from using just the same arguments against Platonism. For it might be thought that Platonists themselves are generally committed to (*A*), in which case using (*A*) to refute Platonism would be a legitimate form of *ad hominem* argument. Nevertheless, if acceptance of (*A*) does drive one to accept (*B*), conceptualism provides a natural home for those of us who hope to be able to provide interesting metaphysical theories.

This link between (*A*) and (*B*) should also serve to answer another worry about the idea that the three approaches I have characterized are fundamental. Someone might say: could we not be conceptualist about some kinds of thing, and Platonist about others? I think the generality of the difficulties with Platonism will show this hybrid conception to be unattractive.

So much for preliminary exposition of what I have claimed are the three fundamental approaches to metaphysics. What we need to do now is to develop a general metaphysical theory (in the sense of 1.2) to provide the constraints that a philosophical theory of content must meet.

I shall put forward a developed form of conceptualism as the best general metaphysical theory. I hope to make it plausible that anyone who hopes to provide a philosophical theory (or analysis, or reduction) of any particular subject should accept this general theory, and reject some familiar alternatives. My proposal depends upon a natural reading of (*A*); that is, upon a certain natural understanding of what counts as an *interesting* metaphysical explanation. That natural understanding derives from Kant.

2

Conceptualism is Kantian

2.1. A Kantian Conception of Interesting Explanations

Conceptualism will already seem broadly Kantian in spirit: the dependence claimed in (B), of the nature of the things we think about upon the concepts involved in our thoughts about them, has a distinctly Kantian smell.

Kant did not make the dependence claims which are analogous to (B) just because they had an appealing aroma. They were put forward as part of his answer to what he took to be a fundamental question: 'How is metaphysics possible?'.[1] More specifically, the question was how we could have a *scientific* metaphysics. For a metaphysics to be scientific it was at least required that metaphysical claims be sufficiently constrained to allow it to be possible in principle to decide non-arbitrarily whether they are true.

I suggest that 'interesting' in conceptualism's tenet (A) (that there can be interesting metaphysical explanations) is naturally read in line with something like Kant's conception of a scientific metaphysics. An *interesting* metaphysical explanation will be one which may issue from and be testable by a *scientific* general metaphysical theory. I define a *scientific* general metaphysical theory as one which incorporates an *operable* condition of adequacy for metaphysical explanations. And I define a condition of adequacy as *operable* if it enables us to test *some* metaphysical explanations effectively, and if it allows us always to *imagine* the testing of any significant metaphysical explanation.

That understanding of what counts as an interesting metaphysical explanation looks likely to be congenial to those who thought initially that tenet (A) of conceptualism was right. Interesting metaphysical explanations have to be informative, in at least the sense that recognizing them to be true is not a condition on counting as understanding the words in which they are couched.

[1] I. Kant, *Critique of Pure Reason*, trans. N. Kemp Smith (London: Macmillan, 1929), B22.

And interesting metaphysical explanations will also have to meet some requirement of explanatory priority. But these two conditions are not enough to sustain interest for long, since they allow whimsically fabricated explanations. What we clearly need is something like what I have proposed: that interesting metaphysical explanations should issue from, or be testable by, a scientific general metaphysical scheme, in the sense I have defined.

In 1.2 I mentioned three defining characteristics of a general metaphysical scheme: a conception of what is required for two sentences to count as expressing the same thought; a conception of what is required for two sentences to count as describing the same fact; and a conception of the condition of explanatory priority which a reduction would have to meet to count as explanatory. It can only be by the second of these three that whimsically fabricated metaphysical explanations can be ruled out. The problem with unconstrained metaphysics appears to be that too much licence is permitted in what are allowed to count as descriptions of the same fact. The crucial constraint of a scientific metaphysics must be that it imposes an operable condition of factual equivalence. (We might call this a criterion of identity for objects, properties, and facts.)

This shows the point of entry for deep versions of the no-theory view. This kind of view is founded in scepticism about the possibility of saying anything explanatory—perhaps even informative—while preserving the right to claim that one is still describing the same facts.

Here is a remark which expresses such a scepticism, in terms which are precisely congenial to my way of setting up the issues:

The limit of language is shown by its being impossible to describe the fact which corresponds to (is the translation of) a sentence, without simply repeating the sentence. (This has to do with the Kantian solution of the problem of philosophy.)[2]

But I cannot see that this presents more than a challenge. If so, it is to be met by actually providing a plausible and operable condition of factual equivalence which permits informative and explanatory metaphysical explanations. That will be the task of Chapter 5.

[2] L. Wittgenstein, *Culture and Value*, trans. P. Winch (Oxford: Blackwell, 1980), 10.

2.2. A Kantian Rejection of Platonism

In this section I want to do three things. First, I shall argue that the demand for a scientific metaphysics is incompatible with Platonism. Secondly, I shall argue that familiar objections to Platonism, in so far as they are effective at all, presuppose a commitment to something like a scientific metaphysics. This reinforces the cohesiveness of conceptualism, since it suggests that tenet (A) of conceptualism is necessary as well as sufficient for tenet (B). Thirdly, I shall try to undermine two intuitive arguments for Platonism.

As a result of these arguments, Platonism will emerge as an extremely foreign position. It might even seem to be a straw man. If that seems like an objection, I have two things to say in reply. First, if Platonism really is a straw man, then so much the better for conceptualism. Secondly, although a thoroughgoing Platonism is indeed a very strange position, some of its characteristic responses are in fact quite familiar. This suggests that some familiar philosophical views are in danger of collapsing into a position which they themselves would regard as very strange.

To begin, then: the demand for a scientific metaphysics (our interpretation of tenet (A) of conceptualism) seems already incompatible with Platonism.

Platonism holds that the nature of the objects, properties, and facts to which our concepts correspond is fixed independently of those concepts. This seems to prevent the Platonist from accepting that there could be an operable criterion of identity for facts. For the criterion to be operable, we would need to be able to tell when it was satisfied, in some cases at least. And we would have to be able to tell in every case, *once fully informed*, whether two expressions describe the same object, property, or fact. Moreover, there must be something which it would be to be fully informed—that must be a position which one can imagine oneself being in.

For the Platonist, being able to tell in the appropriate way whether two expressions describe the same thing would require getting a view of the thing in itself, without any concepts cluttering up the picture, and checking whether the expressions both really fit it. And that is an unimaginable view. The Platonist seems to be committed to this, because, if one holds that the nature of things is fixed independently of any concepts of them, one must hold that it is always an open question whether things really are as our concepts represent them as being. Or if the Platonist thinks (as she might, but need not) that something could not be a *concept* unless it represented things as they are—fitted the real divisions in nature— she will hold that it is always an open question whether what seems to be a concept is really a concept: nothing we could ever do could ever get us any closer.

We can get an idea of the character of the difference between Platonism and conceptualism by noting that despite this the Platonist need not think that the relevant identity claims are always unknowable. She could just think that no truth-related *justification* could ever be given for them, where a *truth-related* justification is one of the kind we normally require when we ask for a justification for a claim to knowledge. (A truth-related justification is distinct, for example, from merely aesthetic or pragmatic considerations which might incline one towards some view.)

With that point made, we can see the substance of the motivation for demanding a scientific metaphysics, and therefore rejecting Platonism. The demand is not just obvious, from some neutral point of view. I think it gets its force from these three beliefs:

(i)   In offering metaphysical explanations, we should be trying to offer something fit to be believed.

(ii) If there can be sensible dispute about something which is offered as fit to be believed, there must be some truth-related justification for believing or disbelieving it.

(iii) There can be sensible dispute about the correctness of metaphysical explanations.

The use in (ii) and (iii) of the unexplained notion of what can sensibly be disputed leaves these claims rough and intuitive, rather than toughly defined; but they can still be used to give the flavour of the difference between Platonism and conceptualism, in a way that shows that the Platonist is not quite such an unfamiliar character as we might have thought.

We can imagine a number of different kinds of Platonist. One might accept (i) and (ii), but, because of her Platonism, deny (iii). Such a Platonist might *look* very like someone who holds a no-theory view, but her motivation will be very different from that of a standard no-theory view. This kind of Platonist is likely to spend her time defusing the pretensions of those who try to argue for metaphysical explanations.

Another Platonist might drop (i), while holding the other two. She might pursue metaphysical explanations in the spirit of a game, or study them in the way that a mathematician might study the properties of formal systems. At any rate, she will hold that the correctness of a metaphysical explanation is not a question of *truth*.

Another might hold (i) and (iii), but deny (ii). Such a person might put forward substantial metaphysical theories, and believe them to be true, but on aesthetic or pragmatic grounds, accepting that she has no truth-related reason for her belief, and that none could ever be provided. This last form of Platonism will be characterized by an air of bravado which is surely familiar. And the bravado is needed, since denying (ii) requires a substantial deviation from normal canons of rationality.

Laying out these different forms of Platonism serves two purposes. First, it shows that Platonism is not entirely unfamiliar. Secondly, it shows the strength of the pressure which pushes one from accepting tenet (*A*) of conceptualism (that there can be interesting metaphysical explanations) to denying Platonism. For it appears that the Platonist cannot seriously engage in the project of providing metaphysical explanations without abandoning the path of ordinary rationality.

That last point should already suggest that there can be no decisive argument in favour of either conceptualism or Platonism, arising from principles and assumptions which are equally acceptable to both. I want now to support that suggestion by considering how certain intuitive arguments against Platonism fare against a peculiarly tough character I shall now introduce: the *hard-boiled* Platonist. The hard-boiled Platonist is prepared to accept anything necessary to preserve consistently (in some sense of 'consistent') the Platonistic conception of the independence of the nature of things from any concepts of them.

The Platonist is likely to be attacked over her acceptance of a classical correspondence theory of truth. What seems to mark out a classical correspondence theory is its view that there are *two* kinds of question of correctness to be answered in considering whether something is true. First, there is the question whether the conditions internal to the concepts involved have been satisfied. Secondly, there is the question whether the concepts themselves fit the world—whether the similarities marked out and presupposed by the concepts correspond to the real similarities in nature. It is distinctive of Platonism to think that this second question of correctness is a real question.

The classic objection to this classical correspondence theory is that the relevant notion of correspondence or fit, which is exploited in raising that second question, is irredeemably mysterious and inexplicable. But the really hard-boiled Platonist should be unmoved by this objection. She should say that this demand for explanation is precisely a demand for an operable criterion of identity for facts. For the relation of correspondence in question is (part of) what is expressed by the 'in virtue of' in the phrase 'true in virtue of'; so the demand for an ultimately demystifying account of that notion will just be a demand for a scientific metaphysics. The mystery of the notion of correspondence is integral to hard-boiled Platonism.

Some might feel that Platonism is objectionable because they hold that we have a right to believe in the well-foundedness of our concepts, and Platonism denies us that right. But, again, the hard-boiled Platonist should not feel disturbed. She can say that perhaps we cannot help behaving as if we had that right, but that that does not mean that we really do have it. Perhaps, even, we cannot help *believing* that we have the right; but then the Platonist can say that in order to have the true view of the independence of things from concepts we have to believe each of two contradictory things. That produces psychological tension, but no deep incoherence; for the Platonist does not hold that reality is contradictory—just that we cannot help, for psychological or pragmatic reasons, denying the truth. This argument does no more than restate the difference between the hard-boiled Platonist and her opponents.

It is true that even the hard-boiled Platonist will have to presuppose the well-foundedness of some concepts (notably those used in the formulation of Platonism itself). But for the hard-boiled Platonist this will seem a merely pragmatic necessity: we must in fact presuppose the well-foundedness of some concepts, but we have no *right* to be confident of their well-foundedness. I cannot see how we could force her to accept that we have this right, without forcing her to accept something like beliefs (i)–(iii), which provide the motivation for insisting on a scientific metaphysics.

Some believe that the very idea of things whose nature is fixed independently of any concept of them is incoherent. It is difficult to be sure what sense 'incoherent' and its allies are supposed to have when this kind of charge is made. What we need to beware of is the kind of predicament Wiggins seems to get into when he makes this kind of accusation. He says, in effect denying Platonism: 'There are no "lines" in nature.'[3] And his comment (on another expression of the rejection of Platonism, which is meant to apply to this too) is this: 'Here (I am aware) I yield to the temptation to try to convey something by issuing the denial of something which is really nonsense.'[4] But if what is denied is nonsense, then its denial will be nonsense too. But that would mean that conceptualism itself cannot be stated, since tenet (*B*) of conceptualism (the claim that reality is not fixed independently of concepts) is just a denial of Platonism. In fact, what is said to be a 'denial of something which is really nonsense' looks to me like a denial of a (metaphorical) truth: nature is just where the 'lines' are. Wiggins's formulation seems to have succumbed to the idealistic understanding of conceptualism.

If Platonism is to be called incoherent, 'incoherent' had better not mean *nonsense*—at least if the charge comes from a conceptualist mouth. What the charge might mean is just this: a Platonist who seriously engages in the project of providing metaphysical explanations is irrational. That charge seems just. But it depends upon the assumption of the desirability of something like a scientific metaphysics, and could hardly be expected to move a hard-boiled Platonist.

In short, I cannot see how a hard-boiled Platonist could be dislodged by argument. But showing hard-boiled Platonism's immunity to argued objection just shows how strange the position is. Its strangeness consists in the fact that, while it is a philosophical position, it fails to acknowledge the desire to make sense of things which gets philosophy going, and leads us to hope for a scientific metaphysics.

On the other hand, there does not seem to be any good argument *for* Platonism. I shall consider two. First, some might think that in order to make sense of progress in science we need to suppose that some concepts are better than others. And this seems to allow us to make sense of that second question of correctness which a classical correspondence theory of truth wants room for.

To this one should reply: in what respect are some concepts shown to be better than others by the progress of science? Better as concepts, or for some other purpose? A conceptualist can perfectly

---

[3] Wiggins, 'On Singling out an Object Determinately', 170.
[4] Ibid., n. 2.

well allow that one concept can be better than another for certain scientific purposes (in virtue of being more precisely defined, for example), or because it picks out some property which has some instances in the actual world. But no more than this seems to be needed to account for scientific progress.

Two examples might help to make this clear. Take first the concepts expressed by the word *water* before and after that word became attached (assuming it did) to some natural-scientific classification. Let us assume that there was no implicit deference in the earlier practice to the scientific classification which underpins the later practice. (This assumption is needed to make the concepts distinct, and so to allow the question of comparative merit even to be raised.) Now the later concept is certainly better fitted to natural-scientific activity than the earlier one, since the earlier one can hardly be said to be so fitted at all. But there is no clear sense in which we can be entitled to say that the later concept is better founded *as a concept* than the earlier one. Both concepts are concepts of liquids which actually exist on earth, though they are different liquids: the essence of one is specified according to what is interesting from a natural-scientific perspective; the essence of the other is not.

Secondly, consider the concept of phlogiston. No modern natural science speaks of phlogiston; the abandonment of phlogiston theory is one of the steps in the progress of science. The concept of phlogiston is clearly worse in some respects than at least some of the concepts of modern science: there is no such thing as phlogiston. But this does not impugn the virtue of the concept of phlogiston as a concept. The word 'phlogiston' remains meaningful, and not merely in a trivial sense; there is presumably some more-or-less determinate condition which something would have to meet in order to count as phlogiston, or else phlogiston theory could never have been determinately rejected.

There seems, then, to be no convincing argument for Platonism from the fact of scientific progress. Indeed, it is hard to see how there could have been. It is part of the Platonist's thesis that we could have no evidence for the goodness or badness of the fit of concepts to reality as it is in itself; and yet this argument pretends to provide just such evidence.

The second attempt to argue for Platonism that I want to consider begins from little more than an appeal to intuition. If we deny the Platonistic conception of the independence of the nature of things from concepts, we seem to allow the following posssibility. There might be beings which could not have concepts anything like ours. It seems, then, that, if such beings thought of anything, they would not think of anything which our thoughts concern, if conceptualism is right. This is what some people's intuitions rebel at. Suppose, for example, that bats are creatures so radically different from us that they cannot have *any* of our concepts. It seems to follow from the denial of Platonism that, if bats think at all, they will be thinking of things quite different from any that we can think of. But surely, it will be said, this is quite implausible. Do we not want some sense in which we can all be said to eat at a common table?[5]

This line of thought has some intuitive appeal, but it needs some work done on it before it can be presented as an argument against conceptualism.

It might help to express the issues here in different terms. A concept can be thought of as a way of thinking of something. The formulation I have offered of the intuitive objection to concep-tualism seems to assume that conceptualism holds that a difference in ways of thinking implies a difference in the things thought about. But conceptualism should not accept that (it is a form of no-theory view), and it need not. What conceptualism is committed to is just the view that, if two ways of thinking are *sufficiently* different, they must be ways of thinking of different things. And a sensible conceptualist will not rush to define what counts as a sufficient difference—not because this makes it easier to evade objections, but because what differences can be tolerated will vary from object to object.

The intuitive line of thought can only provide the basis of an argument for Platonism if it can be used to show that there are some ways of thinking which conceptualism must count as sufficiently different to be ways of thinking of different objects, but which we can see independently must be ways of thinking of the same things.

The only ground which the intuitive line of thought appears to provide for thinking that we and bats, say, must have thoughts about at least some of the same things is the fact that we inhabit

---

[5] I owe this lovely phrase to Gavin Lawrence.

(simply inhabit; not 'feel at home in') the same physical universe. If the intuitive thought is to generate an argument, it must therefore establish two things:

(a) Conceptualism must accept that two inhabitants of the same physical world could have such different conceptual schemes that they do not think about any of the same things.

(b) In fact, any two concept-possessors who inhabit the same physical world must think about at least some of the same things.

Unfortunately, it is not clear why we should accept either claim.

Let us return to bats, and begin from what it is obviously safe to say. It is obviously safe to say that we can describe in terms of our concepts the things with which the bats interact causally, within the classifications of causal interactions that concern us. That gives us a rather minimal, near-literal, sense in which we all eat at a common table. But how can we get from this to the claim that, if bats think, they must be able to think about at least some of the things *we* think about, which is what we need to support claim (*b*)?

One assumption which *would* bridge the gap is the assumption of causal reductionism about reference. I think this assumption is incompatible with a scientific metaphysics, as I shall argue later. If this were the only assumption which could provide plausible grounds for accepting claim (*b*), it would then follow that claim (*a*) would be true. But, again, if this were the only ground for accepting claim (*b*), the intuitive line of thought would hardly have provided an independent argument for Platonism.

As it happens, I cannot see anything very implausible about the view attributed to conceptualism in (*a*). Consequently, I do not feel the force of an 'intuitive' demand that we should see ourselves (the inhabitants of this physical universe) as all eating at a common table, in any sense which would require the possibility of mealtime conversation. Let us put the point as boldly as possible: if we use 'world' to mean what is thought about, there is nothing obviously implausible about saying that, in the circumstances we are imagining, the bat's world might be a different world from ours. On the other hand, it is not obviously something the conceptualist is committed to either.

In conclusion, I can see no convincing argument for Platonism, and no argument which a conceptualist could mount which would dislodge a really hard-boiled Platonist. Does this itself constitute a problem for conceptualism? Is the disagreement between Platonism and conceptualism not itself a sensible dispute? And can the conceptualist offer anything but pragmatic or aesthetic reasons for preferring her view?

The answer is that the dispute between a conceptualist and a thoroughly *hard-boiled* Platonist is *not* a sensible dispute. These two positions differ over such fundamental matters that there could be no argument between them which was not question-begging: they disagree over what needs to be explained, what needs to be argued for, and what kinds of argument are appropriate.

This does not matter, because conceptualism does not need *this* dispute to be a sensible one. The hard-boiled Platonist was not introduced as someone whose view was so obviously refutable that conceptualism can be shown, on utterly neutral grounds, to be true. She was introduced just in order to explain, by contrast, what conceptualism is committed to, and what a thoroughgoing denial of it would look like. Nothing has been (nor, I think, could be) said to show that the hard-boiled Platonist can be refuted on terms which she herself would accept. But enough has been done to show that we are almost all already committed to rejecting her position.

And there is at least one sensible dispute which conceptualism stands on one side of. This is the dispute between conceptualism and those who advocate Platonism without being prepared to accept the consequences of going hard-boiled. Between *these* two positions there can indeed be an argument of the kind which conceptualism demands.

All we need (or can) argue against are those who are already committed to a certain conception of rationality, and to the worthwhileness of certain kinds of project. Within this shared framework, pointing out that to maintain Platonism consistently one has to stay a good deal longer in the pot is itself a way of providing truth-related grounds for conceptualism, for those who share the framework. No one can stand on the ground from which there might be a real choice between conceptualism and Platonism, so there does not need to be an argument for conceptualism from *there*.

With the intimacy of the connection between the demand for a scientific metaphysics and the rejection of Platonism now so securely established, the task is to generate some specific constraints on metaphysical explanations. I shall proceed initially by developing the demands of a scientific metaphysics more explicitly, on the basis of the rejection of some familiar kinds of view about metaphysical explanation. I shall then try to use the lessons learnt from the rejection of those views to argue for constraints of the kind we need.

3

Informativeness

Someone who hopes for a scientific metaphysics needs it to be possible for there to be informative metaphysical explanations. This puts a constraint on the way we individuate facts. If a metaphysical explanation is to be informative, the sentence which provides it must differ in informativeness from the sentence which gave our original description of the same fact. It must, therefore, be possible for two sentences which differ in informativeness to describe the same fact.

We can characterize difference of informativeness quite uncontroversially. I shall want to allow that the very same sentence (roughly, the same type of shape or sound with the same reference) can be used in ways which are differently informative. (This is to deal with what I call 'flexible opacity' in 6.3; see also Chapter 13.) This complicates the account slightly, but it is still easy enough to provide a characterization. We can say:

(I) s_1 and s_2 differ in informativeness, as they are used on a given occasion, if and only if it is possible for someone who understands both sentences as they are then used to believe that s_1 is true without believing that s_2 is true.

That much is uncontroversial. There is also an intuitive characterization of what is involved in believing that a sentence which one understands is true. I shall use '$‹e›$' as a way of indicating a use rather than a mention of some expression e; or, when e contains some perspective-biased expression—demonstratives, indexicals, tensed verbs—a use of an expression exactly like e except that the perspective of the perspective-biased expressions is adjusted to the point of view of the reporter of belief, rather than that of the subject (where these differ). Our intuitive conception of what is involved in believing that a sentence which one understands is true can then be captured by what we might call the *Fregean assumption*:

(FA) It is possible to believe that s_1 is true without believing that s_2 is true, while understanding both sentences, only if it is possible to believe that ⟨s_1⟩ without believing that ⟨s_2⟩.

This is naturally called a Fregean assumption, since (FA) and (I) together capture a fundamental feature of Frege's notion of sense. Frege characterized difference of sense initially in terms of difference of informativeness. He then claimed that the sameness or difference of sense, so characterized, of the words used in the 'that'-clauses of belief reports determined the truth value of such reports.[1] That is, expressions are intersubstitutable *salva veritate* in such contexts if, and only if, they have the same sense. (That is all that need be involved in the claim that words in such contexts *refer* to their senses, since for Frege sameness of reference is just a matter of intersubstitutability *salva veritate*.)

There is a position which holds *both* (I) with (FA) *and* that metaphysical explanations are to be provided only by offering sentences which are *conceptually* equivalent to those which gave our original description of the same facts. That is, for metaphysical explanations, the new sentences must be intersubstitutable with the old within ascriptions of attitude to any subject. Let us call this position the *philosophy of conceptual analysis*—PCA for short. (This is a caricature of conceptual analysis as traditionally practised. But if sentences like 'Bachelors are unmarried men' are taken to be paradigms of conceptual analysis and philosophical explanation, the caricature will not seem unjust. I suspect that traditional conceptual analysis just was not very clear about the condition of factual equivalence which metaphysical explanations have to meet.)

Given this characterization of PCA, one who hopes for informative metaphysical explanations must reject PCA. The reason is that PCA's condition of factual equivalence is defined in terms of intersubstitutivity within belief contexts. That means that, if a sentence s_2 provides a metaphysical explanation of a fact originally described by a sentence s_1, it will be impossible for anyone to believe that ⟨s_1⟩ without believing that ⟨s_2⟩. And since PCA accepts (FA), that makes it impossible for there to be informative metaphysical explanations. The problem here is, in effect, a version

[1] G. Frege, 'On Sense and Meaning', trans. M. Black, in Frege, *Collected Papers on Mathematics, Logic, and Philosophy*, ed. B. McGuinness (Oxford: Blackwell, 1984).

of the paradox of analysis. I take it that the uncertainty whether this paradox really undermines *traditional* conceptual analysis is due to the uncertainty about what exactly the condition of factual equivalence adopted by traditional conceptual analysis was.

If we reject PCA while holding (FA), we will not accept that meaning the same is the condition which two sentences must meet in order for them to describe the same fact, or two predicates to describe the same property, or two singular terms to refer to the same object. This is because, if someone understands a sentence and holds it to be true, they believe what the sentence means. This guarantees that conditions on substitution within meaning-giving contexts march with those for belief contexts. Again, I take this to be uncontroversial. Anyone who denied it would mean something different by 'meaning', just as someone who denied (I) would mean something different by 'informative'.

But there is a position which holds that meaning the same *is* the condition of factual equivalence, but which is strikingly opposed to PCA. The contrast with PCA can be made like this: PCA begins with a richly intensional, intuitive notion of meaning—one suitable for (FA)—and makes the notion of fact fit it; whereas this other position begins with a less richly intensional notion of a fact, and makes the notion of meaning fit *that*. Let us call this other position a *facts-first* theory.[2] A facts-first theory denies (FA).

Facts-first theories are counter-intuitive, because our intuitions support (FA). If we deny (FA), we cannot make sense, for example, of its having been a discovery that Hesperus is Phosphorus, but not that Hesperus is Hesperus. The examples could be multiplied. In the face of that counter-intuitiveness, a facts-first theorist needs to do three things. She must show those intuitions to be mistaken. She must explain why they are nevertheless so widely held. And she must provide an alternative account of informativeness.

Facts-first theories typically argue that our intuitions about belief contexts are mistaken by claiming that they could only be defended within the framework of some clearly false semantic theory. (It is commonly assumed, for example, that a descriptive theory of names is needed to support our intuitions about 'Hesperus' and 'Phosphorus'.) This is an inevitably vulnerable style of argument,

---

[2] This title is meant to embrace both J. Barwise and J. Perry, *Situations and Attitudes* (Cambridge, Mass.: MIT Press, 1983), and N. Salmon, *Frege's Puzzle* (Cambridge, Mass.: MIT Press, 1986).

since there is room for a defender of (FA) to support her belief by means of a semantic theory which is not subject to the same objections. I shall offer such an account in chapter 13. I know of no other way of undermining our ordinary intuitions; should one emerge, it will have to be met as it appears.

It will be natural for a facts-first theorist to explain the prevalence of the intuitions despite their alleged falsity by appealing in some way to conversational implicature. But I cannot see how an explanation of this sort can get off the ground. Such an explanation will have to involve saying that it is at least sometimes misleading to say that someone believes that Hesperus is Hesperus when we could have said that she believes that Hesperus is Phosphorus. But it is hard to see how it could be misleading on a facts-first theory. Is it supposed that there is a general presumption that, if someone believes that Hesperus is Phosphorus, then she will (typically) assent to the sentence 'Hesperus is Phosphorus' (or some suitable translation of it—whatever precisely that might mean) when queried? This would allow that ascription to tell us more than would be conveyed by saying that the person believes that Hesperus is Hesperus. But if this is the suggestion, then we just need to push the question back further: how does that conversational presumption get established, according to a facts-first theory? One can understand the presumption if we take the ordinary intuitions for granted, but I cannot see why it should arise in the first place if the facts-first view is right.

Nor can a facts-first theory plausibly explain the ordinary intuitions by saying that they are the result of commonly held but false semantic theories, like a descriptional view of names. For it is quite implausible to suppose that ordinary users of belief-reporting sentences hold any such theory—or indeed any substantive semantic theory at all.

I cannot then see how a facts-first theory can meet the first two of the requirements which I imposed. It fares no better with the third. The only serious attempt I know to explain informativeness without appealing to something like (FA) is Salmon's.[3] I suspect that the problems with this attempt would also confront any other.

Salmon claims that the function of declarative sentences, both within attitude contexts and outside them, is to 'encode' pieces of

---

[3] Salmon, *Frege's Puzzle*, ch. 8.

information, which he calls *propositions*. Propositions are here individuated much as facts or states of affairs are. Informativeness is then explained by appeal to the notion of the *guise* of a proposition.[4] Someone can believe s_1 to be true without believing s_2 to be true, while understanding both sentences, and where both sentences 'encode' the same proposition, if s_1 and s_2 present that proposition under different guises.

This notion of a guise of a proposition stands in serious need of explanation. Salmon introduces it first by analogy with the different guises under which a material object might be presented. But he then, rightly, points out an obvious disanalogy: propositions are not perceivable in the way that material objects are. (This difficulty might, in fact, be circumvented if a facts-first theorist used the notion of a situation or of a state of affairs instead of that of a proposition, and some notion of reference or correspondence instead of 'encoding'. But even this kind of theory will in the end face the same fundamental difficulty as the one which I shall raise for Salmon's theory.)

In the face of the demand for further explanation of the notion of a guise of a proposition, Salmon simply claims, in effect, that there must be such a notion if we are to reject the ordinary intuitions which underlie (FA), without abandoning differences of informativeness.[5] He appears to hold that one will only find the notion of a guise of a proposition problematic if one accepts one of the false semantic theories which he takes to provide the only ways of accommodating the intuitions he rejects. That means that his defence of the notion of a guise of a proposition is no stronger than his attack on the ordinary intuitions. This is ironic, since it seems that the notion of a guise will itself vindicate an attitude idiom for which the ordinary intuitions about belief are appropriate.

If he is to allow that there can be informative metaphysical explanations, Salmon will need to allow that two sentences can present the same proposition under different guises.[6] Indeed, any theory like Salmon's must allow this if it is to account for the difference between 'Hesperus is Hesperus' and 'Hesperus is Phosphorus' *outside* attitude contexts. Salmon also holds that believing something is believing a proposition under a guise. Again,

---

[4] Salmon, *Frege's Puzzle*, ch.8.104–5.
[5] Ibid. 107–9.
[6] He does; see *Frege's Puzzle*, 113.

he must do this if he is to make error intelligible at all. These two commitments are enough to enable us to reconstruct our ordinary intuitions.

Let us introduce a new three-gap expression, 'Bel$_3$'. We can use it to make reports of belief of this form:

(1) Bel$_3(a, p, q)$.

This is to be read as saying that *a* believes the proposition that *p* under the guise which '*q*' presents.

The proposition that *p* will be the same as the proposition that *q*, even if '*p*' and '*q*' are different. A reasonable economy of notation therefore suggests itself: we do not need the '*p*' position to capture the facts expressed by reports of the form of (1)—we have already fixed the proposition believed (in Salmon's sense of 'proposition') once we have an appropriate guise-capturing replacement for '*q*'.

Let us then move to reports which use a two-gap expression, 'Bel$_2$', of this form:

(2) Bel$_2(a, p)$.

This says that *a* believes some proposition under the guise which '*p*' presents.

If 'Hesperus is Hesperus' and 'Hesperus is Phosphorus' present the same proposition under different guises, they will not be automatically intersubstitutable within the '*p*' position of reports of the form of (2). This means that Salmon's own notion of a guise of a proposition, if it is to allow room for two sentences to encode the same proposition under different guises, must allow to be legitimate a form of locution to which the ordinary intuitions may properly be applied.

And surely (2) is just a fancy way of writing what we would normally express by means of belief-reporting sentences. Salmon's provocative view seems, within this picture, to be the result of unmotivatedly choosing to regard the '*p*' position in reports of the form '*a* believes that *p*' as being subject to the constraints appropriate for the '*p*' rather than the '*q*' position in reports of the form of (1).

That means that we should be able to explain the notion of a guise of a proposition within the framework provided by (FA). And we can. Let us say, following Frege, that the things individuated by

---

[7] The quotation marks here, and in the explanation of (2) below, are used to refer to whatever replaces the quoted letter, in line with the Notational Convention.

the intuitive substitutivity conditions on attitude contexts are *thoughts*. Then a guise of a proposition will be a thought. The problem of explaining how a sentence can present a proposition under one guise rather than another will then be the same as the problem of explaining how a sentence can express one thought rather than another. This is not yet solved, of course: that is a task for a theory of content. But what we can see is that, if a facts-first theory is to avoid the problems faced by PCA, it will have to legitimate the very notions it claims to undermine.

Salmon's own discussion comes to the very brink of re-introducing the Fregean notions it claims to be abandoning.[8] What marks the difference between us? The point seems to be this: for Salmon, the conditions on substitution in the 'p' position in (1) are determined by *semantics*, whereas those in the 'q' position in (1) (or the 'p' position in (2)) are merely *pragmatic*. Infringing the semantic conditions, I take it, leads to *falsehood*; whereas infringing the pragmatic conditions produces no more than infelicity, or uninformativeness, or something like that. But this distinction does not seem ultimately sustainable. Presumably it is a question of fact whether a particular belief report is infelicitous, or misleading, or whatever. I must then be able to introduce a new kind of attitude report whose *truth* depends upon its pragmatic felicity. And the conditions on *truth*-preserving substitution within this new kind of context will then match those we all already thought applied to ordinary belief contexts.

That should be enough to deflate the claims of a facts-first theory to provide an alternative to our intuitive acceptance of (FA). But one might wonder whether facts-first theories are not also objectionable from the perspective of a scientific metaphysics, in being committed to Platonism.

I shall not pursue this far, but there are at least hints of Platonism about a facts-first theory. First, the way that the metaphor of a guise is used in Salmon's version suggests that a guise can be lifted, like a veil. This would imply that we can make sense of a proposition, in Salmon's sense, stripped of all guises, guiselessly naked; the nature of propositions would then be fixed independently of their guises. This is just a guise-talk version of Platonism.

A stronger hint of Platonism comes from the general conception of language which seems to be presupposed by facts-first theories.

---

[8] *Frege's Puzzle*, 115–18.

We should ask why it should seem plausible to suppose at the outset that the function of declarative sentences is just to 'encode' propositions, in Salmon's version, or, in an alternative terminology, to refer to situations or states of affairs. It is hard to think of a motivation for this very direct form of realism which does not involve the idea that the relations between language and the world are fixed in advance of, or at least without essential reliance upon, any considerations to do with what it would be to think about the world. And that again sounds Platonistic.

These hints of Platonism are suggestive, but I shall not develop them here. (I shall return to them briefly in 13.2.) What matters for the moment is what we learn from the failure of PCA, and the collapse of a facts-first theory's attempt to provide an alternative account of informativeness. A scientific metaphysics requires the individuation of facts to be different from the individuation of thoughts: it must be possible for two sentences to describe the same fact while expressing different thoughts.

4

Scientism

4.1. Scientism as a General Metaphysical Scheme

One way of trying to secure informativeness in metaphysical explanation is to align metaphysics with natural science. The general idea will be to use the manifest informativeness of natural-scientific explanations to provide the basis for informative metaphysics, and to use experimental testing as the method for determining the truth of proposed metaphysical explanations.

I shall consider a particular version of this basic idea, which I call *scientism*. In fact, I think that the criticisms of scientism will undermine any attempt to develop a scientific metaphysics by aligning metaphysics with natural science. That should serve to justify the use of the word *scientism* as the name of a particular target of attack.

I define scientism as the thesis that every expression which can genuinely be correctly applied—which can be used in saying something true—is reducible to some expression of a natural science.

If scientism is offered as a way of providing a scientific metaphysics, we can understand how it imposes *part* of a condition of adequacy upon metaphysical explanations. It fixes a conception of explanatory priority for reductions by isolating a certain class of statements, or a certain vocabulary, as basic. These statements, the words of this vocabulary, are prior to all others, and all other statements stand in need of reduction to them.

Since this is the way in which the conception of explanatory priority is fixed, scientism cannot allow that all expressions are expressions of natural science. There must be some non-scientific expressions, or else there would be nothing to reduce, and no conception of priority. In particular, if scientism is to provide a scientific metaphysics within which one might propose a philosophical theory of conceptual content, no discipline which involves expressions of conceptual content can be counted as a natural science. Thus, sociology, anthropology, economics, and conceptual-level psychology will not be counted as natural sciences for the purposes of a scientism which hopes to provide a theory of content.

In fact, it is plausible to think that these disciplines would have not to be counted as natural sciences anyway, whatever the purposes to which one might put scientism. For it seems that, if ascriptions of conceptual content are to be counted as within the domain of natural science, then so will the concepts which might be ascribed in such ascriptions—which would again leave nothing to be reduced.

We are concerned, then, with a theory which counts as basic the expressions of just those natural sciences which do not deal in ascriptions of conceptual content. Particular brands of scientism may also embrace the thesis of the unity of science, in effect just counting the expressions of *physics* as basic. But I shall just be concerned with the general view, which need not be committed to the unity of science.

Scientism, as I have characterized it, is a familiar and very widely held view. Sometimes it is called 'naturalism', by those who want to present it as plausible ('natural'). But for all its popularity, I think it is vulnerable to decisive objections.

As I have noted, scientism provides a fairly clear conception of the condition of explanatory priority which reductions have to meet. But this is only half of what a scientific metaphysics needs to provide in the way of a condition of adequacy for metaphysical explanations. Scientism is silent about the condition of factual equivalence which adequate reductions must meet. This is no accident. I shall offer two arguments to show that scientism can provide *no* operable condition of factual equivalence, and so *cannot* support a scientific metaphysics.

This is the place to anticipate an objection. Many of those who will appear to be the target of the arguments of the next two sections will not like to think of themselves as concerned with 'metaphysics' at all; so they might feel unconcerned that scientism cannot support a scientific metaphysics. My arguments might even serve to reinforce their view that 'metaphysics' is bunk.

This bolt-hole does not exist. Any view which places restrictions on the kinds of vocabulary which can be used to say something true thereby places a restriction on the kinds of fact there can be. There is no serious sense of 'metaphysical' in which that is not a metaphysical commitment. Moreover, the view I have called scientism makes explicit use of the notion of reduction. There is no serious sense of 'reduction' which does not rest on some conception of the 'true in virtue of' relation. So scientism is explicitly committed to the idea of metaphysical explanation in my sense (the sense of 1.2). There is no room for scientism to pretend that my criticisms do not apply to it.

4.2. The First Argument Against Scientism

What is distinctive of the natural sciences which form the accredited base for scientism? A plausible suggestion is something we might call the *non-a-priori requirement*:

(NAP) Where an explanatory connection is describable in terms of an accredited natural science, it is impossible to argue a priori from the nature of the *explanandum* to the nature of the *explanans*.

There are one or two exceptions to this, and some might feel some reservations. I will return to these later.

(NAP) is certainly at least initially plausible. More important, scientism itself seems to be committed to its truth.

The way in which scientism hopes to provide *informative* metaphysical explanations is by providing a posteriori explanations, and the way it hopes to check the correctness of metaphysical explanations is by testing them a posteriori, in experiments. The scientistic philosopher characteristically wants to cut free from a priori 'speculation' (which she will generally dismiss with a condescending chuckle), and get down to the hard facts which can be discovered in the laboratory or 'in the field'.

We need only a few short steps to get from here to a problem for scientism. First, if scientism is to provide a scientific metaphysics, it must accept that statements of the following form can be *true*:

(T) It is true that *p*, because *q*.

Given that, it follows from scientism that the concepts involved in such statements must either be, or be reducible to, expressions of the accredited natural sciences. In particular, the 'true in virtue of' relation, which is an explanatory relation after all, must meet the condition imposed by (NAP). The general point of scientism requires that anyway: that is how it secures informativeness and testability in metaphysical explanations.

It follows from this that whatever account is provided of thoughts or concepts, the nature of a thought can provide no a priori constraint on the nature of that in virtue of which it is true; and the nature of a concept can provide no a priori constraint on the nature of that of which it is a concept. For example, we can infer nothing from the concept of causation about the nature of causation itself (the real relation in the objective world).

That means that there can be no a priori constraint on what counts as a description of the same fact. Might there be an a posteriori discoverable constraint? It is hard to make sense of a posteriori discovery without a priori constraint. Here is one way of making the point.

We can only make sense of a posteriori discovery where we can make sense of a posteriori refutation. What is involved in the refutation of an empirical theory T can be expressed schematically very simply. We have, first, some conditional of the following form:

(1) If T is true, then p.

And, secondly, we discover by experiment:

(2) It is not the case that p.

If there are no a priori constraints on our theories, (1) will be a posteriori. But if (1) is a posteriori, it will be refutable only empirically. What would an empirical refutation look like? Well, it would look like accepting (2) on empirical grounds, while still insisting on the truth of T.

This means that, faced with the demonstrable fact expressed by (2), we still have a choice between two options:

(i) Holding that T has been refuted.
(ii) Holding that (1) has been refuted.

And given that (1) is not a priori, it is hard to find anything but pragmatic grounds for the choice. It becomes a merely pragmatic matter whether an absolutely perfectly run experiment even counts as evidence against a theory.[1]

---

[1] This puts in question Quine's right to the notion of 'recalcitrant experience' in 'Two Dogmas of Empiricism' (in his *From a Logical Point of View* (New York: Harper and Row, 1953)), 20–46, given his abandonment there of the a priori. For a similar worry, see G. Forbes, *The Metaphysics of Modality* (Oxford: Clarendon Press, 1985), 225–6.

This view is unacceptable. It is also at odds with the practice of the sciences to which the scientistic philosopher defers. And its abandonment of belief in the power of reason is incompatible with the motivation for a scientific metaphysics.

It was shown, first, that, given (NAP), scientism could provide no a priori constraint on what counts as a description of the same fact. It now appears that there can be no a posteriori constraint either. Given (NAP), scientism cannot offer an operable condition of factual equivalence for reductions. As far as anyone can tell, anything goes.

Might we question (NAP)? There are two kinds of apparent exception. First, it seems likely that all we could ever say about some kinds of cause is that they are the causes of a certain kind of effect. The only possible characterization of the cause is precisely as the cause of its typical effects. This might have been believed of gravity, for example. This kind of counter-example to (NAP) will hardly help scientism, though. That there are *some* causes whose nature can only be described in terms of their effects seems inevitable in any science which has a range of *fundamental* explanatory properties or theoretical primitives. Those fundamental properties will only be characterizable in terms of their characteristic effects. But *which* causes can be described only in this minimal way will depend upon which theory is empirically confirmed. So, although there will be exceptions to (NAP), it will be an a posteriori matter which they are. And that seems bad enough for any scientistic attempt to provide constraints on what counts as a description of the same fact.

Secondly, it might seem that *this* claim could provide the basis for exceptions to (NAP):

(3) Physical effects have physical causes.

On the basis of that we might claim to know a priori of the cause of any given physical effect at least that it is physical.

(3) can be read in two ways: on one it is a priori, but makes no substantial claim about the causes of physical effects, and so says nothing about their nature; on the other, it does make a substantial claim, but it is not a priori. There is no reading which generates counter-examples to (NAP). On the a priori reading, (3) simply asserts the definitional completeness of physics; it means, in effect, that our physics will need to be revised in whatever way is necessary

to keep (3) true. This reading makes no substantial claim about the causes of physical effects, since it is not committed to any view about what physical causes are like. To take (3) as making a substantial claim, we need to take it as a claim about *our* physics, in which case it is probably false, and certainly not a priori.

4.3. The Second Argument Against Scientism

The first argument against scientism depends on the specific character of the accredited natural sciences to which all significant concepts must be reduced. The second argument is more general.

I have already argued that scientism must hold that not all expressions are expressions of natural science, if it is to provide any conception of explanatory priority for metaphysical explanations. So it must accept that there are two categories of expression: those which are natural-scientific, and those which are not. This is enough to create a serious difficulty.

If it is to support a scientific metaphysics, scientism must provide a condition of factual equivalence for reductions. Such a condition of factual equivalence can be formulated in terms of a sentential context: intersubstitutability within that context will be the condition for two expressions counting as describing or referring to the same object, property, or fact. Let us suppose that the standard of factual equivalence for scientistic reductions is set by some context '$R \ldots$'.

Scientism now faces a dilemma. Is the expression 'R' which introduces that context an expression of natural science, or not? If it is, then it is hard to see how it can be well defined except for substitutions within the context it introduces of expressions which themselves belong to natural science. But if it is well defined only for those, it cannot provide any significant constraint upon the reductions we are interested in—reductions of non-scientific expressions to the expressions of natural science.

If, on the other hand, 'R' is *not* itself an expression of natural science, it too stands in need of reduction. But that gives us an insuperable difficulty. For this reduction cannot be carried out in any significantly constrained way. The constraints on reduction are precisely what the reduction is needed to legitimate. So scientism can acknowledge no significant condition of factual equivalence. Whether '*R*' is an expression of natural science or not, scientism can provide no basis for a scientific metaphysics.

I can imagine a worry about the first horn of this dilemma. Someone might be unhappy about the assumption, that, if '*R*' is an expression of natural science, it can be well-defined only for substitutions within the context it introduces by expressions which are themselves expressions of natural science. Why should this be so? The answer is that, unless this were true, it would be hard to see what could be meant by calling '*R*' an expression of natural science. If it was well defined equally for scientific and non-scientific intersubstitutions, what grounds could we have for calling it a scientific expression?

This second objection to scientism seems to me to be good. Its speed is slightly astonishing; to make it convincing, we need to explain how such a swift objection could strike home.

4.4. Further Remarks on Scientism

These two arguments against scientism are likely to be met with some incredulity. It seems surprising that a position which seems to have such general appeal should be capable of such swift refutation. What is it about scientism which makes it so quickly vulnerable?

The reason why the two arguments can work so quickly is that they both exploit the same basic defect in scientism. It is required of a general metaphysical theory that it should apply to itself. The two arguments show that scientism fails when its demands are applied to itself. But it is not surprising that scientism should fail in this way, since those sciences which scientism can recognize as accredited natural sciences differ from metaphysical theories precisely in that respect: they do not have to apply to themselves. That fact ought to have been taken into account before it was proposed to treat metaphysical issues as issues of natural science.

The explanation of the swiftness of the arguments is therefore this. Scientism is only plausible because of a basic oversight. The arguments can be swift because they work by drawing attention to what has been overlooked. We can make this vivid if we characterize scientism, reasonably enough, as being committed to the truth of this:

(1) There are only scientific facts.

If (1) is true, it states a fact which is not itself a fact of natural science. So if (1) is true, it is false.

Another way of explaining why scientism is unsuitable as the basis of a scientific metaphysics is to suggest that it is covertly Platonist. In fact, the general position is reasonably represented as a rather arbitrary form of Platonism. Scientism seems to hold that just one kind of vocabulary—the vocabulary of natural science—is suitable for describing the world as it is in itself. Any other vocabulary can only really describe the world if it is reducible to that basic vocabulary. This sort of distinction between kinds of concepts seems already Platonist. But if it is, scientism is a rationally unmotivated form of Platonism, since, from a Platonistic perspective, there can be no truth-related reason for thinking that one set of concepts fits the world better than another.

Suppose it is granted that scientism is a Platonistic view. How does that relate to the arguments I have presented? If what is wrong with scientism as a basis for a scientific metaphysics is that it is Platonistic, those arguments ought to be exploiting that fact if they get to the heart of the matter.

The first argument rests on scientism's commitment to the claim that the relation between a concept and what it is a concept of is an a posteriori relation. Does that commitment itself involve Platonism?

I think it does. Conceptualism holds that the nature of concepts at least partially determines the nature of the objects, properties, and facts to which they correspond. If this is not to be an idealist position, concepts have to be thought of as timelessly existing things, and the kind of determination involved will also have to be atemporal. But it is hard to understand an atemporal determination except as being a priori knowable. That is, conceptualism seems to be precisely the view that the nature of a concept imposes a priori constraints on what it can be a concept of.

In fact, this seems to mean just that there are a priori truths. For an a priori truth is a truth which meets something like this condition: an understanding of the concepts involved is a sufficient basis for knowing that it is true, given just enough logic to make the relevant derivations. A priori truths seem to be of two vaguely demarcated kinds which we might describe as the *obvious* and the *unobvious*. The *obvious* a priori truths meet this condition: one does not count as possessing the concepts involved if one does not hold them to be true. (Very elementary arithmetical truths— '2 + 3 = 5', say—are clear examples.) *Unobvious* a priori truths meet this condition: they can be derived from obvious a priori truths by means of principles whose validity is itself *obvious*. If this traditional conception of the a priori is anything like correct, conceptualism seems to demand little more than this: to count as possessing a concept, one must get at least something right. And Platonism emerges as the view that concept possession is not constrained by any requirement that one must get things right in order to count as possessing a concept.

This point is illuminating about both scientism and Platonism. Scientism is shown to be Platonistic, because of its abandonment of a priori constraints on the 'true in virtue of' relation. And we can understand clearly the sense in which Platonism leaves it an open question whether our concepts really 'fit' the world: the nature of concepts puts no constraint on the nature of the world of which they are concepts.

This in turn reinforces two connections which have already been made. First, it underlines the link between the two tenets of conceptualism. The first argument for the claim that scientism cannot provide a scientific metaphysics turns out to be inextricable from the charge that scientism is Platonistic. Secondly, it confirms the connection between conceptualism and Kant. Kant held that a scientific metaphysics was only possible if there could be synthetic a priori truths of a certain kind.[2] What does 'synthetic' mean here? Kant's official definition seems to make 'synthetic' mean almost the same as 'non-trivial' or 'potentially informative'.[3] But in the larger context of what he actually does, a synthetic truth seems to be one which is in a sense *genuinely about* the world which we experience. The requirement that there must be synthetic a priori truths then becomes the requirement that there must be a priori truths which are genuinely about the world.

But that is in effect just what conceptualism is insisting on, when it insists that the nature of concepts imposes some a priori constraint on the nature of the things of which they are concepts. We can, therefore, see the first argument against scientism as an

---

[2] Kant, *Critique of Pure Reason*, B19–20.
[3] Ibid., B10–11.

argument for the Kantian claim that a scientific metaphysics requires there to be synthetic a priori truths.

What is it about scientism that makes it vulnerable to the *second* of the two arguments I gave? It must be some more general, structural feature of scientism which causes the problem here, since the argument does not depend on anything specific to the natural sciences.

I think that what causes the trouble is the fact that scientism is a potentially revisionary form of foundationalism. By 'potentially revisionary' I mean that it could, in principle, tell us that some concept which had previously seemed perfectly in order was not in fact properly regulated at all. It seems that any potentially revisionary form of foundationalism will be subject to just the same kind of argument. In so far as it is foundationalist, it will distinguish between two sorts of concept—those which belong to the foundation, and those which do not. And, if it is potentially revisionary, any concept which does not belong to the foundation runs the risk of being shown not to be properly regulated, until it has been reduced to the foundation concepts. We can then ask whether the concept which defines the standard of equivalence for reductions itself belongs to the foundation, or not; and this will create just the kind of dilemma with which scientism is faced in the second argument.

A potentially revisionary foundationalism seems inevitably Platonistic. It must hold that it might turn out that not all concepts fit the world. This in itself requires a conception of the world as fixed independently of any concept of it. There has to be a conception of a standard of genuine correspondence to the world which a concept does not meet just in virtue of being a concept.

The moral of this is that we should reject any kind of potentially revisionary form of foundationalism, if we are hoping for a scientific metaphysics. In fact, I think we should reject foundationalism altogether. We can certainly make sense of a non-revisionary foundationalism, but it is hard to see how it could support a scientific metaphysics.

Non-revisionary forms of foundationalism are in fact quite common.[4] They start by taking for granted the whole range of our concepts, and adopting a provisional list of basic vocabulary. They

---

[4] This appears to be the kind of position adopted in P. F. Strawson, *Individuals* (London: Methuen, 1959).

then attempt to reduce the non-basic to the basic, with the difference that, in this kind of theory, where reduction fails, the concept shown to be irreducible is counted not meaningless, but *basic*. When this happens, the foundation simply expands. Alternatively, it may turn out that some of the concepts originally taken to be basic are actually reducible to others; in that case, the foundation will contract.

A non-revisionary foundationalism may be a useful position to adopt in an *ad hominem* argument against a revisionary foundationalist, but it is hard to make it both a position of interest and a suitable support for a scientific metaphysics. Foundationalist systems fix their conception of explanatory priority by reference to a class of basic propositions or concepts, which are thereby deemed to be prior to all others. The trouble with a non-revisionary foundationalism is that this basic class is flexible, and that makes it hard to see what conception of explanatory priority is involved, unless it is simply guided by the thought that those concepts which can be non-circularly defined are basic, while those which cannot are non-basic. But if we have *no* conception of explanatory priority, we have no metaphysical system; and if the criterion of basicness is just not being non-circularly definable, the class of basic concepts seems likely to so far outnumber the class of non-basic concepts that there will be little for philosophical explanation to do. For example, if two concepts can each be defined only in terms which involve the other, both will have to be counted as basic, but the definitions which run from each to the other will not be counted as metaphysical explanations, unless we appeal to some non-foundationalist conception of explanatory priority.

So it seems to me that a general metaphysical scheme which is intended to provide a scientific metaphysics should not be foundationalist. Some people who are impressed by the regress argument for foundationalism will be worried by this. They should not be: the regress argument is invalid.

The regress argument for metaphysical foundationalism begins with the premiss that all explanations must come to an end somewhere, and concludes that there must be a set of basic propositions or concepts in whose terms all other concepts or propositions must be explained. But this argument is just invalid: it rests, in effect, on an ambiguity in the apparent scope of the quantifiers involved.

The only sense of the premiss in which we have any reason to believe it may be expressed like this:

(2) For each explanation, there must be somewhere where *that* explanation ends.

This expresses the primitive but intuitive thought that an explanation does not count as an explanation until it is finished, until the demand for explanation which prompted it is met. But the conclusion needed for foundationalism is this:

(3) There must be a single place (a set of basic propositions or concepts) where *all* explanations end.

And (3) just does not follow from (2). It is therefore safe to drop foundationalism. (How we make sense of an alternative is another matter: I shall return to it in 5.3.)

There is still something surprising about the thought that adherence to the project of a scientific (properly constrained) metaphysics should lead one away from foundationalism. The idea of metaphysics having to be scientific if it is to be done at all seems naturally associated with a tough-minded dismissal of fantasy and mumbo-jumbo, which in turn is naturally associated with certain forms of foundationalism. There is an irony here, of course: it is the irony brought out by saying, with heavy emphasis on the words involved, that *scientism* cannot support a *scientific* metaphysics.

I shall conclude this section with one further moral to be drawn from the failure of scientism. Since the notion of aboutness (or of reference, in the case of language) is derivative from the notion of a thought's being *true in virtue of* a fact, the failure of scientism means that there cannot be a causal theory of reference, or, more generally, a wholly a posteriori theory of aboutness. That will have significant consequences for any theory of content.

But it should be emphasized that the conclusion is that there cannot be a *wholly* a posteriori theory of aboutness or reference. Conceptualism is consistent with the recognition of natural-kind terms. I take a natural-kind term to be one which is not itself a technical term of a natural science, but for whose application some natural science is authoritative. There will be an a posteriori, genuinely empirical, specification of the essence of what a natural-kind term refers to. All that conceptualism requires is that it must be fixed a priori—as knowable just in virtue of a lay understanding of the term—both that some natural science is authoritative about its application, and what kind of natural science is authoritative. There can be natural-kind terms, but it cannot *just turn out* that a term is a natural-kind term. That seems intuitive enough anyway: how else could one claim that the natural-scientific specification gives the essence of the very same thing that the lay people were talking about before?

5

A Proposal for a Scientific Metaphysics

5.1. The Knowledge Constraint

We now need to supply a condition of factual equivalence for reductions, and a conception of explanatory priority for metaphysical explanations. I shall begin with the condition of factual equivalence.

The condition of factual equivalence for reductions determines what it is for two expressions to count as expressions for the same object, property, or fact. If we are to allow for the possibility of informative metaphysical explanation, this cannot be conceptual equivalence. We need to allow that two expressions for the same thing may nevertheless express different concepts or ways of thinking.

Let us try to construct a condition of factual equivalence using just that thought. We want to define a notion of sameness which has precisely this property: the same thing can be thought of in different ways.

How can two concepts or ways of thinking of the same object be different? How do we have to think of concepts or ways of thinking to make sense of that possibility? It should not be thought that there is no issue here. What we need to balance are, on the one hand, sufficient closeness between concept and object to allow the concept to be properly *of* the object, and, on the other, sufficient distance to allow room for several concepts of the same object.

There is only one natural suggestion in response to this: Frege's. Frege thought of what we call a concept as being determined by a 'mode of presentation of the object'—as the technical translation has it—or, more naturally, as the way in which the object is given.[1] The idea is simple: a particular way of thinking of an object is

---

[1] Frege, 'On Sense and Meaning', in Frege, *Collected Papers on Mathematics, Logic, and Philosophy*, ed. B. McGuinness.

characterized by a particular kind of epistemological access to that object.

This makes natural sense of the fact that there can be different ways of thinking of the same thing. On the one hand, there is a tight connection between concept and object—the connection of knowledge—which makes sense of one being genuinely *of* the other. And, on the other hand, it seems that anything *objective* can be known about in more than one way, or under different conditions. The planet Venus can be sighted in the morning or in the evening; the same colour can be observed in different lighting conditions; the same number can be the value of different functions. If this were not possible, it would be hard to make sense of error. That is the sense in which the point applies to anything *objective*, since it is a fair definition of what is objective that it is something one could be wrong about.

So a way of thinking of something, a concept, is naturally aligned to a kind of epistemological access to that thing, or a way of knowing about it. Given the basic conceptualist thought that the nature of a thing is not fixed independently of concepts of it, this means that the nature of a thing is not fixed independently of the ways there are of knowing about it. In short, the nature of an object, property, or fact is determined by what it would be to have knowledge of it.

At this point there will be immediate protests that we have ended up with a rather old-fashioned form of verificationism. I shall return to that issue in the next section, pausing here just to note that the kind of old-fashioned verificationism which comes to mind here was itself designed precisely to constrain free-wheeling metaphysics. In the meantime, let us press on and try to fix a condition of factual equivalence for reductions.

The general idea here is that it is distinctive of each particular kind of thing that there are certain particular ways of knowing about things of that kind. The basis of the condition of factual equivalence I want to propose is this thought: two expressions count as expressions for the same object, property, or fact just in case there are precisely the same ways of knowing about the things they are expressions for. That basic idea is quite simple. We now need to make it a bit more formal so that we have a concrete proposal for a criterion of equivalence.

The suggestion is that what is distinctive about each fact is what it would be to know that fact in particular. Here is a dummy claim about what it would be to know something:

(K1) For any '*p*' and any *x*, there is a '*q*' such that, if *x* were to know that *p*, *x* would believe that *p* because, in fact *q*.[2]

This is just a dummy claim, since the 'because' here is to be read as standing for that explanatory relation, whatever it is, which must hold between a belief and a fact for the belief to count as knowledge of that fact.

Dropping the quantifiers from (K1), we get the following schema:

(K2) If *a* were to know that *p*, *a* would believe that *p* because, in fact, *q*.

Given the definition of 'because' here, the replacement for '*p*' in any instance of the schema will always be a suitable replacement for '*q*' too. It is quite all right to say, for example, that, if I knew that rats are rodents, I would believe that rats are rodents because, in fact, rats are rodents. No alternative description of the fact is *needed* in the 'because'-clause.

It is at least arguable that the explanatory relation expressed by 'because' in (K1) and (K2) is the same whatever kind of fact is at issue. If it is the same, a general analysis of knowledge might be possible; if it is not, it will not be. But if the explanatory relation is invariant across different kinds of fact, we cannot use it directly to fix the condition of equivalence for reductions that we are after. What we want is precisely something that does vary between different kinds of fact, if it is to operate as a criterion of identity for facts.

Suppose, then, that this explanatory relation is constant. It might be characterized in terms of reliability, or whatever. Nevertheless there are differences between the ways in which this explanatory relation is realized in the case of different kinds of fact. I may know that my flask is red, and that 9 is the square root of 81, in virtue of my reliable connection (say) with the fact that my flask is red, and the fact that 9 is the square root of 81, respectively. But the realization of the reliable connection will be quite different in the

---

[2] The quotation marks here indicate substitutional quantification, in line with the Notational Convention.

two cases: it will be dependent on vision in one case, for example, but not in the other.

Let us call what are differently described to account for the different kinds of knowledge here *realizing connections* between beliefs and facts. Now let '*R*' be a schematic letter restricted to replacements by fullish descriptions of realizing connections. We can give the form of a description of the relation between a belief and a fact, when someone knows something, as follows:

(1) *R* [*a* believes that *p*, *q*].

An instance of (1) will give some fairly full description of the connection between a particular person and a fact, in virtue of which that person's belief counts as being explanatorily related to a fact in the way required for the belief to count as knowledge of the fact. Naturally, replacements for '*R*' will vary with differences in the replacements for '*p*' (since different things are required for different beliefs to count as knowledge), and may also vary with differences in replacements for *a* (since different people can know the same thing in different ways). They should also vary between *some* replacements for '*q*'.

Realizing connections, which vary from fact to fact, do seem to be the right kind of thing to exploit to produce a condition of factual equivalence for reductions. To be able to exploit them, we will need appropriate transformations of (K1) and (K2).

Let an asterisk prefixed to an expression indicate the subjunctive transformation of that expression which is appropriate to the context in which it occurs. Thus, if I wrote,

(2) If I were drunk, *[I am happy],

that would mean:

(3) If I were drunk, I would be happy.

Using that device, we can make a claim analogous to (K1), involving the notion of a realizing connection:

(K3) For any '*p*' and any *x*, there is some '*R*' and some '*q*' such that if *x* were to know that *p*, *[*R* [*x* believes that *p*, *q*]].

Dropping the quantifiers, we get this schema:

(K4) If *a* were to know that *p*, *[*R* [*a* believes that *p*, *q*]].

This schema has a property it inherits from (K2). Any replacement for '*p*' in an instance of (K4) will always be an appropriate replacement for 'q' too. This follows from the definition of a realizing connection.

We are now in a position to state a condition of factual equivalence in line with the initial thought that the nature of a fact is determined by what it would be to have knowledge of it. First, recall the schema used to characterize metaphysical explanation:

(T) It is true that p, because q.

The idea is that the constraints on substitution within the 'q' position in (T), when (T) is used to characterize metaphysical explanation, are the same as those within the 'q' position in (K4). More formally, the condition is this:

(TK) An instance of (T) is true if and only if the replacement for 'q' in that instance of (T) is also an appropriate replacement for 'q' in all instances of (K4) which have the same replacement for 'p'.

This formulation allows that there may be a range of different kinds of realizing connection supporting knowledge of the same truth. It exploits the fact that the range will be different for different kinds of fact.

Let us call this condition of factual equivalence the *knowledge constraint*. It seems to me to have a number of things going for it, from a conceptualist point of view. I shall mention five.

First, something like it seems to be required by the combination of two things to which conceptualism is committed: the dependence of the nature of things upon the nature of the concepts of them; and the fact that thoughts must be individuated differently from facts if there are to be any interesting metaphysical explanations. The only natural account of concepts which makes sense of there being different concepts of the same thing precisely aligns concepts with ways of knowing about things.

Secondly, the knowledge constraint permits uninformative metaphysical explanations. (Why is it true that she is mowing the lawn? Because, as a matter of fact, she is mowing the lawn.) These are permitted because replacements for 'p' in (K4) are always suitable replacements for 'q' too.

Thirdly, although the criterion allows thoughts and facts to be individuated differently, the metaphysical theory which is partially expressed by (TK) makes sense of the interdependence between metaphysical theories and theories of content with which I began (in 1.1). The condition of factual equivalence for reductions is stated in terms which involve the notion of belief, even though factual equivalence is not defined as conceptual equivalence.

Fourthly, on plausible assumptions, the knowledge constraint allows there to be a priori constraints on what can count as expressions for the same thing. All that is required is that, just in virtue of possessing a concept, one knows something about how one must be situated in order to know facts describable in terms of that concept. That is extremely plausible in the case of language. In learning a word, one does not just learn its extension (how *could* one learn *just* that?): one learns also when the word can be used with confidence, when one can easily be fooled, and so on. A conception of what is involved in acquiring a concept which is like that would be enough to ensure that (TK) permitted a priori constraints on whether two expressions count as expressions for the same thing.

Fifthly, (TK) demands no more from the difference between thoughts and facts than is safe from a conceptualist point of view. The difference is basically one of individuation: several thoughts may be made true by one and the same fact. All that is added to that is something which seems a requirement of objectivity: the same thing can be known about in different ways. There is no basis in (TK) for the metaphor of a spatial distance between thoughts and facts which leads to Platonism.

All this, however, is entirely abstract. How does the knowledge constraint actually work? How does it *constrain* proposed metaphysical explanations?

A simple example of its application is provided by 'Hesperus' and 'Phosphorus'. If I say that Hesperus is Phosphorus, I have given the basis of a whole series of metaphysical explanations, in the sense of 1.2. It follows from the identity that facts about Hesperus can be redescribed as facts about Phosphorus, and vice versa. To make sense of this, each of the names, 'Hesperus' and 'Phosphorus', must be associated with a different kind of epistemological access to the same thing. One name might be associated with evening access, the other with morning access. What the knowledge constraint requires is this: what makes morning access, for example, count as a way of knowing about an object must itself show that the object known is the kind of thing which evening access might also provide knowledge of. The condition is met: what makes morning access count as a way of knowing about an object also determines that the object known is a persisting celestial body, which could in principle appear at other times. (We think of Phosphorus as something which appears in the morning, not as a morning appearance.)

That is just a simple example. We can see how the knowledge constraint works in more interesting cases by considering the view that 'water' is a natural-kind term, and that the essence of water is revealed by the chemical formula 'H_2O'.

The claim that water is H_2O is a reductive proposal within the spirit of the conception of metaphysical explanation I have been concerned with. Here is the kind of test which the knowledge constraint recommends. We generally count ourselves as being able to tell when we are, for example, *drinking* water. That is, we allow our sense of taste to be a good judge of water, particularly when combined with our sense of the feel of it in our mouths and throats. The first question to ask is this:

(a) If water were H_2O, would the faculties which we take to be reliable discriminators of water actually be reliable?

I take it that in order to answer this question we would have to know something about correlations between questions of taste and feel, on the one hand, and molecular structure, on the other. The function of question (*a*) is chiefly exploratory, however: its purpose is to get us to focus on the kinds of circumstance in which we take ourselves to know whether what we are drinking is water. The crucial question is this one:

(b) Should we be prepared to discount the authority of our intuitive judgements in any circumstances in which they were at odds with the judgements of the chemist?

This question tests our conception of what is involved in knowing that something is water. If our confidence in our judgements of taste relies upon a belief that taste is a reliable indicator of something of chemical interest, then it will seem safe to say that water is a natural, indeed a chemical, kind. But if it does not, the issue at least will not be clear. That seems exactly what is in question when we consider whether water is H_2O. In that case, the knowledge constraint seems to do just what we wanted.

A way of putting the effect of the knowledge constraint is this: in considering whether a proposed analysis of a property-term, say, is adequate, what we need to consider is whether we are prepared to count the perspective adopted by the analysis as *authoritative* about the property in question. That seems to capture exactly the heart of the worries we feel when confronted by crass reductions of anything. It also captures the natural feeling that a threat is posed by scientism: why, we ask, should natural science be authoritative about all that we do and think?

This is the beginning of an answer to another question: does conceptualism, developed in the way of the knowledge constraint, apply to itself? This is a fair question, since it was precisely its failure to apply to itself that undermined scientism. Under the knowledge constraint the question becomes: does the condition of factual equivalence which the knowledge constraint supplies match our conception of when we count as knowing that two expressions are expressions for the same thing? It seems to me to work for simple cases like that of 'Hesperus' and 'Phosphorus', but then it was designed specifically with those in mind. Its treatment of the claim that water is H_2O seems to me to confirm the knowledge constraint's self-applicability in harder cases. There remains a more general question of whether the knowledge constraint provides us with a robust enough conception of facts. I shall turn to that next.

5.2. Is the Knowledge Constraint Verificationist?

Some people will be inclined to reject the knowledge constraint immediately on the grounds that it is verificationist or more generally anti-realist. This kind of charge is too vague to be assessed as it stands. There are different shades of verificationism, and different hues of anti-realism. It needs to be shown that the knowledge constraint is verificationist or anti-realist in a way that is objectionable independently of swift associations with familiar bogies.

Certainly, if it is verificationist to say that for there to be a fact that p there must be something which it would be to know that p, then the knowledge constraint is verificationist. If there is nothing which it would be to know that p, then (TK) will impose no constraint on metaphysical explanations of the alleged fact that p. Anything whatever—even a falsehood—could be used to give a metaphysical explanation of such a supposed fact. If we accept the rather plausible principle that the truth condition of a truth cannot be given by a falsehood, we will find this intolerable.

But this does not make the knowledge constraint obviously objectionable. It does not, for example, make it equivalent to any standard or implausible version of verificationism. Standard forms of verificationism hold that there can be no unknowable (perhaps in principle unknowable) truths, or, at any rate, they do not accept that there might be such truths.

The reason it is not clear that the knowledge constraint involves us in any such verificationism is that the knowledge constraint is formulated using a *subjunctive* conditional, and it is not clear that subjunctive conditionals with impossible antecedents are merely vacuously true. Indeed, so far from this just not being clear, initial indications suggest that it is false.

The reason is that we generally explain why something is impossible by entertaining that impossibility as the antecedent of a subjunctive conditional, and then showing what that would require. (Suppose that Goldbach's conjecture is true; then consider what it would be to know it, if it does not follow from the axioms of arithmetic: now you can see why it is impossible to know it, if it is true but does not follow from the axioms of arithmetic.)

This point even extends to subjunctive conditionals whose antecedents are conceptually or more narrowly logically impossible. (For a case relevant to (K4), consider a replacement for 'p' of the form: p and nobody knows that p.) Most conceptual or logical impossibilities can be proved, non-trivially, to be impossible. (The proof would not settle serious *doubt* in most cases; but it would still explain why the impossible was impossible.) The proof will generally take the form of assuming the impossibility and deriving a contradiction. But it is hard to see how assuming an impossibility in order to derive a contradiction differs in the relevant respects from entertaining that impossibility as the antecedent of a subjunctive conditional whose consequent is the derived contradiction.

That seems to me to be a good initial reason for thinking that subjunctive conditionals with impossible antecedents—even logically impossible antecedents—are not just vacuously true, and hence for thinking that the knowledge constraint does not amount to any standard form of verificationism. This initial reason will not satisfy all of those who analyse subjunctive conditionals in terms of possibility, and therefore are committed to thinking that such conditionals are vacuously true if their antecedents are impossible. I shall consider three manifestations of the kind of disquiet these people might feel.

The first kind of worry has already implicitly been dealt with just in providing the specific condition of factual equivalence for reductions which I have. It is still worth dealing with explicitly, though. Surely, it will be thought, *some* subjunctive conditionals are going to be vacuously true; we might suggest that conditionals beginning 'If green were not green, . . . ' (where that does not mean the same as 'If what is actually green were not green . . . ') are completable in any way we like. The difference between these conditionals and some of those which we seem prepared to countenance seems to lie just in something like the *blatancy* of the impossibility. The difference is surely just *epistemic* at least.

A natural conception of what is required for two expressions to count as expressions for the same object or property holds that they must be intersubstitutable in both antecedents and consequents of subjunctive conditionals. If the substitutivity conditions on any part of any subjunctive conditionals are epistemic, we surely get a seriously anti-realist conception of the individuation of objects and properties.

So runs the worry. It should be clear how it has been implicitly anticipated. If we adopt the knowledge constraint, we do not hold that the condition for any two expressions to count as referring to the same object is just that they be intersubstitutable anywhere within subjunctive conditionals. The condition is rather that they be intersubstitutable just in a specific place in a specific kind of subjunctive conditional—namely, instances of (K4). And it is just not plausible that that position is subject to the restrictively epistemic conditions which might lead to this kind of worry.

Another objection might be put like this. We can explain the initial appearance of significant constraint on the consequents of conditionals whose antecedents are impossible *without* denying that they are vacuously true. If so, the initial argument I gave is powerless. The explanation is simple: these conditionals are vacuously *true*, but they are *not* vacuously *assertible*. Thinking that the initial argument has any weight is just a matter of confusing truth with assertibility, in characteristic anti-realist fashion.[3]

---

[3] This objection, and the next, were suggested by remarks made to me by Tim Williamson.

This objection, like the first, has the nice property that it claims that anti-realism only appears to be avoided in one place if it is covertly assumed in another. But I think it can be met. I do not think that the conditionals I had in mind are only non-vacuously *assertible*. I doubt if anyone else would think they were who was not already committed to the view that they must be vacuously true.

Consider again the hackneyed case of Goldbach's conjecture, on the assumption that it does not follow from the axioms of arithmetic. We would say:

(1) If anyone knew that Goldbach's conjecture is true, she would have completed an infinite check.

According to the objector, this is vacuously true, but non-vacuously assertible. That is, given that antecedent, we could have continued with any consequent we liked, *salva veritate*. But not every continuation would have had the point that this does. The point of this continuation is that it has particular relevance for a *demonstration* of the impossibility of the antecedent.

This does not seem to me to be the function of that consequent, and the point of the conditional is not to demonstrate, merely, that Goldbach's conjecture is unknowable. It seems to me that the incoherence of the idea of completing an infinite check is what *makes* Goldbach's conjecture unknowable. That is, we do not seem just to be being given a reason for *thinking* that it is unknowable; we are being told why it *is* unknowable.

This point looks as if it will generalize. The objector seems committed to denying that there can be genuine explanations of the necessity or impossibility of certain states of affairs. An explanation of the necessity of its being the case that *p* will commit one to something of this form:

(2) If it had not been the case that *p* . . .

And an explanation of the impossibility of its being the case that *p* will commit one to something of this form:

(3) If it had been the case that *p* . . .

The antecedents of the relevant instances of both (2) and (3) are, by hypothesis, impossible. The objector seems committed to regarding such conditionals as providing the basis just of a *demonstration* of the necessity or impossibility of something's being the case; there cannot be *explanations* of such things.

The difference between me and the objector here looks as if it will affect our whole conception of philosophy. Philosophical truths will be both necessary and a priori. According to this objector, they will, therefore, be demonstrable (with luck) but not explicable. According to me, they are explicable too. Indeed, I think we can make out a contrast between kinds of demonstration of philosophical truths: some merely demonstrate, but the deep ones also explain. If this is the kind of thing that is at stake in holding that the knowledge constraint is not verificationist, it seems to me that the knowledge constraint is as safe as anything of this kind can be. Moreover, the knowledge constraint seems on this reading to be entirely in tune with the spirit of conceptualism, which is motivated precisely by the thought that things should be explained.

The last kind of objection I shall consider is a challenge to a kind of trial by logic. It might be said, for example, that those logical systems which make subjunctive conditionals with impossible antecedents vacuously true are far more 'powerful' than those which do not.[4] It will then be suggested that we should accept the diagnosis favoured by the most 'powerful' available logic.

'Powerful' here must mean something like: capable of explaining the validity of intuitively valid arguments. It is claimed that logics which make subjunctive conditionals with impossible antecedents vacuously true are capable of explaining the validity of a far greater range of intuitively valid arguments than those which do not. One might be a little uncertain about the kind of explanation involved, but suppose we accept the claim. What follows?

Perhaps if there was a logical system which explained the validity of every intuitively valid argument, and which involved no semantic infelicities, we should accept its analyses. But there is no such logical system; nor could there be. Why should we then feel driven to accept what the most powerful available logics recommend, given that they are hardly complete?

The only argument I can see for doing this is by analogy with empirical scientific theories. Even if we are aware of faults in a physical theory, for example, we stick with it until we find a better and more comprehensive theory. Similarly, the argument would go, even if we are aware of faults in a logical system, we should stick with it until a better, more comprehensive system is developed.

---

[4] For such a system, see, e.g., D. Lewis, *Counterfactuals* (Oxford: Blackwell, 1973), especially pp. 24–6; Lewis is himself very liberal-minded on the issue.

This seems to me a weak argument in two respects. First, it is not entirely clear what 'sticking with it' amounts to, even in the case of a physical theory. No doubt it involves using it in engineering projects, and giving it a presumption of benefit of doubt in the interpretation of some experiments. But it is not clear that it requires *believing* it.

Secondly, the analogy between an empirical theory and a logical system seems dubious. The fundamental reason for sticking with an empirical theory seems to be that there are empirical tasks to be achieved, and some theory is needed to achieve them. In these circumstances, it seems obviously rational to use the best theory one has, even if one knows that it is flawed. But what is the analogy for a logical system, when no empirical project is at issue? The task to which a logical system might be put, outside of empirical science, is testing the validity of arguments. But it is hard to see how a logical system could strictly be *needed* for such a test. How would one know whether to trust the answer it gave?

The point of disanalogy here arises from the basic role of prediction in shaping and motivating empirical theories. It is because we need to make *some* prediction for every empirical project that we need to use some theory, even if we know that our best theories are flawed. There is no analogous need for prediction which a logical system could serve, when it is not itself being employed within an empirical science. I therefore see no reason to be pushed by an appeal to the 'power' of a logical system into accepting an otherwise counter-intuitive analysis of subjunctive conditionals.

It seems legitimate, then, to allow that subjunctive conditionals with even logically impossible antecedents are not always vacuously true. This allows the knowledge constraint to be distanced from standard forms of verificationism. It is also important for another reason. In 1.3 I pointed out that to make sense of either conceptualism or Platonism we needed to be able to allow that subjunctive conditionals with impossible antecedents could be non-vacuously true. Platonism accepts, and conceptualism denies, that there would have been just those objects, properties, and facts—the ones to which our concepts correspond—even if there had not been those concepts. Once concepts are thought of as existing atemporally, the antecedent of this conditional seems impossible. If the defence I have given here of non-vacuous subjunctive conditionals with impossible antecedents is right, the central claims of both Platonism and conceptualism are intelligible.

The knowledge constraint also differs from standard forms of verificationism in not being foundationalist. Most forms of verificationism have been foundationalist, often because they are attempting to construct a defensible conception of reality while taking seriously the threat of radical scepticism. The Logical Positivists, for example, insisted on verification in terms of sense data. There is a suspicion of a similar stance among more recent *semantic* anti-realists, who are sceptical of a 'verification-transcendent' conception of truth. Some semantic anti-realists are inclined to regard knowledge of the finite, for example, as comparatively secure; quantification over infinite domains then seems problematic, because of the supposed difficulties of 'extending' our knowledge that far.[5] The knowledge constraint remains neutral on all this, and so does not lead to implausible scepticism about particular kinds of fact.

But, for all the contrasts, there is obviously some overlap between the motivations which lead to the knowledge constraint and those which support traditional verificationism. I think the knowledge constraint expresses these more effectively. Consider, for example, perceivable objects—that is, things of the right kind to be perceived (by us). The class of perceivable objects, in this sense, presumably includes things which cannot in fact be perceived by us—or by any sentient being, if there are any others. The thought common to verificationism and the knowledge constraint is that the way such things are to be known, if they are to be known, is essential to them. Verificationists standardly accommodate perceivable objects which cannot be perceived by saying that it is *in principle* possible to perceive them. But this formulation, whatever exactly it means, must run into trouble with Goldbach's conjecture, which surely could not be known to be true, even in principle. The knowledge constraint, by contrast, has no such difficulties with Goldbach's conjecture. There may be other grounds for doubting whether it could be true, if it does not follow from the axioms of arithmetic; but in principle unknowability is not itself ground enough.

[5] See, e.g., C. Wright, 'Strict Finitism', *Synthèse*, 51 (1982), 203–82.

In the light of all this, it seems to me to be largely a terminological matter whether to call the knowledge constraint verificationist. If the description is fair, it is not obviously the description of an offence.

Is the knowledge constraint, or conceptualism more generally, anti-realist? I cannot see that it is committed to an intuitionistic logic, or to the semantic anti-realism which is associated with it by Dummett and his followers.[6] Beyond that, asking whether the position is anti-realist is unhelpful. It simply invites posturing and banner-waving.

In general, there is a range of questions concerning the independence of the world from thoughts, and favouring greater rather than less independence in response to any one of these questions can qualify one as some kind of realist. Conceptualism allows that the mountains of Skye were awesome, craggy, and volcanic long before any thinker existed. In virtue of that it is not idealist, and so counts as realist. But it opposes Platonism, the most extreme form of realism; in that respect it counts as anti-realist. It allows unknowable truths, unlike standard forms of verificationism or semantic anti-realism; in that respect it counts, once again, as realist.

In this connection, it is worth distancing conceptualism from some features of Kant's view. Conceptualism is a broadly Kantian position, but it is not committed to such things as this, for example: 'Thus the order and regularity in the appearances, which we entitle *nature*, we ourselves introduce.'[7] That would result from an idealistic reading of conceptualism, which the timeless existence of concepts was used to avoid. (It is not an accident that *introducing* something is a temporal process.) Nor does conceptualism accept that we cannot have knowledge of things as they are in themselves. When we know something, what we know is precisely something about how things are in themselves. Conceptualism is, therefore, not a form of *transcendental* idealism.

But is it realist or anti-realist *really*? There is no answer to that question. This is not sitting on the fence; there is just no single fence here.

---

[6] See, e.g., M. Dummett, *Elements of Intuitionism* (Oxford: Clarendon Press, 1977), Ch. 7.

[7] Kant, *Critique of Pure Reason*, A125.

5.3. Explanatory Priority

Every general metaphysical theory needs some conception of explanatory priority for reductions. For a foundationalist theory, the shape of such a conception is clear enough. We have a class of basic terms, the terminus of all complete metaphysical explanations; and the direction of explanation is the same for all explanations, with terms closer to the base explaining those further away. We get a nice simple picture to hold in mind.

If conceptualism is opposed to foundationalism, it cannot appeal to this simple picture. What makes the picture simple from the point of view of a conception of explanatory priority is the fact that the direction of explanation is the same for all metaphysical explanations. If we reject foundationalism, we can only maintain that simplicity of explanatory direction if we accept non-terminating (that is, regressive) explanations.

But foundationalist metaphysics does seem to be right in its rejection of regressive explanations—in metaphysics at least. (There might be no need of a first *cause*, but that is another matter.) I think, then, that we want each explanation to terminate, satisfying the demand which it is designed to meet. That means that we cannot insist that the direction of explanation be the same for all metaphysical explanations. In effect, we may explain *A* in terms of *B* (together with other things) in one explanation, but *B* in terms of *A* (together with some other things) in another.

This is likely to seem puzzling, or merely an exercise in making patterns, unless some substance is added. So let us add some substance.

We can think of metaphysical explanation as directed towards this question: what sort of fact is this? But that question itself is not motivated just by a desire for classification. Rather, it is driven by some such further question as this: how is this the kind of thing which we can have a conception of? For any given property, or kind of fact, we can explain how it is the kind of thing of which we can have a conception of by relating it clearly to something else, assuming, for the moment, that we can have a conception of *that*.

In some ways, this gives the philosophical project very much the flavour it has traditionally had, even under the empiricists (even though other features of the picture look more like rationalism).

But there are two important differences from many traditional conceptions of philosophy. First, no severe restrictions are placed on how we can conceive of things. The empiricists, for example, demanded a strictly sensory base, where what counted as strictly sensory seems to have been a matter of what each of the senses might be thought to provide authoritative information about in the absence of the other senses. It is not clear that any restriction like this can be well motivated. We ought to allow our conception of how we can conceive of things to adapt to fit the range of things of which we can conceive. This is what conceptualism demands, since restricting in advance our view of how we can conceive of things will lead to a form of potentially revisionary foundationalism.

Secondly, the stance we adopt when pressing for an explanation need only be temporary. There is a frame of mind which we sometimes enter into, in which we can find it unproblematic that we can conceive of physical properties but find the apprehension of moral facts puzzling. But again, caught off our traditional philosophical guard, nothing seems more natural than to find a face malicious or kind, and the world of physics seems puzzling and foreign. Both perspectives are legitimate. Each demands a different explanation. There is no reason why there should be just one direction of explanation.

The guiding idea here is the thought that the kinds of facts we can conceive of form a unified network. There are no two properties we can conceive of which are explanatorily unrelated. The relation may be indirect, but there will always be some connection. On this conception, the task of philosophy is to make sense of the unity of the network. Given that conception of the task, there is no need to insist, with foundationalism, that we must always work in the same direction.

It appears from all this that we can impose no *general* condition of explanatory priority beyond *non-circularity*. Particular projects demand particular explanatory directions. And there may be more local priorities, involving other notions of explanation, which we should also respect.

Is the resulting picture a *coherentist* conception of the world? Not on a usual understanding of coherentism. First, it is still required that every explanation must terminate somewhere. There will always be some kinds of fact or property taken for granted, even if only temporarily, as being unproblematic. It is only in contrast with what we take for granted that we have a conception, even if only a temporary one, of something else as requiring explanation. Coherentism is generally thought of as trying to legitimate every kind of fact all at once, taking nothing for granted until the whole picture is complete.

Secondly, coherentism, as generally understood, claims that there is a single property of world-views—coherence—whose possession by any particular world-view is necessary and sufficient for its adequacy. This suggests that there is some perspective, outside any particular world-view, from which world-views can be compared for adequacy. Conceptualism is certainly committed to no such thing.

These two points are clearly manifestations of the same thing: coherentism, as it is generally understood, is a Platonistic view. Conceptualism insists that we must always work within some conception of things. There cannot be a decisive argument in favour of a whole world-view. All arguments in the end are *ad hominem*.

PART II

The Shape of a Theory of Content

6

What is a Theory of Content?

6.1. The Topic

It is noticeably easier to evaluate a theory if we know what the theory is meant to do. The aim of Part II is to make as explicit as possible the constraints which I take a theory of content to be required to meet. This should serve both to delineate the topic, and to locate the theory proposed in Part III within current debates.

A philosophical theory need not be a reduction, but a reduction is the simplest kind of theory. Let us suppose that we are after a reduction of content, in the sense of 'reduction' which was defined in 1.2. That is, we are looking for an account of that in virtue of which content-reporting statements are true, which provides necessary and sufficient conditions (subject to a criterion of factual equivalence) for their being content-reporting, and which is at least non-circular.

The kind of content we are concerned with is the content of propositional attitudes—what is believed, desired, hoped, feared, expected, known, and so forth. If we are to have a reduction of this kind of content, we will have a reductive account of what it is to possess a concept, since possessing the concept "C" is just a matter of having some propositional attitude that . . . C . . . (for some filling of the blanks).

The assumption implicit in singling out the content of propositional attitudes is that there is another type of content, or another way of having content, with which propositional attitude content—conceptual content—is to be contrasted. This might be called *informational* content. Computers may be said to register and process information; so, perhaps, may parts of organisms, like parts of the visual systems of mammals, for example.

I am assuming, then, that there is a difference between possessing concepts and registering or processing information. This ought to be uncontroversial. Most people are inclined to believe that people have beliefs; hardly anyone really thinks that an adding machine or an eye can really think. This is the minimal condition for a theory of content. Nothing will count as an adequate theory of content unless it meets this constraint:

> (C1) Being describable as registering or processing information is not sufficient for possessing concepts, and having propositional attitudes.

Call this the *minimal condition*. Some people think that some existing computers (chess computers, for example) really think, in the only sense of 'really think' which we can really ground. Some of the same people also think that slot-machines really think, in the only real sense of 'really think'.[1] I shall not argue against these theories here. They depend upon their own theory of thinking being well founded, and upon there being no other available. It is extremely doubtful that their own theory is well founded, and Part III will make another theory available.

I shall just take it as a basic principle that any theory which counts a slot-machine as a thinker is mistaken. This does not mean that it is not possible that some day someone may build a machine which really does have concepts. All that matters is that it will not count as being a concept-possessor just in virtue of being describable as an information-processor.

I am also obviously assuming that *people* really do have concepts and beliefs and desires. This sets me against the surprisingly popular view of the eliminativists.[2] There are two familiar kinds of objection to eliminativism, which seem to me not to have been satisfactorily answered. I shall summarize them briefly.

The first is an objection to the *arguments for* eliminativism. The general form of these arguments is this:

> (1) Beliefs, if they exist, have properties *A*, *B*, *C*, etc.
> (2) Nothing could (or at any rate does) have all those properties.

So;

> (3) There are no beliefs.

The first premiss of such arguments is generally vulnerable: it will depend upon some analysis of belief which is controversial. I shall myself be providing an account of belief which the eliminativist

---

[1] Thus, apparently, D. Dennett, 'Evolution, Error, and Intentionality', in his *The Intentional Stance* (Cambridge, Mass.: MIT Press, 1987) 287–321.

[2] See, e.g., P. Churchland, 'Eliminative Materialism and the Propositional Attitudes', *Journal of Philosophy*, 78 (1981), 67–90.

would find hard to use to support her conclusion. In particular, eliminativists tend to think of belief-talk as naïve proto-science, or would-be science. On my account that gets the point of belief-talk completely wrong.

There is an absolutely general weakness about these arguments. A good argument needs its premises to be jointly more plausible than the denial of the conclusion. It is not clear that this condition can ever be met when the conclusion is that there are no beliefs. This is related to the second familiar kind of objection to eliminativism.

The second familiar kind of objection to eliminativism is that it is incoherent to accept the conclusion. This form of objection will reach its target most quickly if we can establish that we could not make sense of anything being *true* if there were no beliefs. Since the eliminativist puts her own theory forward as being *true*, the theory would then be pragmatically self-defeating. The theory proposed in Part III seems to make the notion of truth inextricable from that of belief, in which case it could form part of an objection to eliminativism of this second kind.

It should be emphasized that this second kind of objection to eliminativism does not constitute a *proof* that we have beliefs, in any interesting sense of 'proof'. It agrees with Descartes that we cannot coherently doubt that we have beliefs; but it disagrees with Descartes in not supposing that this counts as *establishing* that we have beliefs. A position from which we could make sense of the *need* to establish that we have beliefs would be a position from which it could not be established.

It is important to be clear about this so that we are not vulnerable to a worry that might be felt about the argument.[3] It might be thought that the argument requires that we cannot be mistaken about whether we—and no doubt a good number of the people around us—have beliefs. And this in turn might be thought to require an analysis of belief which makes it impossible for us to be mistaken about whether others have beliefs: that is, it might seem to force us into a very superficial form of behaviourism. So it might seem that we ought to analyse belief in such a way that eliminativism might turn out to be right.

I think there are several confusions here. First, it is true that I cannot be mistaken about whether I have beliefs. But this is not

---

[3] This worry is due to Martin Davies.

because my own state of mind is particularly obvious to me ('clear and distinct' in Descartes's phrase); it is just because to be mistaken is itself a matter of having (false) beliefs. This relates to the point I made about the second kind of argument against eliminativism not being a *proof* that we have beliefs.

As for the beliefs of other people, we need to distinguish between two claims:

(4) For each of the other people whom I take to have beliefs, it is in principle possible that I am mistaken in thinking that that person has beliefs.

(5) It is possible that I am mistaken about *all* the other people whom I take to have beliefs.

Our attitude to these two will depend upon how large an error in my judgement we think is compatible with my still counting as possessing the concept of belief: if I do not even possess the concept of belief, I cannot mistakenly think that other people have beliefs, since I cannot think that anything has *beliefs* at all. (5) seems to me to contemplate *too* large an error, unless some very fancy story is told. (4) does not seem so bad, although my possession of the concept of belief might be cast in doubt if my mother or my wife turned out not to have beliefs.

But, again, the point does not depend upon any indubitable obviousness of belief possession. It is just a matter of what can be made sense of while still allowing me to count as *mistaken*.

Suppose, though, that we allow both (4) and (5) to be true: we have managed, suppose, to tell a fancy enough tale to make it clear that I would still have the concept of belief in the circumstances imagined. Now consider this suggestion:

(6) I am mistaken in thinking that any of the other people I know has beliefs.

It seems to me that I could not rationally accept this. Given (5), there is a sense in which it might be true, but I cannot accept it without throwing in doubt all my capacities for judgement. If I thought I was as wrong as that, then I cannot see what I could sensibly have confidence in. Again, the resting point is not the kind of indubitable obviousness of belief possession which might support a superficial behaviourism.

Does this mean that we need to acknowledge that eliminativism might turn out right? No, because eliminativism only says anything at all—if the original second objection was right—if it is the expression of some belief. The second objection seems not to force us into anything like a superficial behaviourism. We are not faced with a choice between countenancing the possibility of eliminativism's being true and a crass philosophy of mind.

I have merely summarized two familiar kinds of objection to eliminativism. I have not argued for them. The rest of the book will constitute a kind of support for the two objections, by producing a conception of what we are doing in reporting beliefs which will make it hard for the eliminativist to get her argument running, and by linking truth to belief in a way which will make it hard for the eliminativist to avoid pragmatic self-defeat. At that point the onus of proof will rest rather heavily upon eliminativism.

6.2. Content and the Knowledge Constraint

Some constraints on a theory of content follow directly from conceptualism, as it was elaborated in Part I. Here is one obvious one:

(C2) A reduction of the concepts of content must meet the condition of adequacy imposed by the knowledge constraint.

Call this the *knowledge-constraint constraint*. It means that a reduction of content must describe facts which are subject to precisely the same conditions for knowledge as the facts described using the concepts of content.

Here is another obvious conceptualist constraint;

(C3) A theory of content must explain how it is that the nature of concepts determines the nature of reality.

Conceptualism must give a special importance, among metaphysical theories (in the sense of Part I), to a theory of content, because, according to conceptualism, content has a special role as a determinant of reality, and hence of the constraints on metaphysical explanations in general. Call (C3) the *determination constraint*. Its effect is that, in addition to *meeting* the condition of adequacy imposed by the knowledge constraint, a theory of content must itself *vindicate* that condition, as it were from the inside.

What this means is this:

(C4) A theory of content must be capable of generating a theory of knowledge.

Call this the *analysis-of-knowledge requirement.* The need for (C4) can be explained quite simply. According to conceptualism, the nature of concepts determines the nature of the things of which they are concepts (see 1.3). According to the knowledge constraint, the nature of a thing is determined by what it would be to have knowledge of it (see 5.1). What we require of a theory of content, then, is that it should show how the nature of a concept of something determines what it would be to have knowledge of that thing. It is hard to see how this can be done unless the theory of content itself is capable of generating an analysis of knowledge. But then, *if* a theory of content does generate an analysis of knowledge, it will thereby have explained how the nature of concepts determines the nature of the things of which they are concepts.

The result of (C2), (C3), and (C4) is that a conceptualist theory of content must itself generate the condition which it has to meet. This might seem to make it inevitable that a theory of content will be vacuously self-confirming. But this is not so. For we have an antecedent, if rough, conception of what effective metaphysical explanations must be like; we have an independent conception of what is required for knowledge; and we have some idea of what is involved in possessing a concept. All of these things provide an independent fix on a theory of content.

These last three constraints help us to make a decision. Since possessing a concept is a matter of having some propositional attitude involving that concept, a reduction of the notion of possessing a concept will inevitably involve a reduction of at least one propositional attitude. It is not clear that any one kind of propositional attitude is intrinsically more fundamental than any other. But if we are concerned with the connections between a theory of content and metaphysical explanation (explanation of that in virtue of which true thoughts are true), then we will be concerned in particular with attitudes which can be true or false. That makes belief the obvious attitude to concentrate on, since beliefs can be true or false, and knowing something is believing it under the right conditions. So, like most theories of content in the analytical tradition, our theory will focus on belief; but in our case, at least, this is not because of any commitment to the view that belief is somehow the basic attitude.

6.3. Sense and Meaning

We all know that despite the obvious similarity between the statement that my mother's car is red and the statement that set theory is not about making jam—both are true—it is possible to believe that my mother's car is red without believing that set theory is not about making jam, and vice versa. Although all and only students of a certain university are required to go through a certain procedure, we all know that it is possible to believe that someone is a student of that university (whichever it is) without believing that she is required to go through that procedure. And with facts-first theories now removed (see Chapter 3), we all know that it is possible to believe that Plum is Plum without believing that Plum is P. G. Wodehouse, although in fact he is.

These mundane facts are the essence of content. What they reflect can be put formally like this. If we assume that names, predicates, and sentences have the kind of semantic value assigned to them in extensional (that is, truth-functional) logic, we have to recognize that expressions with the same semantic value cannot always be intersubstituted *salva veritate* in the gap following '*a* believes that . . .'. So an elementary requirement of a theory of content is this:

(C5) A theory of content must generate the right substitution conditions for belief contexts.

Conceptualism, as I developed it in Part I, requires that the individuation of thoughts be finer-grained than the individuation of facts or states of affairs (see Chapter 3). So part of what (C5) involves is this: it must be clear how it is possible for two names which refer to the same object, or two predicates which correspond to the same property, or two sentences which report the same fact, not to be intersubstitutable *salva veritate* within belief contexts.

I shall, in fact, demand something more. I think that there is no single, uniformly correct condition on substitution within belief contexts.[4] The condition is determined by the context in which the belief is reported, and can vary. I call this flexible opacity. Its significance can be seen by considering the case of Kripke's Pierre,

---

[4] See Morris, 'The Varieties of Sense', *Philosophical Quarterly*, 38 (1988), 123–44.

who learnt about London in his youth in France, and now lives
there, though without realizing that the city he is living in is the city
he was told about as a child.[5] We can make each of these two
claims compelling:

  (1) Pierre believes that London is pretty.
  (2) Pierre does not believe that London is pretty.

Unfortunately, we seem then to be stuck with a contradiction. I
think that there are at least two legitimate readings of these reports,
taken in abstraction. First there is a reading on which they are
genuinely contradictory. A second reading can be represented by
rewriting the reports with an aside added, so that (1) and (2)
become these two, respectively:

  (3) Pierre believes that London [whispered aside: the city he
       heard of in his youth] is pretty.
  (4) Pierre does not believe that London [whispered aside: the
       city in which he is now living] is pretty.

If (1) and (2) are taken properly in the context of the story, then the
right way to hear them will be the way which (3) and (4) present.
Then there will be no contradiction. But this clearly requires a
difference in the role the word 'London' plays in these reports from
the role it is assumed to play in the interpretation which makes (1)
and (2) contradict each other.

And if both readings are legitimate in principle, in abstraction
from any particular circumstance of utterance, then we have what I
call flexible opacity.

A theory of content should then explain the special intensionality
of conceptual content. That involves distinguishing it from the
special intensionality involved in the idea of factual equivalence.
But a theory of content must provide the materials for explaining
the intensionality of factual equivalence too, since we have already
accepted the determination constraint:

  (C3) A theory of content must explain how it is that the nature
        of concepts determines the nature of reality.

What does explaining some kind of intensionality involve? It means
explaining constraints upon the use of words in certain contexts,
subject to these two conditions:

---

[5] S. Kripke, 'A Puzzle about Belief', in A. Margalit (ed.), *Meaning and Use*
(Dordrecht: Reidel, 1979), 239–83.

(i) The constraints must actually restrict intersubstitution in the right ways.

(ii) The constraints must be of a kind that words can actually be subject to.

The second condition can make it seem difficult to meet the first condition. Facts-first theories, for example, have a conception of the functions and properties of words which makes it impossible for the constraints on intersubstitution which we all really believe in to work: words just refer to objects, properties, and states of affairs; they do not have enough in them to be sensitive to the further constraints required for a plausible account of conceptual content.

The effect of this is that an account of intensionality must be supported by a plausible theory of meaning, in the sense of an account of what words are, and what it is for something to be a meaningful word. But it is natural enough to require that a theory of content should combine with a theory of meaning, in this sense, anyway. First, for an utterance to be an utterance of a meaningful word is for it to be a certain sort of expression of a concept. (This requires a harmless generosity in one's conception of a concept. Roughly, a word is capable of expressing a concept if it can occur genuinely within the context of the 'that'-clause of a report of an attitude, or at least is such that its use in an utterance makes a difference to the attitudes that can be ascribed on the basis of that utterance.) And, secondly, conceptual content was characterized initially (1.1) as essentially the right sort of thing to be expressed in words. Conceptual content is *what* is believed or desired when someone believes or desires something. And *what* is believed is what we might say was believed in saying that the person believed *that* something or other, where 'something or other' is informally schematic for a verbal expression.

We can make all this explicit in this constraint, which we might call the *word-meaning constraint*:

(C6) A theory of content must explain what it is for words to be meaningful in the way they are.

It is worth pointing out that this is not a request for a semantic theory in the sense of a theory which explains how the meaning of sentences is a function of the meaning of words, by assigning semantic values to words in axioms, from which the assignment of semantic value to sentences can be derived in theorems. Semantic theories, in this sense, sidestep by stipulation (assignment) the question which is of first importance to us: what it is for something to be a meaningful word at all. The task is to answer that question in a way which permits words to be subject to constraints which could provide the right restrictions on substitution.

Meeting condition (i) is demanding enough in itself, particularly since we are trying to construct simultaneously *two* kinds of intensionality—that appropriate to conceptual content, and that involved in factual equivalence. That means that neither kind of intensionality can be question-beggingly presupposed in a theory of content.

What kind of presupposition of intensionality would be question-begging? Concepts themselves must not be described in terms which are only intelligible in the light of the intensionality of conceptual content. And concepts cannot be defined, within the theory, in terms of correlations with objects or properties, since that would presuppose the intensionality of factual equivalence. It is natural then to accept this constraint (the *extensionality constraint*):

(C7) A theory of content must be extensional at base.

This means that a theory of content should begin with attributions of significance which can be defined extensionally.

It is important to note two things which this does *not* imply. First, it does not imply that significance in general should be defined extensionally. It is quite all right for much richer notions of significance to be appealed to, provided that those richer notions can be explained ultimately in terms of what has to obtain for there to be extensionally-defined significance. (There is therefore no commitment here to anything like a Davidsonian truth-theory for a language.[6])

Secondly, it is not supposed that extensional notions are more fundamental, in any general way, than those intensional notions that need to be explained. The priority for us of extensional notions is simply the priority imposed by the explanatory demands of a certain project. For that project extensional notions count as basic, but that does not mean that they are in any sense absolutely basic,

---

[6] D. Davidson, 'Truth and Meaning', in his *Inquiries into Truth and Interpretation* (Oxford: Clarendon Press, 1984), 17–36.

and does not prevent them being explained in turn in a different project which took for granted those intensional notions which need to be constructed here.

The extensionality constraint provides another point of contact with theories which are already familiar within the analytic tradition. Those other theories are partially vindicated—there is a point in beginning with the extensional. But there is no endorsement here of a lifelong commitment to the cloistered purity of extensionality. It is not supposed that intensionality is *in fact* constructed out of extensionality; it is just that a particular kind of *theory* needs to construct intensionality.

A further consequence of the extensionality constraint is that we cannot give an atomistic account of word-meaning. That is, we cannot explain word-meaning in terms of certain items being paired or associated with concepts, or with objects or properties. For any such pairing or association will presuppose at least one of the kinds of intensionality which our theory must explain.

The extensionality constraint therefore seems to make the following demands of a theory of content. Significance must be attributed to whatever it is that is held to form the basis of concept-possession *in sentence-length units*. And the context in which sentences are used to attribute significance in the first place must be extensional.

The first seven constraints already make the task of a theory of content toothsome enough. And these are the relatively uncontroversial conditions. In the next two chapters we will have to abandon such bland plausibility.

7

Unified Externalism

7.1. The Basic Argument

'Externalism' has become the name of a range of views about content. It remains the best term to locate the kind of position I shall argue for in debates about content, but it now needs to be defined. This, then, is what externalism states:

(E) Sameness of truth condition is essential to sameness of thought (belief content), even for thoughts expressed by means of singular terms.

An externalism will count as *unified* if it also accepts this:

(U) There is no division within content such as that alleged between 'narrow' and 'broad' content, or between an 'internal' and an 'external' component of content.

Two points are worth noting about the definition of externalism I have given. First, the spatial metaphor has been stripped away. The term 'externalism' itself belongs to a long tradition of representing the relation between thoughts and the world in spatial terms. In such a picture, the mind and mental content are 'inner', while the world is 'outer'. This picture is bad enough to begin with, since it suggests and encourages a misunderstanding of the contrast between introspection and one's awareness of one's current state of mind, on the one hand, and one's knowledge of other things, on the other. The suggestion is roughly that introspection is a matter of swivelling the eye-ball inwards and contemplating one's mind close to, which makes the special status of first-person avowals depend upon a special back-door access: as if other people see only the puppets, but we ourselves can see the puppeteer.

But the spatial metaphor also makes externalism very hard to understand. If we preserve the metaphor, externalism becomes the thesis that certain inner items would not have been the items they are, if they had not been connected in an appropriate way to the outer environment. This is highly counter-intuitive without some thesis of essentiality of causal origin. The classification of states of mind as 'inner' seems precisely to preclude the 'outer' from being relevant to their individuation.[1]

So the definition of externalism in (E) is abstract. But it is firmly connected with the use which the notion of the external has been put to in the tradition. A fair working definition of the 'external' world—the world that Descartes had such trouble giving us knowledge of—might be this: it is a world about which we might be wrong. (I used essentially the same definition as a definition of 'objective' in 5.1.) A world about which we might be wrong is just the kind of world whose states might provide the *truth conditions* of our thoughts, since it is the only kind we might be right about. So a definition of externalism in terms of truth conditions preserves the legitimate connections across issues which are enshrined in the traditional use of the word *external* itself.

The second point that needs to be made about (E) is that it does not justify belief in an explanatory asymmetry between content and the world. It therefore does not support the (Platonistic) thesis that states of the world determine content, if that is taken to be incompatible with mutual interdependence. (E) therefore contrasts with the characterization of externalism given by McGinn, for example. McGinn begins with an informal description of externalism which issues in this rough definition: 'The environment is thus held to be constitutive of the very nature of mental states, determining what they *are*'.[2] A little later we have this illuminating sequence of remarks:

Externalism holds that mental distinctions (distinctions of content) are grounded in worldly distinctions, that the former depend upon the latter, that mental individuation is to be explained by reference to worldly conditions. It thus regards the direction of individuation as running from the world to the mind. Accordingly, this individuation-dependence is deemed asymmetrical: the world is not likewise individuation-dependent upon the mind.[3]

We see here a gradual, but unargued, slide from a claim about what is essential to content to a claim of an asymmetrical dependence of content upon the world. This position looks Platonistic.

---

[1] McGinn seems exercised by the puzzle which this creates; see C. McGinn, *Mental Content* (Oxford: Blackwell, 1989), 3–4.

[2] Ibid. 3.

[3] Ibid. 10.

Curiously, McGinn motivates his view by means of the very puzzle which provided initial support for the *denial* of Platonism (in 1.3 above). McGinn calls it the 'matching problem'. Here is how he sets it up:

There are properties of objects in the world, and there are concepts in the minds of persons: how do these get to match up? How do our concepts come to have extensions that coincide with the instantiation classes of real properties? How do our subjective mental acts manage to latch onto the objective properties of things? By what miracle is the taxonomy of concepts in a mind not hopelessly mismatched with the taxonomy of properties in the world?[4]

This is an effective way of enlivening the issue. The imagery is quite properly Platonistic, since the problem is the problem of Platonism. But the problem set here is not one to which externalism can be the solution.

There are, in fact, *two* matching problems, posed by these two questions:

(Q1) Taking the world for granted, how could these concepts be appropriate to it?

(Q2) Taking our concepts for granted, how could there be a world to which they are appropriate?

And they are answered, respectively, as follows:

(A1) It would not have been *this* world, if these concepts had not been appropriate for it.

(A2) They would not have been *these* concepts, if they had not been appropriate to this world.

(A1), the answer to (Q1), is, in effect, tenet (B) of conceptualism (see 1.3). (A2), the answer to (Q2), is, in effect, externalism.

The first difficulty for McGinn is that the problem he sets up so vividly is that expressed by (Q1), which needs conceptualism for an answer, not externalism. The second is that, since one presumably wants to be able to answer both questions, one should not define externalism in a way which makes it incompatible with conceptualism, as McGinn does.

In fact, there is an intuitive argument that conceptualism *requires* externalism. Conceptualism requires that the nature of a concept determines the nature of that of which it is a concept. The argument

---

[4] Ibid. 11.

might be thought to be an inference to the best explanation of conceptualism, or else as the claim that conceptualism would be unintelligible otherwise. Here it is, in the form of a question. How could the nature of a concept determine the nature of that of which it is a concept, unless it is essential to its being *that* concept that it is a concept precisely of *that*? I can see no way of making sense of conceptualism without externalism.

Let us call this argument *the basic argument* for externalism, emphasizing in the title both that the argument is fundamental, and that it is fairly direct. In the rest of this chapter, I shall try to argue for unified externalism in more detail. (E) makes particular mention of thoughts expressed by means of singular terms, reflecting an area of recurrent anxiety. In order to secure this version of externalism, I need to argue against those who are hostile to the idea of singular thoughts. I then need to argue against various forms of dual component theory. Once that has all been done, some fairly uncontroversial points about word-meaning ought to be enough to secure unified externalism in full.

7.2. Objections to Singular Thoughts

My definition of externalism specifically included reference to thoughts expressed by means of singular terms. This is because, although there has been persistent anxiety about such thoughts, what I called *the basic argument* for externalism allows no obvious room for treating these thoughts any differently from others.

The reasons for the common disquiet about singular thoughts may be epistemological; they may concern the explanation of behaviour; or they may have some other source. I shall be concerned just with the views which that disquiet produces. I shall argue that they are hardly coherent.

We are dealing with thoughts which at least appear to be expressed by means of singular terms. What is a singular term? I shall say that a singular term is an expression for a particular object, whose meaningfulness depends upon there being that particular object to refer to. With that rudimentary definition in hand we can examine those positions which object to singular thoughts.

Consider a report like this one:

(1)   Ralph believes that Ortcutt is a spy.[5]

On the face of it 'Ortcutt' is a singular term, and expresses part of what Ralph believes. Let us call someone who accepts this a *singular-thought theorist*.[6] Those who do not accept it are my targets now. Let us call them *opponents of singular thought*.

Opponents of singular thought must give some account of what it is that Ralph really believes when we say (1) truly. I can think of just two options. On the first, the content of Ralph's belief would be better expressed like this;

(2)   Ralph believes that *x* is a spy.

In general to capture the *content* of a belief normally reported by means of a 'that'-clause which contains a singular term (or something which is apparently a singular term), we should replace the (apparent) singular term by a free variable. The content is properly expressed by means of a schema or open sentence. Let us call this *the schema view*.[7]

The other option is to regard the content of such beliefs as being properly expressed by means of sentences containing quantifier expressions instead of singular terms. Thus the content of the belief reported in (1) would be more accurately represented by some such report as this:

(3)   Ralph believes that there is something which is *F*, and which is a spy.

(Someone advocating this kind of view ought not to insist on a uniqueness clause here, since uniqueness can only in general be guaranteed by incorporating a demonstrative reference, which is incompatible with opposition to singular thoughts.) Let us call this kind of view *universalism*, following Blackburn.[8]

There are several difficulties which confront both kinds of opponent of singular thought equally. I shall mention two. The first is that it is hard to make sense of their 'accurate' reports of the content of beliefs, if singular terms do not express content.

[5] This example is derived from W. V. Quine, 'Quantifiers and Propositional Attitudes', in his *The Ways of Paradox and Other Essays* (2nd edn., Cambridge, Mass.: Harvard University Press, 1976), 185–96.

[6] The most visible example of such a theorist is J. McDowell; see, e.g., his '*De Re* Senses', *Philosophical Quarterly*, 34 (1984), 283–94.

[7] This appears to be the view of T. Burge, 'Belief *De Re*', *Journal of Philosophy* 74 (1977), 338–62, and G. Segal, 'The Return of the Individual', *Mind*, 98 (1989), 39–57.

[8] S. Blackburn, *Spreading the Word* (Oxford: Clarendon Press), Ch. 9.

Consider the schema view first. The content of a putatively singular belief is supposed to be accurately expressed using a free variable rather than a singular term. But what role is the free variable playing? There seem to be two possible views.

On the first, a free variable merely marks a place for a singular term. But, in that case, if a free variable can occur genuinely within the 'that'-clause of a belief report, so can a singular term. But surely that means that singular terms can express parts of thoughts, and that there can be singular thoughts.

On the second conception of the role of free variables, a free variable functions as a kind of temporary name.[9] But this means that a free variable is a singular term already, albeit one with only temporary reference. So once again it must be possible for there to be singular thoughts.

There is a very similar difficulty with universalism. The content of an apparently singular belief is supposed to be properly expressed by a quantified sentence. The question then is: can we make sense of quantifiers where we cannot make sense of singular terms? In standard predicate calculus, a quantifier is an expression which binds a free variable in an open sentence. This ought immediately to incline one to expect an argument like that against the schema view. And that inclination is supported by the standard account of the truth conditions of quantified sentences. On this account, an existential quantification, for example, is true just in case there is at least one true instance of the embedded open sentence—where an instance has a singular term in the position of the relevant variable (perhaps the variable itself, on the 'temporary-name' conception of variables). This account obviously requires that we can make sense of singular terms wherever we can make sense of quantification. If the universalist is to sustain her position, she will have to find some other account of quantification.[10]

But it is more than unlikely that she will succeed. It is hardly an accident, for example, that standard English (singular) quantifiers ('someone', 'something', 'there is a . . . which', etc.) occupy positions which singular terms can occupy. There is an essential link between quantified sentences and sentences containing singular terms. How could we claim that 'Someone was ugly' involved an

<hr />

[9] H. Field, 'Tarski's Theory of Truth', *Journal of Philosophy*, 69 (1972), 349.

[10] This is a relative of the argument in G. McCulloch, *The Game of the Name* (Oxford: Clarendon Press, 1989), 22–9.

existential quantifier, if we did not think it could be supported by something like 'Socrates was ugly'? How could we claim that 'Everyone is drunk' involves a universal quantifier, if it does not imply 'Arthur is drunk'?

This reveals in a non-technical way the problem the universalist faces in allowing quantifiers to express content while banning singular terms. She has no right to count these quantifiers as quantifiers: they become uninterpretable. The same problem also affects the *subject* of belief. If we allow quantifiers but not singular terms to express content, we seem to be crediting subjects with a conception of 'all' and 'some' without any conception of an *instance* of a quantified claim. And that seems unintelligible for the same reason.

The second difficulty faced by both kinds of opponent of singular thought is that they seem to be committed to a form of Platonism: the world we think about seems forever inaccessible. It is impossible, on these views, to know what one is thinking about just in virtue of knowing what one is thinking.

To see this, consider a rule of inference which singular-thought theorists will accept, but their opponents will reject. Call it the rule of *singular-term exportation*, or (SE). Here is a version of it:

(SE) If '*b*' is a singular term, then from

   (i) *a* believes that *b* is *F*,

you may infer

   (ii) *a* believes of *b* that it (/she/he) is *F*,

with no additional assumptions.

This characterization follows the convention that expressions written within the 'that'-clause of a belief report express the content of the belief reported, whereas those written outside need not. (This convention is actually questioned in 13.4.)

This rule of inference is unproblematic for a singular-thought theorist for the following reason. If '*b*' functions as a genuine singular term in (SE)(i), we are already committed to there being something, *b*, which the belief is about. And (SE)(ii) does no more than make that commitment explicit.

As for the opponents of singular thought, we should note first that neither kind of opponent can accept the propriety of either (SE)(i) or (SE)(ii). In the case of (SE)(i) the reason is obvious: a singular term occurs genuinely within the scope of the 'that'- clause. It is not difficult to see the problem over (SE)(ii) either. For the universalist, the problem is that the 'it' (or 'he' or 'she') cannot be construed as a quantifier. For the schema view the problem is that the 'it' (or 'he' or 'she') cannot be treated as a *free* variable: its reference is fixed by anaphoric connection with '*b*'. But that anaphoric connection would be unintelligible if the inference from (SE)(i) to (SE)(ii) were not legitimate; and the schema view cannot even accept the form of the premiss of the inference.

That means that opponents of singular thought need to find some alternative to (SE)(ii) if they are to make any sense of belief being about objects at all. They will suggest something like the following (for universalism and the schema view respectively):

(ii*a*) *a* believes of *b* that there is something which is *G*, and which is *F*;

(ii*b*) *a* believes of *b* that *x* is *F*.

In both cases the belief will be related to its object by means of some external (for example, causal) connection.

The problem is that the opponents of singular thought can find no counterpart to (SE)(i) from which we could infer (ii*a*) or (ii*b*). And that means that we cannot know what we are thinking about just in virtue of knowing what we are thinking.

The objects of our thoughts become endlessly fugitive. Suppose I think I have discovered what my thought was about: I think it was about *n*, say. Now what is *that* thought—the thought that my previous thought was about *n*—about? Another investigation is required, to link the presence of the '*n*' component of this latest thought to something in the world. But this second investigation concerns the object of my *first* thought: we have made no progress. Nothing I can ever think quite gets me in touch with things.

Some might feel that this argument is weak because of a weakness in (SE). Surely, it will be said, a report of the form of (SE)(i) can be true, even if '*b*' refers to no existing object; but if '*b*' does not exist, we surely cannot accept (SE)(ii). So the rule of inference is not generally safe.

This kind of worry ought not to drive anyone into the arms of the opponents of singular thought. There are at least three ways of preserving (SE) and singular-thought theories.

The first way accepts that the move from something of the form of (SE)(i) to something of the form of (SE)(ii) is not legitimate when there is no actually existing object to which '*b*' refers; but it insists that in these cases '*b*' is not properly speaking a singular term, whatever the superficial appearances. Since (SE) is explicitly restricted to singular terms, it is not threatened. This means that not all expressions which look like singular terms are to be treated uniformly; and that we might turn out to be wrong in thinking that some expressions are singular terms. It will also follow that we might be wrong about what we think, and not merely because we are not very good at discerning our own motives. These consequences might be initially counter-intuitive, but that is no objection in itself.

The second way allows that there can be singular terms which refer to no actually existing object, but holds that such terms are only meaningful when used with connivance in a kind of fictional discourse.[11] (SE) will be legitimate even when '*b*' has no really existing referent—provided that the reports of the forms of (SE)(i) and (SE)(ii) are both made connivingly. But when there is neither a really existing referent nor connivance, the attempted reports of the forms of (SE)(i) and (SE)(ii) will not even be meaningful, so no threat to the legitimacy of (SE) can arise.

I prefer the third way. This accepts (SE), even when '*b*' refers to no actually existing object, and when there is no special or deliberate connivance on the part of the person reporting the belief. This means, of course, that reports of the form of (SE)(ii) cannot be existentially committing.

The difficulty this seems to raise is this. If a singular term can be exported in the manner of (SE), it must occupy a position one can quantify into. But then existential generalization should legitimate a move from (SE)(ii) to this:

(SE)(iii) There is something such that *a* believes of it (/he/she) that it (/he/she) is *F*.

And here we seem to be existentially committed after all.

My own inclinations run the other way. Suppose we know this:

(4) Ralph believes that Pegasus is a winged horse.

That seems quite natural, and does not seem to involve us in any kind of pretence. (SE) immediately licenses the move to this:

(5) Ralph believes of Pegasus that he is a winged horse.

---

[11] This is the view of G. Evans, *The Varieties of Reference*, ed. J. McDowell (Oxford: Clarendon Press, 1982), Ch. 10.

And that seems reasonable: after all, if Ralph knows anything about the subject, he will not believe that of Bellerophon. Existential generalization takes us to this:

(6) There is something of which Ralph believes that it is a winged horse.

Of course there is: Pegasus. Does that commit us to *this*?

(7) There is a real thing of which Ralph believes that it is a winged horse.

Not obviously.

If we adopt this third way of preserving (SE), we incur some explanatory debts. We need to explain existential quantification without appeal to real existence. We need to explain real existence in terms other than existential quantification. We need to explain reference without presupposing the real existence of the thing referred to. We need to explain why phrases like 'There is a . . . ' can often be used to imply real existence. But these tasks are not obviously insuperable.

There are two morals to be drawn from this. First (relevant to my general concerns here), there is no problem involved in accepting (SE) which looks anything like as serious as that involved in its Platonistic denial. Secondly (relevant to the more particular issue of presenting singular-thought theories), we should be careful how we characterize singular terms. It is one thing to say that the meaningfulness of some terms depends on their having reference. It is another thing (even if one thinks it is true) to insist that the thing referred to by a meaningful singular term must really exist.

Let us return, finally, to the opponents of singular thought. Both kinds of opponent introduce what seems to be an unmotivated asymmetry between their treatment of singular terms and their treatment of predicates. Why should predicates be allowed to express content if singular terms are not?

Blackburn seems to recognize that this asymmetrical treatment needs justification. He attempts to provide some by representing us as facing a choice between two opposing asymmetries. The dispute between singular-thought theorists and their opponents, he says,

really gets its steam from this old clash: the opposition between theories taking the notion of a thing as somehow fundamental to our way of conceptualizing the world, and those which believe we can think best in terms of manifestation of properties, with the world of enduring and reidentifiable things a secondary conceptual construction on top.[12]

But this just misrepresents the issue. The choice is not between two asymmetrical views, but between both asymmetrical views and a symmetrical one. A singular-thought theory is not committed to thinking that properties are somehow secondary: the theory merely insists that the contribution of singular terms to the truth conditions of sentences be given the *same* status as the contribution of predicates.

And this seems clearly the right line to adopt anyway. It seems unintelligible that one could conceive of an object without thinking of it as having properties, or that one could conceive of a property without thinking of it as a property which some object might have. (In particular, what are we to make of Blackburn's 'manifestation of properties' without things whose possession of the properties *is* their manifestation?)

In fact, this looks as if it is just a 'material-mode' transposition of the difficulty for the schema view in making sense of variables, and for the universalist in making sense of quantification. If you can make sense of properties (or predicates with singular verbs) you are thereby committed to making sense of objects (or singular terms).

Blackburn may be right in thinking that opposition to singular thoughts gets its steam from that old clash; but it is not obvious that this enhances its status.

7.3. Dual Componency

The idea that content might be divided into an 'internal' and an 'external' component seems to have originated with Putnam.[13] It is suggested by a certain way of describing the 'Twin Earth' cases which he taught us to imagine.

The fundamental point of Twin Earth cases, when they are used in connection with the content of beliefs, is to show that the truth conditions of one's thoughts are essential to the identity of those thoughts, or, more crudely, that what one is thinking depends on what one is thinking about. There is room for doubt about whether

---

[12] Blackburn, *Spreading the Word*, 328.
[13] H. Putnam, 'The Meaning of "Meaning" ', in his *Mind, Language and Reality* (Cambridge: Cambridge University Press, 1975), 215–71.

they really *show* this, rather than just illustrating the point vividly for those who are already convinced.

The usual way of setting up Twin Earth cases is something like this. Take some expression '*e*' (singular term, common noun, adjective, predicate, or whatever), and imagine that you have some belief expressible by means of that expression. Schematically, we may say:

(1) You believe that . . . *e* . . .

You, of course, are on Earth. We now suppose that somewhere else in the universe there is another planet, which we call Twin Earth. Twin Earth is almost exactly like Earth, and it has on it someone (Twin You) who is physiologically and 'qualitatively' indistinguishable from you: that is, as far as your bodies go, you and your Twin are exact duplicates, and everything 'feels just the same' to both of you. Twin Earth, however, does differ slightly from Earth: there is no *e* (or nothing *e*, or whatever—depending on what part of speech '*e*' is) there. But '*e*' is an expression which applies to something on Earth. If there is no *e* (or nothing *e*, or whatever) on Twin Earth, Twin You has no access to *e* (or anything which is *e*, or whatever), and cannot therefore think about *e* (or anything which is *e*). Twin You cannot then have thoughts which are properly expressed using '*e*'. So Twin You's thoughts are different from yours.

This way of describing the cases makes it appear that 'the way things seem' to someone is dependent only on their physiology (or neurophysiology), and that this is crucial to the effectiveness of the examples. It then appears that there is a common factor, a constant element, in what you and your Twin think in Twin Earth cases. This might be thought of either as a common kind of content (so-called 'narrow' content), or as a common ingredient which makes a uniform and determinate contribution to the thoughts you both think.

But this belief in a common component is something which is injected into Twin Earth cases, and cannot be derived from them non-question-beggingly. Mention of physiology is in fact irrelevant to the fundamental point.

What Twin Earth cases really do is just make vivid what one is accepting when one accepts these two claims:

(2) Sameness of truth-conditional contribution is essential to sameness of word-meaning (in the relevant sense of 'word-meaning').

(3) If sameness of truth-conditional contribution is essential to sameness of word-meaning, then sameness of truth condition is essential to sameness of thought.

Twin Earth cases simply show that in accepting these two claims one is committed to a realist (in the sense of *non-solipsistic*) conception of thought. The important point is just this: if two people are thinking about different things, then their thoughts are different, even if neither would notice if you swapped them.

That means that the fundmental conditions for Twin Earth cases are just these two:

(i) Your thoughts have different truth conditions from your Twin's.

(ii) Neither of you would notice if you were miraculously swapped.

One would expect to be able to construct cases which meet these two conditions for almost any kind of thought. If we can speak of truth conditions at all, we must be able to make sense of error. But intelligible error is a matter of things seeming to one just as they would if one were right, even though one is wrong. And that possibility seems to be all we need to set up a Twin Earth example meeting condition (ii).

For any kind of thought for which one can get both of conditions (i) and (ii) met, a Cartesian conception of privileged access to one's own mind becomes problematic, if we accept (2) and (3). On that conception (shared, of course, by empiricists like Russell too), one cannot conceivably be wrong about what one is thinking. But where (i) and (ii) can be met, if we assume (2) and (3), what one is thinking will depend upon factors which could be varied without one noticing, that is, which one could be wrong about.

The untenability of that Cartesian conception of privileged access ought to be the moral made vivid by Twin Earth cases. But this moral gets lost in the standard presentations of the cases—the presentations, that is, which seem to favour dual componency. We should now be able to see what distortions those presentations make.

First, conditions (i) and (ii) make no mention of physiology. Of course, once one has accepted (2) and (3) it should be obvious that where physiological indistinguishability is irrelevant to the truth condition of a thought, it will be insufficient for its identity. No elaborate Twin Earth examples are needed to make that vivid. Indeed, the standard presentation of the examples, which insists on physiological indistinguishability between you and your Twin, is likely just to muddle matters where physiological indistinguishability *is* relevant to the truth conditions of the thoughts. (Thus Putnam's original example, about water, is awkward because of the quantity of water in the constitution of human beings.)

In fact, the situation is worse than that. The standard presentation of the examples certainly shows physiological indistinguishability to be insufficient for identity of thought (provided one has already bought (2) and (3)); but it perpetuates the assumption that it is *relevant*. This assumption should be questioned. If the crucial 'indistinguishability' between you and your Twin is that captured by condition (ii), then all *kinds* of physiological variation can be tolerated, provided that they make no difference to what you and your Twin would notice if you were swapped.

The second important feature which the standard accounts misrepresent is the kind of indistinguishability which *is* involved in condition (ii). It is supposed that, in Twin Earth cases, things 'seem just the same' to you and your Twin. It is unclear what sense can be given to the notion of 'the way things seem' that is required here. Intuitively, the notion is essentially comparative: things seeming a certain way is their seeming *like this* or *like that*. But if that is so, we will not be able to make things seem just the same to you and your Twin, because some of the terms of some relevant comparisons will be different.

Thus suppose we set up a Twin Earth case for which the fundamental difference between the two Earths is that there are no roses on Twin Earth. There is a botanically unrelated plant there, which neither you nor your Twin could tell from a rose, but there are no roses. This will be used to point out that while this may be true:

(4) You believe that roses are red;

this cannot be:

(5) Twin You believes that roses are red.

But by the same token, this will be true:

(6) Various things seem to you to resemble and differ from roses;

while *this* surely cannot be:

(7) Various things seem to your Twin to resemble and differ from roses.

If the identity of beliefs depends on their truth conditions, so surely does the identity of seemings.

The upshot of this, is that although Twin Earth cases have suggested to many that there are separable components of content, they in fact give no support to that view. It is imagined that there is some common core of content, which is shared by you and your Twin in the cases. We can certainly stipulate a physiological commonality, but it is unclear that this is sufficiently systematically related to commonalities of content to count as a *component*. And it is not obvious that there is a common feature expressible in terms of 'the way things seem'. There is no clear inference from the fact that neither you nor your Twin would notice being swapped to the claim that there is some isolable core common to both of you.

So much for the pedigree of dual-componency theories. Is the resulting position plausible? It is essential to any dual-componency view that content is made up of two independent, potentially isolable, contributory factors.[14] After that, there is a divergence between two versions. In one version, the 'internal' component is itself a kind of content: so-called 'narrow' content. In the other, neither component is a kind of content: content is the result of combining the two.

Let us take the 'narrow-content' version first. The obvious problem specific to this version is this: even if there is some kind of common component, why should it be counted as a kind of *content*?

It is tempting to dismiss this kind of dual-componency theory by stipulation. I have assumed throughout that content is, for example, what is believed when someone believes something. What someone believes is precisely what we say that she believes, when we say truly that she believes that roses are red, for example. In the sense of 'expression' involved when I say that I express your belief when I say what you believe, it is hard to make sense of beliefs without making sense of expressions of them. I take it that this

---

[14] The *locus classicus* for such views remains C. McGinn, 'The Structure of Content', in A. Woodfield (ed.), *Thought and Object* (Oxford: Clarendon Press, 1982), 207–58. McGinn seems to be ambivalent between the two versions of the view which I distinguish in the text.

means that we cannot make sense of there being a certain belief, if we cannot make sense of there being meaningful words which would express it. It is also not easy to make sense of words which make no contribution of truth conditions. Not only that, but the standard truth-conditional contribution of particular uses of particular words is essential to their role in expressing beliefs. Thus, when I say,

(8) I believe that I am right,

you, speaking to another, report my belief by saying:

(9) He believes that he is right.

That is, the perspective of indexicals is adjusted precisely in order to preserve ordinary reference. It seems, therefore, that there cannot be a kind of content which is neutral with respect to truth conditions in the way this version of dual componency requires.

That dismissal is based on my assumption of what is meant when we talk about content. That makes it sound as if I am doing no more than stipulating the 'narrow-content' version of a dual-componency theory off the field. But the stipulation is not arbitrary, and dual componency theories seem to be committed to it too.

The stipulation is not arbitrary because the notion of content is of philosophical interest just because of the links between content and aboutness and truth. In particular, without these links conceptualism would not have been stated in terms of content.

More crushingly, it seems clear that a dual-componency theory must itself accept this conception of content, since a dual-componency theory is itself a form of externalism. Recall the Twin Earth cases. We are faced with the fact that you and your Twin have thoughts with different truth conditions. Why should this mean you have different *thoughts*, beliefs with different *content*? The reasoning surely depends on the two principles I mentioned before:

(2) Sameness of truth-conditional contribution is essential to sameness of word-meaning (in the relevant sense of 'word-meaning').

(3) If sameness of truth-conditional contribution is essential to sameness of word-meaning, then sameness of truth condition is essential to sameness of thought.

I have just provided an argument for these two claims, on the basis of the idea that we must be able to make sense of a belief being expressed. I cannot see any other argument. The dual-componency theorist seems to need to resort to it too. But that argument depended on taking content as being just what is believed when someone has a belief. So that is how the dual-componency theory must think of content too. In that case, it seems quite arbitrary for a dual-componency theory to call something 'content' for which this externalist argument does not work.

Stipulating the notion of 'narrow content' away does not seem arbitrary, then. In fact, the point is not all that important, because there is a more general argument against dual-componency theories which also undermines the other version. Let us turn to the other version, then. There are two difficulties, which both turn on the sense that has to be given to the notion of a *component* here.

The idea must be something like this. We can make a division among the facts which make it true that a person has a belief with a given content. The facts on each side of that division each make a determinate contribution to the content of that belief. That puts it vaguely; the first difficulty arises over what is meant by a 'determinate contribution'.

How must we think of the facts on each side of the division if we are to make sense of the division as being a division between components? The obvious model makes the facts on each side of the division function as something like *ingredients*. That suggests that the following condition must be met: systematic variation in either kind of fact leads to systematic variation in content.

The problem with this is that it leads to a severe difficulty over the 'internal' component, once we actually fill in the roles the two components are meant to play. The external component is meant to consist of those facts which determine the truth condition of the thought which we get when we combine the two components. This set of facts will indeed meet the ingredient condition we imposed, if we follow anything like the standard view of Twin Earth cases, since variation in truth condition does lead to variation in content. But what is there left for the internal component to do?

It is natural to appeal here to the Fregean distinction between sense and reference, which has in effect been adopted in the distinction between the individuation of thoughts and the individuation of facts (see 5.1). Two different thoughts can have the same truth condition: famously, the thought that Hesperus is bright and the thought that Phosphorus is bright are both true if and only if

Venus is bright. The natural suggestion for a dual-componency theory is that it is a difference in the 'internal' component which is responsible for the difference between these thoughts.[15]

This suggestion, however, is incompatible with the version of conceptualism which I developed in Part I. What makes the thoughts different is that they embody different modes of epistemological access to the planet Venus: one embodies an evening route, the other a morning route (these hardly look like 'internal' facts, incidentally). But it is a tenet of the version of conceptualism which was developed in Part I, combined with the basic argument for externalism of 7.1, that the mode of epistemological access embodied in a concept determines what the concept is a concept of. And, therefore, more generally, the nature of the kinds of epistemological access embodied in a thought determines the truth condition of the thought. Or, to put the point briefly: sense determines reference.

The consequence of this is that the role assigned to the 'internal' component has now been swallowed up by the 'external' component. What determines the truth conditions has turned out to determine content in general.

This problem looks as if it will recur whatever role we attempt to reserve for the 'internal' component. Thus one might suggest that the 'internal' component is responsible for the *explanatoriness* of the content of beliefs. But this would require that the explanatoriness of beliefs be independent of both their sense and their reference, given that sense determines reference; and that seems absurd. The first difficulty that the idea of there being two *components* of content raises is just this, then: there seems no role at all for the 'internal' component.

Given the argument I have just offered to show that the role of an 'internal' component will inevitably have been absorbed by the 'external' component, the other difficulty that the notion of a *component* of content creates should come as no surprise. The problem is that dual componency is Platonist. The 'external' component could only be a *component* of content, if the facts in which it consists could obtain without the existence of the content which they are held to constitute. That means that the objects thought about must be capable of existing independently of any

---

[15] See, e.g., McGinn, 'The Structure of Content', 239–40.

concepts of them. And that is Platonism. The dual-componency theorist might object that her position is being misrepresented here. All that is being claimed, she might say, is that in order to have a belief someone must both have her physiology suitably arranged, and have her physiology suitably related to an appropriate environment. And one could imagine the physiology being so arranged in the absence of any particular environment, or the physiology being so related to the environment without being arranged internally in that way.

If this is the view we are to consider, then, whatever other faults it may have, it at least has *this* virtue: it is not a form of dual-componency theory. A dual-componency theory holds that there are two components to *content*. This view merely holds that there are (at least) two components to someone's thinking something on a particular occasion. Nothing has been done here to suggest that each of these components makes a determinate contribution to the *content* of her beliefs.

We could summarize this second difficulty for dual componency in the form of a dilemma. If what the components are components of is *content*, the view is Platonistic. If, on the other hand, what the components are components of is not content, but, say, someone's having a particular belief on a particular occasion, then the proposed theory is no threat to unified externalism. Either way, unified externalism seems to be required if we are to reject Platonism.

In dismissing dual componency, it is important to emphasize that we are not rejecting the thought that the beliefs of the two Twins in Twin Earth cases are *similar*, and indeed similar in content. But two things can be similar without having any *component* in common. A careless slide might lead to confusion over this: if two things are similar, then there is a feature common to both; someone might think that means that there is a component common to both. It does not, of course.

7.4. Unified Externalism and Causal Reductionism

In the course of this chapter we have found two arguments for externalism, the thesis that sameness of truth condition is essential to sameness of thought. The first was what I called the *basic argument* in 7.1, which states, in short, that conceptualism is unintelligible without externalism. The second, which might be called the *linguistic argument*, emerged in the consideration of dual componency. This insists that content is essentially something which meaningful words might express. But the meaningfulness of words depends upon their making some contribution to the truth condition of sentences, and words whose truth-conditional contributions are different must have different meanings, in the sense of 'meaning' relevant to the expression of beliefs. It follows that sameness of content cannot be preserved across difference of truth conditions.

These two arguments seem to me enough to establish externalism. Opposition to singular thoughts, which might have limited externalism, seems scarcely coherent, and to involve a form of Platonism. Dual componency, which might have led to a divided externalism, seems inconsistent with conceptualism too. We should embrace a unified externalism. Let us enshrine that as a constraint on a theory of content:

(C8) A theory of content must be consistent with unified externalism.

We can also derive a further, not insignificant constraint, by combining externalism with one of the conclusions of Part I. If we accept externalism, we hold that what a thought is about is essential to its identity. In 4.4 it was claimed to follow from the demise of scientism that there could not be a causal, or more generally natural-scientific, reduction of reference or aboutness. It seems to follow from this, together with externalism, that there can be no causal, or more generally natural-scientific, reduction of content. That seems to me to make an explanatory demand of a theory of content:

(C9) A theory of content should explain why there can be no natural-scientific reduction of content.

It seems to me that it should be apparent, from a proper description of the nature of content itself, what it is about content which makes scientistic reduction impossible.

8

The Explanation of Behaviour

8.1. An Anodyne Constraint

Everyone can agree on this constraint on theories of content:

(C10) A theory of content must be harmonious with a plausible account of the way in which contentful states of mind are properly cited to explain behaviour.

(We might call this the *explanation condition*.) And there will be little controversy over this reason for the constraint: we explain behaviour by citing contentful states of mind; so our account of content should make that intelligible.

But this constraint and this reason for it have the flavour of a communiqué after an international summit. They blandly state the banal common ground between widely differing views.

The constraint has a more striking significance within conceptualism. It is hard to make sense of having knowledge of content without having knowledge of contentful states of mind. And we have no conception of a way of knowing about contentful states of mind which is not a matter of finding them explanatory of behaviour. The same holds even for our own case: the most direct form of awareness of our minds is in our own avowals of our states of mind; but those avowals are themselves behaviour, and they truly reveal our state of mind only if they are to be explained by the states of mind they avow.

According to the version of conceptualism which I developed in Part I, the nature of a thing is determined by what it would be to have knowledge of it. Since contentful states are only to be known as explanatory of behaviour, and content is only to be known by knowing of contentful states of mind, the nature of content is determined by the way in which contentful states of mind are explanatory of behaviour. An account of the explanation of behaviour must, therefore, be at the heart of a theory of content.

Even this conclusion would be widely accepted, with or without explicit support from conceptualism. The controversy begins over what counts as a *plausible* account of the crucial explanatory relation. Unfortunately, current orthodoxy favours what seems to me a quite implausible conception of the kind of explanation involved.

8.2. The 'Folk-Psychology' Myth

The current orthodoxy about the ways in which contentful states of mind explain behaviour can be presented from two perspectives. One perspective stands outside our use of propositional attitude terms and describes their function from there: call this the *external* view. The other perspective is from within the practice of using such terms; it makes substantial claims about what contentful states of mind are. Call this the *internal* view. I shall begin by characterizing the orthodoxy from the external point of view.

The terms *belief* and *desire*, and their associates, we are told, are theoretical terms in a scientific (or quasi-scientific, or proto-scientific) theory which is designed to explain behaviour.[1] The theory may be called the 'belief-desire theory', if we want to remain neutral about its merits, or 'folk psychology', if we want to associate it with the rag-bag of superstition, folklore, and old wives' tales which (it is well known) swamped the human mind before the popularization of modern science.

The other version of the orthodoxy describes things from within the theory. Objects cause experiences in us. Experiences cause feelings and beliefs. Beliefs give rise to other beliefs, and combine with desires to cause movements of the body—behaviour. Beliefs and desires are internal states, in a more-or-less literal sense of 'internal'. They combine to produce behaviour in accordance with certain fundamental psychological laws, of which the most frequently cited is this:

(BD) If *a* desires that *p*, and believes that if *a* Bs then *p*, then, other things being equal, *a* Bs.

I think that the external view and the internal view are both ways of presenting what is in important respects the same conception of the mind. I shall call that conception the *'folk-psychology' myth*. I think

---

[1] This is the kind of description congenial to eliminativism; see, e.g., P. Churchland, 'Folk Psychology and the Explanation of Human Behaviour', *Aristotelian Society Supplementary Volume*, 62 (1988), 209–21.

it is a myth that talk of belief and desire constitutes a 'folk psychology', or indeed a psychology of any kind. (If one wants an example of a genuine piece of folk psychology, one might consider the widespread belief that the death penalty is an effective deterrent. Whether that belief is true or false, it is clearly not the kind of thing we are committed to just in virtue of talking of thoughts and feelings.) The prevalence of the orthodoxy is manifest in the fact that the term *folk psychology* is used as if it were an uncontroversial way of referring to the whole practice of talking of thoughts and feelings. In fact, I think, its use is a connivance in a mistaken conception of the mind.

What I think is common to both the external and the internal versions of the myth is the idea that beliefs and desires are causes of behaviour, in a certain strong, and fairly specific, sense of *cause*. To begin with, I shall not fuss about the use of the word 'cause' itself. (I shall return to that later.) At the outset, let us just try to get clear about the specific commitments of the 'folk-psychology' myth.

No doubt there are all sorts of ways in which beliefs, desires, and other contentful states of mind may be explanatory of behaviour. (My beliefs may have a certain kind of effect on what *you* do, for example.) We are concerned here just with a particular kind of explanatory relationship, the one involved in such statements as 'She did it because she thought it would help', or 'He shrank back because he was afraid it was going to explode'. Statements of this kind cite thoughts and feelings to explain behaviour in what we think of as the 'standard' way. Let us say that, when beliefs and desires, and the rest, are properly cited to explain behaviour in this 'standard' way, they stand in the *special relationship* to behaviour. The 'folk-psychology' myth takes the special relationship to be a certain sort of causal relationship.

What sort of causal relationship? The 'folk-psychology' myth holds that beliefs and desires figure in the special relationship as causes, in a sense of 'cause' for which *at least one* of the following obtains ('FC' for 'feature of causation'):

(FC1)   Content is causally inert.

(FC2)   It is not ruled out a priori that there could be all the behaviour which we take to be 'caused' by beliefs without there being any beliefs at all.

(FC3)   The discovery of the mental 'causes' of behaviour is directed towards prediction.

(The scare-quoted use of 'cause' in (FC2) and (FC3) is meant to signal that the explanatory relationship involved is the special relationship.)

I say, cautiously, that the 'folk-psychology' myth is only committed to at least one of these three claims being true. In fact, I suspect that most actual adherents to the myth are committed to all three. But since I shall be claiming that all three are false, I can fall back on the cautious statement.

How might the myth get committed to (FC1)? I think this is clear enough on the internal view. It is essential to the internal version of the myth that beliefs and desires are internal states in a more-or-less literal sense of 'internal': they are states of the inside of the head, on most views. (They might have properties which involve a connection with an extra-cranial environment, but those will not standardly be thought of as essential properties of the mental states in question.) Why should anyone think that beliefs and desires are in the head? Because the causes of the bodily movements involved in action are inside the head. This requires a certain conception of the notion of a 'cause of bodily movement'. What we have to have in mind to think that the cause of a bodily movement is inside the head is a certain *mechanical* conception of causation. But if we have a mechanical conception of causation, the causally efficacious properties will be mechanical properties. But *possessing a certain content* cannot be a mechanical property of anything. So content must be causally inert.[2] (This is not to say, of course, that content is not explanatory in some other way, or that content is not a useful way of *identifying* the causally efficacious properties; but being about something will not itself be that in virtue of which a state is the cause of muscular activity.)

The internal version of the myth seems fairly clearly committed to (FC1). There is no direct commitment to (FC1) in the external version of the myth. But in so far as the external version shares the internal version's conception of the behaviour which needs explaining, it will at least be likely that it too will be driven to a mechanical conception of the causal relationships involved.

Both versions seem clearly committed to (FC2). The external version is committed to it because it counts the behaviour which is explained in special-relationship explanations as *evidence* for the

[2] This is a way of stating the motivation for what Fodor calls 'the Formality condition', in 'Methodological Solipsism Considered as a Research Strategy in Cognitive Psychology', *Behavioral and Brain Sciences* 3 (1980), 63–110.

theoretical postulation of thoughts and feelings; descriptions of the behaviour are observational for this theory. And the theory is supposed to be an empirical theory. That just means that there can be no a priori argument to the truth of the theory from the truth of the relevant observational statements. Since, on this view, the existence of beliefs and desires, and the rest, depends on the truth of the theory (they are supposed to be theoretical posits), we cannot rule out a priori that there might have been all that behaviour and no beliefs at all.

The internal version gets to the same conclusion by another route. We have seen that it is committed to a mechanical conception of the causation it takes to be involved in the special relationship. That means that it must have a mechanical conception of the behaviour which is the mechanical effect of these mechanical causes. To have a mechanical conception of the behaviour is to regard the mechanical properties of the behaviour as its essential properties. Unless one holds a rather restrictively reductionist view of action, it will appear that being action—or, more generally, being the kind of behaviour which is apt for explanation in terms of thoughts and feelings—is inessential to the behaviour. So there could have been all of that behaviour—the behaviour which we take to be caused by beliefs—even if there had been no beliefs. One might try to block this by appealing to some thesis of essentiality of causal origin, but this will look like a rather *ad hoc* move, which is not easily motivated from within the position itself. But even if one did that, on any normal view of causation, the nature of the cause of something is not a priori discoverable from the thing itself, or from just its intrinsic properties. And that will be enough for (FC2).

Now to (FC3). What does 'directed towards prediction' mean? The idea is this. If someone was asked why she was engaged in a particular science, her motivation would not be sufficiently explained if she said just that she wanted to understand the world: that could be a motivation equally for reading poetry. Clearly science provides a particular *kind* of understanding. It is then hard to characterize what is distinctive about that kind of understanding of the world without making some reference to prediction. The natural suggestion is something like this: the special virtue of the understanding provided by *science* is that one who understands things in this way will be good at predicting. In a certain sense, one might say, the goal of science is prediction.

This has to be handled quite carefully. There are two things in particular which do not follow from it. First, it does not imply that scientists themselves are predominantly motivated by the desire to predict accurately. It is not claimed that the sole virtue of science is predictive accuracy, merely that the goal of prediction sets science apart from various other ways of understanding things. One would expect the orientation towards prediction to be taken for granted by scientists, and not to occupy their minds all the time.

Secondly, the view that science is directed towards prediction does not imply an instrumentalistic philosophy of science, according to which the truth of scientific theories simply consists in their predictive adequacy. We can insist that the truth of a scientific theory depends on its providing *understanding*, and that will require at least that it gets the predictions right *for the right sort of reason*.

If this is right, then it seems clear that the internal version of the 'folk-psychology' myth will be committed to (FC3), in virtue of its commitment to a mechanical conception of the causal relation which it takes to be involved. It is also surely clear that the external version's conception of a scientific theory is a conception of a theory directed towards prediction. (FC1), (FC2), and (FC3) seem to characterize familiar positions: it hardly seems arbitrary to see them all as manifestations of a single kind of conception of the mind, the 'folk-psychology' myth.

8.3. Unpicking the Myth

I think that the 'folk-psychology' myth is wrong in every particular. In this section I shall try to argue that the special relationship cannot be characterized as causal in a sense of 'cause' for which *any* of (FC1), (FC2), and (FC3) holds.

Recall the first of the claims:

(FC1) Content is causally inert.

This kind of claim is implicit in representationalist theories of the mind.[3] Such theories assume both (FC1) and that the special relationship is causal.[4] The result is that contentful states of mind

---

[3] See, e.g., J. Fodor, *Psychosemantics* (Cambridge, Mass.: MIT Press, 1987), ch. 4.

[4] Fodor tries to distance himself from (FC1) in 'Making Mind Matter More', in his *A Theory of Content* (Cambridge, Mass.: MIT Press, 1987) but on the more liberal view of causal efficacy which he urges there, the assumption of representationalism is unmotivated.

have to be thought of as being individuated in content-neutral ('syntactic') terms. A representation is just something which is individuated independently of content, but which nevertheless has content. Davidson's argument that mental events are physical events is tactically similar: he assumes that the special relationship is causal; he then imposes conditions on the proper grounding of causal relations which amount, in effect, to an abstractly conceived version of (FC1).[5] On both theories, the possession of content by the things which we describe as mental states turns out to be incidental to their true nature.

This is a dramatic result; but we should expect no less from such fantastic assumptions. Believing in (FC1) ought to be an almost decisive reason for believing that the special relationship is not causal. Special-relationship explanations are explanatory precisely in virtue of their content. There are, therefore, two things seriously wrong with any view which holds that special-relationship explanations are causal, in a sense of 'cause' for which (FC1) is true. First, the account provided of the explanatory relationship which we are concerned with is useless, since it fails to explain what is explanatory about it. Secondly, since the account fails to explain what needs to be explained, the connection it posits is one we have no reason to believe in. If we hold (FC1), we have no reason at all to think that the special relationship is causal.

This, in turn, has further serious consequences. Since the mechanical conception of causation requires that we hold (FC1), there can be no motivation for thinking that beliefs are mechanical causes of behaviour. That then means that there is no motivation for thinking that the behaviour which beliefs are cited to explain is the kind of thing that might be a mechanical effect of a mechanical cause: in short, the behaviour does not need to be individuated mechanically. And since the only reason for thinking that beliefs are in the head seems to be that this is required if they are mechanical causes of bodily movement, there seems to be no motivation for thinking that beliefs are in the head.

None of this, of course, is a *proof* that beliefs are not mechanical causes of behaviour, or, more generally, that they are not causes of behaviour in a sense of 'cause' for which (FC1) holds. That view

---

[5] D. Davidson, 'Mental Events', in his *Essays on Actions and Events* (Oxford: Clarendon Press, 1980), 207–25.

would be quite arbitrary, could not be adopted in any properly scientific spirit, but it is not ruled out (yet).

Now to the second distinctive feature of causation:

(FC2) It is not ruled out a priori that there could be all the behaviour which we take to be 'caused' by beliefs without there being any beliefs at all.

(FC2) assumes that the nature of the behaviour which we explain by citing thoughts and feelings is itself neutral as to whether it is really properly explained in terms of thoughts and feelings at all. But this is certainly not how it seems. The behaviour seems to present itself to us as apt for such explanation before we ask which particular thoughts and feelings explain it. We only ask why someone did something when we have already assumed that what was done was motivated by *some* beliefs and desires.

This is true even of the most localized and blatant forms of behaviour, forms which seem most easily characterizable as bodily movements. Kicking a ball is not just a matter of having one's leg move in a certain geometrically describable way. Knitting is not just a matter of having one's fingers twitch. Smiling is not just having one's mouth widen and one's eyes narrow. And beliefs are cited to explain much less easily localizable behaviour: negotiating with diplomats all round the world for months; taking a course in philosophy; lazing around for a year.

When one considers the full range of kinds of behaviour which might be explained in terms of thoughts and feelings, it seems that we generally abide by a principle which is almost the opposite of (FC2):

(FC2*) Behaviour is only explicable in terms of belief, desire, and the rest, if it is correctly conceived in such a way that, so conceived, it is *inconceivable* that there should have been this behaviour and no beliefs at all.

A photograph once appeared in a newspaper which seemed to show a policeman kicking someone in a crowd. In fact, he had lost his balance and was falling over: the extended leg which seemed to be kicking had looked like that just because of the way he was toppling over. If you had asked, 'Why did he kick that person?', you would have presumed there was some motive explaining the action; which is why, if I know what really happened, I cannot answer that question: I first have to say that what you saw was not a kick. And at the same time, the various features of the position of the policeman's body, and its relation to the person who had seemed to be being kicked, lose their coherence: we are left with a series of things of which there is no unitary explanation.

There is a familiar response to this kind of point. Someone might say that the behaviour which we explain by citing beliefs is in fact the mechanical effect of mechanical causes, which we simply *describe* in intentional terms. There is a purely mechanical description of the very same behaviour which actually reveals its true nature. It is true that we only look for explanations of behaviour in terms of belief and desire, and the rest, once we have conceived of the behaviour in intentional terms. But thinking of the behaviour like that, and explaining it in those terms, are both part of adopting a certain kind of *stance* towards it (the 'intentional stance').[6] And what we take this stance towards is still the very same behaviour whose nature a mechanical science could reveal.

The proper reply to this response has already been anticipated, to some extent, in widening our gaze to include the full range of kinds of behaviour that might be explained by citing a single belief. The crucial point is that the response requires that the mechanical properties of the behaviour should be essential to it: it is the mechanical properties which determine the identity of the behaviour.

There are two reasons for finding this extremely implausible. First, the behaviour explained by a single belief need have no mechanical coherence at all. Why should any mechanical science single out as a unitary event the behaviour involved in someone's starting a war, for example? Secondly, it seems indeterminate which mechanical events, precisely, constitute any given piece of intentionally characterized behaviour. Suppose I walk purposefully across a lawn? Where did that occur? Wherever the lawn is, presumably; but that is hopelessly imprecise from a mechanical point of view, and there seems no basis for any further precision. When did it begin? I could give the time as a witness, say, if I happened to look at my watch; but that will hardly reveal the kind of precision which would satisfy someone concerned with events in the brain and their bodily consequences.

In the face of such apparent implausibility, we need some good reason to think that the behaviour is really only *described* in

---

[6] D. Dennett, 'True Believers', in his *The Intentional Stance* (Cambridge, Mass.: MIT Press, 1987), 13–35.

intentional terms, with its true nature being revealed by some causal science. What reason might there be? One reason might be that beliefs figure in special relationship explanations as mechanical causes of behaviour, so what they explain must have a mechanical essence too. But this does not look a good reason, now that the view that beliefs are causes of behaviour, in a sense for which (FC1) holds, has been discredited. Alternatively, one might think that there are really only mechanical events and mechanical objects: all other vocabularies, in so far as they are well-founded at all, simply redescribe those very same things. But this looks just like a version of the scientism which was attacked in Chapter 4. There seems no good reason to doubt that it is essential to the very nature of the behaviour which we properly explain in terms of thoughts and feelings that it is apt for such explanation.

Once we have abandoned the insistence that intentional behaviour is really just mechanical events redescribed, we can open our eyes to another difficulty for (FC2). There is not the neat division between behaviour and states of mind which it presupposes. This division is essential to the external version of the 'folk-psychology' myth, since it marks the division between observation and theory. But if we are not just trying to maintain a thesis, it should seem very implausible. Consider, first, the following brief dialogue:

'Why hasn't she done anything?'
'Because she's waiting to see what happens.'

It is true, of course, that 'waiting to see' does not usually figure on the rather short lists of theoretical terms that the 'folk-psychology' myth generally acknowledges. But the explanation here seems not vastly different from one which we might express more laboriously like this:

'Because she doesn't want to move until she's seen what's going to happen, and she hasn't yet seen that.'

But is *waiting to see* a kind of behaviour or a state of mind? Once the question is raised with one example, further problem cases are easy to imagine. Suppose someone is sitting anxiously: is the sitting behaviour, while the anxiety is a state of mind? Which category do decisions and choices belong to? If I think aloud, is that a kind of behaviour—whereas if I think to myself it is merely mental? None of these questions has a good answer.

In short, (FC2) seems extremely implausible. I have not *disproved* it, of course. It flies in the face of the presumptions of the whole practice of explaining behaviour in terms of thoughts and feeling, and it appears to have no good motivation; but there is nothing to stop someone holding it, if they are sufficiently determined. (Not yet, at least.)

Finally, let us turn to the third feature of causation assumed in the 'folk-psychology' myth's view that the special relationship is causal:

(FC3) The discovery of the mental 'causes' of behaviour is directed towards prediction.

The assumption here is that the distinctive virtue of the kind of understanding provided by knowledge of someone's beliefs and desires is that it enables one to predict her behaviour. I have three objections to this, which I shall present in ascending order of technicality.

The first objection is brutally simple, but I think it ought to be compelling for all that. It is just that it is *immoral* to regard the virtue of the kind of understanding provided by special-relationship explanations as being that it enables one to predict people's behaviour. It involves not treating them as people, but as strange interveners in our projects, whose interventions we need to be able to anticipate in order to further our own ends. The reason it has this consequence is that, if prediction is the point even of finding out what someone else *thinks* and *feels*, there is no place left for any other concern with other people to have any basis. We may *find* ourselves feeling sympathy, compassion, revulsion, or admiration; but these feelings will become peculiar incidental accompaniments of the larger project of working out what other people are going to do. If even understanding what other people think and feel is directed towards prediction, we have no room left for our understanding of other people to be directed towards the question whether these feelings towards other people are appropriate or just.

It seems no accident that this attitude cannot be adopted towards one's own thoughts and feelings. It seems absurd to suppose that the virtue of understanding my own motivations is that it enables me to predict what I am going to do. I might make such predictions, of course; I might predict that I will fail to do something because of the feebleness of my resolve in certain matters. But this cannot be what my understanding of my own motivation is directed towards;

if I value an understanding of myself, this cannot be the reason. What I am much more likely to be concerned with is whether what I have done is to be admired or despised—or, in short, whether the kind of feelings mentioned in the last paragraph are appropriately directed towards me. The impossibility of adopting a thoroughly predictive attitude towards myself seems to confirm the first thought about what is wrong with thinking that understanding other people's thoughts and feelings is directed towards prediction. The simple thought was that it involves failing to treat other people as people; and it is impossible not to treat oneself as a person.

Although I think that kind of simple consideration ought to be compelling reason to reject (FC3), it may seem to some a little crude, and the wrong kind of thing to be appealing to in determining a theoretical question. So let us now turn to the second reason for rejecting (FC3). This is that our predictions of what people will do are not in fact based just on our knowledge of what they think and feel, but also depend upon our knowledge of other things, which we do not know just in virtue of knowing even quite a lot about people's thoughts and feelings. This makes it hard to claim that predictive power is the distinctive virtue of just knowing about other people's states of mind.

A favourite example of the alleged predictive gain afforded by insight into the minds of others is the appointment. This is a nicely everyday kind of practice, which seems to rely on our ability to have confidence in our expectations of other people. But if one thinks about what these expectations are based on, in plausible detail, it turns out that it is not the mere knowledge of thoughts and feelings which is important. Suppose, then, that I make an appointment with a colleague to meet somewhere at some time. If it is the right colleague, I can predict with reasonable confidence that he will be there then. I know that, if he has said he will be there, then it is very likely that he will. But this knowledge seems to me to precede any detailed knowledge of his thoughts and feelings, rather than to depend upon it. Does he really want to see me about that business? The over-riding impression on the telephone was of irritation at a further interruption in an already busy day. But perhaps I was over-reading his naturally brusque manner. Still, since he has said he will be there, and I know that if he has said he will be there he *will* be there, and I imagine he will be there on purpose if he is there—since all that is true, there must be a *sense* in which he wants to see me about it. Does he think that turning up at the agreed place and the agreed time is a good way of seeing me? I had not thought about it, but if he is there on purpose, that will show that he does, and I am sure he will be there, so I suppose he does. The fundamental factor in my ability to predict my colleague's behaviour is not my knowledge of the detail of what he thinks and feels, but my knowledge of the kind of person he is. And that knowledge in turn does not exploit any supposed predictive advantage to be had by knowing just that he thinks one should turn up to appointments—for one can have that belief and be disorganized or lazy enough to be unreliable. What I know that makes the difference here is just that my colleague is the sort of person who keeps appointments.

There are plenty of cases, of course, in which knowing someone's thoughts and feelings can be directly helpful in prediction. If I know that someone thinks she is being persecuted, I may be able to say that there is a significant risk that she will do something dangerous. (I do not know if this is actually true.) But there are two points to be made about this. First, the predictive claim is in fact just a claim of *significant risk*; this seems to me quite typical, though not inevitable, in predictive claims made directly on the basis of knowledge of thoughts and feelings. Secondly, if it is true that the fact that she thinks she is being persecuted means that there is a significant risk that she will do something dangerous, this is not something I know just in virtue of knowing that she thinks she is being persecuted. I could perfectly well know that she has this belief, and see no reason to fear—perhaps I would be inclined just to feel sorry for her.

In general, it does not in fact seem to be knowledge of people's thoughts and feelings which explains our ability to predict others, such as it is. That ability seems to depend rather on ancillary knowledge, which is independent of knowing about any particular person's thoughts and feelings.

This leads on to the third objection to (FC3). If a set of terms is *directed towards* prediction, it is not enough merely that they can be *used* to make predictions; otherwise every kind of vocabulary would be directed towards prediction. What is required is that the use of the terms should involve some specific a priori predictive commitments. That is, one would not count as understanding such a term unless one recognized that the failure of some predicted consequence was a decisive demonstration that there was no such thing present as the term applies to. (Nothing can count as a *particle* which goes through two slits at the same time in the way that the famous experiment shows.)

This seems to me a general requirement on the theoretical terms of a predictive science. If one did not accept it, nothing could count as refuting a theory—even under perfect experimental conditions—and one could not argue that any theory provided a good explanation of any particular piece of experimental evidence.

If this is right, then if 'belief' and 'desire', and the rest, are theoretical terms in a theory which is directed towards prediction, the very use of such terms must involve certain specific a priori predictive commitments. If that is what we are looking for, it is hard to think of anywhere better to look than the alleged predictive law which I mentioned before:

(BD) If *a* desires that *p*, and believes that if *a* B*s* then *p*, then, other things being equal, *a* B*s*.

My worries about this as a predictive law are diametrically opposed to those which are most frequently voiced. Some have thought that a problem is created by its being a priori:[7] I think the 'folk-psychology' myth can only be saved if it *is* a priori. Some have felt that the vagueness of the 'other-things-being-equal' clause disqualifies (BD) from counting as a proper law.[8] I think that it is only the insistence on the vagueness of that clause which has preserved the illusion that (BD) is predictive at all.

Certainly the trouble is with that 'other-things-being-equal' clause. But the trouble is not that it is hard to say what 'other things being equal' amounts to, because it is not hard. This is what it means.

(*a*) Her belief and desire must end up 'combined' in order to become active.

(*b*) She must not end up wanting, more than she desires that *p*, something whose obtaining she thinks would be incompatible with its being the case that *p*.

(*c*) She must not conclude that there is a better way of bringing it about that *p* than B-ing.

[7] See, e.g., C. Taylor, *The Explanation of Behaviour* (London: Routledge and Kegan Paul, 1964), 33.

[8] e.g., S. Schiffer, 'Ceteris Paribus Laws', *Mind*, 100 (1991), 1–17.

(d) She must not end up thinking that B-ing is beyond her power.

(e) She must not be distracted while finally making up her mind.

(f) She must not change her mind between decision and action.

(g) When she tries to B, she must succeed.

It certainly seems a priori certain that, if someone desires that p, and believes that if she Bs then p, and all these conditions obtain, then she will B. The problem is that this 'law' cannot be predictive.

The reason is simple: there is no test of the obtaining of *any* of the conditions covered by the 'other-things-being-equal' clause apart from an action of trying to B. This is evident from the fact that the first five conditions have to make some reference to the *final* stage of the deliberation. But the final stage of the deliberation is just (to be defined as) the stage which is acted on unless the person changes her mind. And it is essential that reference be made to the final stage of deliberation: without it none of the conditions gets us any closer to what the person will decide. As for the sixth condition, (f), once again the only test of a change of mind is whether or not the person acts.

This seems to make (BD) useless as a predictive law. One should have been suspicious of the predictive pretensions of talk of beliefs and desires the moment it became apparent that something like condition (f) was needed. It would be a very odd predictive psychology which allowed its claims to be insulated from refutation by such an unexplained appeal to changes of mind. One does not have to be rabidly Popperian to feel that this is shying away from falsification a little too much.

Not only is action the only test of the *obtaining* of all the relevant conditions. Failure to act is the only test of any of them *not* obtaining. And that fact is surely what explains the conditions themselves. The conditions are, as it were, the residue of different flavours of failure to act. Their contraries are just ways in which one may both desire that p and believe that if one Bs then p, while not actually B-ing. The obtaining of each of the contraries seems to have a distinctive phenomenology, which is more than can be said for the conditions themselves.

That seems to dispose of the claim that (BD) is a predictive law. I have assumed that (BD) is an a priori predictive law if anything involving the concepts of special-relationship explanation is.

Perhaps an upholder of the 'folk-psychology' myth will be able to produce a better candidate. Until then, the third objection to (FC3) looks good.

When the three objections to (FC3) are taken together, they seem to me to make the claim clearly unacceptable. Again, though, no absolutely decisive proof has been provided. There is still room for dogged perseverance with the myth (for the moment).

The 'folk-psychology' myth as a whole ought now to seem altogether wrong about the way in which beliefs and desires, and the rest, are standardly cited to explain behaviour. The whole conception should clearly be abandoned. But I doubt if it will be given up yet. The curious resilience of the myth is something which needs to be explained.

8.4. The Onus of Proof

Here is a splendid way of finishing a paper:

I'm not really convinced that it matters very much whether the mental is physical; still less that it matters very much whether we can prove that it is. Whereas, if it isn't literally true that my wanting is causally responsible for my reaching, and my itching is causally responsible for my scratching, and my believing is causally responsible for my saying . . . if none of that is literally true, then practically everything I believe about anything is false and it's the end of the world.[9]

Thus Fodor. And here is the target of the first sentence of that quotation, no less obstinate, even if more urbane:

In this paper I want to defend the ancient—and commonsense—position that rationalization is a species of causal explanation. The defence no doubt requires some deployment, but it does not seem necessary to abandon the position, as has been urged by many recent writers.[10]

Davidson states his view a little more robustly later on:

One way we can explain an event is by placing it in the context of its cause; cause and effect form the sort of pattern that explains the effect, in a sense of 'explain' that we understand as well as any. If reason and action illustrate a different pattern of explanation, that pattern must be identified.[11]

[9] Fodor, 'Making Mind Matter More', *A Theory of Content*, 156.
[10] D. Davidson, 'Actions, Reasons, Causes', in his *Essays on Actions and Events*, 3.
[11] Ibid. 10.

These three passages summarize the main arguments for the view that the special relationship is causal. They are:

(i) A whole conception of the world would have to be abandoned if the causal view was rejected.

(ii) The causal view is ancient and common sense.

(iii) The causal view does not need to be abandoned.

(iv) If beliefs cause behaviour, we can understand how citing beliefs might explain behaviour.

(v) No satisfactory alternative account of the special relationship has been provided.

These arguments seem rather a long way short of being decisive. On (ii): although one cannot deny the age of the causal conception, it is not obvious that the view is plain common sense, given the arguments of the last section, which suggest that at least one version of the causal conception does considerable violence to the whole practice of providing special-relationship explanations. On (iv): it is not clear that counting beliefs as causes of behaviour does explain how citing beliefs can explain behaviour; on any conception of causation which is committed to (FC1) it would remain entirely mysterious how citing beliefs could explain behaviour. On (v): the absence of an alternative to the causal conception is only an argument in favour of the causal conception if the causal conception itself is adequate, which seems at least doubtful; otherwise the absence of an alternative to the causal conception should lead us to think just that we do not understand the special relationship. (In any case, I shall be providing an alternative in Chapter 12.)

I think the most compelling considerations are in fact (i) and (iii) (even if it was mischievous to single out (iii) as a separate argument in the first place). Point (iii) amounts just to an insistence that the onus of proof will always rest on any opponent of the causal conception; and point (i) incorporates the same thing, although in a different style. Point (i) seems to me to be the strongest, and to do something towards justifying the insistence that the onus of proof is always on the opposition.

The power of these points ought to have been severely weakened by the arguments against the 'folk-psychology' myth. But I will bet that the onus of proof will still be thought to lie on anyone who opposes the causal conception of the special relationship. If one argument seems to work, that will be taken to show that the nature of causation has not been properly understood, or that the causal relation *here* is not to be so easily assimilated to causation elsewhere: perhaps causation demands *less* than we had thought.

Viewed dispassionately, it should be clear that this is just fudging the issues. There are two morals to be drawn from that, I think. First, if we are persuaded by the arguments against the 'folk-psychology' myth, we should not attempt to evade them by supposing that the special relationship is causal in a special sense of 'cause': the special sense can be expected to turn out to be a Pickwickian sense. Secondly, we need to do something to dig out whatever it is that makes us want to keep the special-relationship causal, even by fudging if need be.

What could it be? One suggestion might be that it is the lure of scientism which makes us want to treat every explanatory relationship on the model of the fundamental kind of explanation afforded by the (predictive) natural sciences. Perhaps that is a contributory factor. I want to suggest, however, that there is another, possibly deeper motive. I suspect that the causal conception of the special relationship has its roots in a conception of the self which is most familiar to us through Descartes, although it is much older than that.

This is a cheeky suggestion, of course: all modern philosophies of mind define themselves by their opposition to Descartes. But it is not just an insult. I shall try to argue in 8.6 that the Cartesian conception gives the *best* version of a causal theory of the mind. Modern theories, by being more prosaic, are less coherent than Descartes's version.

8.5. Descartes's Ghost and 'The Mind–Body Problem'

According to the 'folk-psychology' myth, Descartes's conception of the mind faces an insuperable problem, known as 'the mind–body problem'. On a modern conception, the problem arises over Descartes's commitment to something like these two theses:

(1) The mind is the mechanical cause of behaviour.

(2) The mind is not a mechanical object.

The resulting position is incoherent. The 'folk-psychology' myth denies (2) while accepting (1).

This conception regards the problem as arising specifically over the notion of *mechanical* causation. The incoherence may be demonstrated on the basis of the fact that (1) and (2) together seem to involve a denial of the completeness of *physics*, specifically; or on the basis of the fact that they require the violation of conservation principles in *physics* specifically (this was Leibniz's argument[12]).

But the basic positions here do not need to be stated in terms of the apparently precise notion of *mechanical* causation. Any notion of causation will do: any notion of the source or origin of change, or of something which *makes* something happen. However generously we conceive of causation, as long as we are still dealing with a notion like this, Descartes is still committed to a position which is incoherent. Descartes is committed to these two theses:

(1*) The mind is the origin/source/producer of behaviour.
(2*) The mind is not the sort of thing which *could* be the origin/source/producer of behaviour.

The reasoning within Descartes's position which leads to (1*)—however generously we interpret the causal notions involved—also requires (2*). This suggests that it is (1*) which is the problem, not (2*). I shall be suggesting in 8.6 that there is a good sense in which a position which holds both (1*) and (2*)—or (1) and (2)—together is indeed more coherent than a position which holds just (1*) or (1).

The source of (1*) within Descartes's view is, I think, a certain conception of the self. This conception dates back to Plato, at least.[13] We might call it the conception of a *disengaged* self, to emphasize one aspect of it, or the conception of the self as *spectator*, to emphasize another. Here is a way of getting the feel of it.

Within this conception, you think of yourself as essentially a spectator. There before you is the passing show, the world and its events. *You* are over here, watching. That is the crucial divide: the world over there, you over here. (Note the spatial language.) Everything which can come beneath the spectator's gaze is part of the world, and not part of you. You look down: there are your

---

[12] See, e.g., G. Leibniz, 'Explanation of the New System', in Leibniz, *Philosophical Writings*, ed. G. H. R. Parkinson (London: Dent, 1973), 129–30.
[13] See, e.g., Plato, *Phaedo*.

hands, quaint and foreign. You hear the sound of your voice, echoing in your mouth and whistling between your teeth. All the time you yourself are to one side, observing. The picture can seem absurd, but it can be compelling enough when you sit late in your office, all quiet, sniffing your pen; or, like Descartes, in your dressing-gown, by the fire, at night, alone.[14]

The image has familiar and startling consequences. Your body is part of the world you observe, and so not part of you. There is no more to you than what is needed for you to be a spectator. You are a mind: that is, you and your mind are the same thing. The mind *is* a thing—a substance, an object with properties—because you are.

You, your mind, are not part of the world you gaze on. But your behaviour *is* part of the world, since you can observe it. There can, therefore, be nothing mental about your behaviour: the behaviour itself gives no hint of a mind. The distinction between the subject and the world becomes the distinction between mental and non-mental. The self and the world are each complete in themselves, independent of one another. The world is alien to you, even if it is familiar.

There is a certain poetic coherence in this conception. But it leads quite quickly to both (1*) and (2*). Among the events in the world, you distinguish some as *your* behaviour. You must, or else you make no difference in the world. But how can this behaviour be *yours*? How can we make sense of this personal attachment? We can only suggest that these events count as *your* behaviour because they are *caused* by you: you, your mind, are their source and origin; you make them happen. This seems satisfying: you can make some impact on the world. So we get (1*): you, your mind, are the cause of behaviour.

But, of course, you (your mind) cannot possibly cause anything in the world you observe. The world is complete without you: you merely watch it. Every event in the world follows from some other event, from which it flows with distant inexorability. (That is an exact enough description just of the phenomenology of the spectator conception.) And, on your side, there is no power you could conceivably have as a mind and nothing more, in virtue of which you could affect the world around you. No part of you could

---

[14] R. Descartes, *Philosophical Writings*, ii. *Meditations on First Philosophy*, trans. J. Cottingham, R. Stoothoff, and D. Murdoch (Cambridge: Cambridge University Press, 1985), 13.

ever open the can without being part of the world, and so *not* part of you. The pure spectator conception of the self is quickly committed to (2*). The conception is incoherent, but then the poetry lies precisely in the inconsistency.

I shall not be claiming that modern theories of the mind are evidently committed to exactly the spectator conception of the self. I shall argue just that they would be better if they were. As a preliminary to that argument, there are two features of this Cartesian route to a causal theory of the mind which are worth noting. First, the mind is only the cause of behaviour because the mind and the person are one and the same thing. Secondly, on the Cartesian conception, the mind is the cause of behaviour in a sense of 'cause' for which an analogue of (FC2) is true: it is not ruled out a priori that there could have been all the behaviour which we take to be 'caused' by a mind without there being any mind at all. These two features will echo through the arguments of the next section.

8.6. The Rediscovery of Descartes's Ghost

In this section I shall argue for two claims:

(I) If anything is the cause of behaviour in a way that is relevant to the special relationship, then the person is.

(II) If the person is the *cause* of her behaviour, then there is no more to the person than a Cartesian mind.

The argument is meant to work for *any* notion of causation which even the most generous view might entitle us to. I take it to be an absolutely minimal condition on a conception of an explanatory relation which is entitled to count itself a conception of *causation* that causal explanation is a species of empirical explanation. This will then be a necessary condition for a relation counting as causal:

(NAP*) If *a* is a cause of *b*, then it is impossible to reason a priori to the nature of *a* from knowledge of the nature of *b*.

This is evidently just a special case of the general condition for an explanatory relation to count as empirical, which was formulated as (NAP) in 4.2. It is also clearly linked to (FC2) of 8.2.

One point needs explaining. If someone believed in the essentiality of causal origin, then they would think it was possible to reason a priori from the *essence* of an effect to the nature of its cause, since a full description of the essence of an effect would include a specification of the cause. When we think of the *nature* of an effect, in the sense required for (NAP*), we must, therefore, think of what might be called its *intrinsic* nature, which specifically excludes anything to do with its cause. It will, therefore, follow that a phrase of the form 'the thing caused by *a*' does not count as a description of the nature of an effect, in the sense of 'nature' required for (NAP*).

Conversely, if we allowed a phrase of the form 'the cause of *b*' to give us a priori knowledge of the nature of a cause, it would obviously be possible to reason a priori from the nature of an effect to the nature of its cause. So if a phrase of that form does really describe the nature of a cause—if there is simply nothing else to say about it, for example—then it cannot be known a priori that it does. It will be safe to assume, for the kind of example that I shall be considering that that kind of phrase does not describe the nature of any of the relevant causes. (These two restrictions on our conception of what can count as the nature of something seem quite natural to the project of empirical enquiry.)

It will be helpful in what follows to have an example before us. I shall choose a very simple piece of behaviour. Once, as a child, I bought a wind-up gramophone at an auction. Let us focus in very close on part of that. I raised my hand to attract the auctioneer's attention. We have here: an action—my raising of my hand; a desire—to attract the auctioneer's attention; and a belief—that raising my hand would be a good way of attracting the auctioneer's attention. There was a further important feature of this behaviour: I used no pulleys or levers to get my hand up; no helpful friends lifted it for me; I just raised my hand. With that example now vividly in mind, we can begin on the argument.

Here are two truths about that situation:

(1) I raised my hand.
(2) My hand rose.

And there are two things we can say about the difference between (1) and (2), as they are to be understood here:

(i) (1) implies that what was done is explicable in terms of belief, desire, and the rest, while (2) does not.
(ii) (1) implies that what was done was something someone was responsible for, whereas (2) does not.

(ii) needs to be treated quite carefully. The sense of 'responsible' here does not allow us to assume that the person responsible is the person to be praised or blamed if praise or blame is due. For (1) could be true, even if this was true:

(3) He made me raise my hand.

This is because (3) does not imply—indeed it is inconsistent with— this:

(4) He raised my hand.

A sense of the difference between (3) and (4) should give some understanding of the sense of 'responsible' relevant to (ii). It is worth noting that, although I would not have been strictly to blame if (3) had been true (and raising my hand had been a bad thing), nevertheless an apology from me might have been in order. A way of putting the point is this: if I am responsible for something in the sense required for (ii), then, if praise or blame is due at all, it should fall on me unless I can properly pass it back to someone else.

It should be clear from this that (i) and (ii) require each other. Citing someone's beliefs and desires explains behaviour for which she is responsible, in the sense relevant to (ii). If she were not responsible in that sense, there could be no point in citing *her* beliefs and desires to explain the behaviour. Conversely, someone can only be responsible for something if it is explicable—and perhaps excusable—in the light of knowledge of her beliefs and desires.

There are, of course, people who deny that we are ever truly responsible for what we do.[15] Am I not just begging the question against them? I am not sure their thesis can be maintained in the face of these observations, but I do not think I am begging the question. All I am asking from a notion of responsibility is enough to make sense of action. It is a noticeable feature of actions that they are attributable to agents. The notion of responsibility I want is just whatever is needed to make sense of that attribution— whatever is needed to make it true that I am the doer of my deeds, even when someone makes me do them.

This minimal sense of responsibility seems needed if we are to be able to talk about beliefs, desires, and the rest, at all. Unless we have the idea of someone being the doer of what she does, we have

---

[15] e.g. G. Strawson, *Freedom and Belief* (Oxford: Clarendon Press, 1986).

no conception at all of what is distinctive of the kind of behaviour which calls for explanation in terms of belief and desire. If someone who thinks that we are never truly responsible for what we do thinks the question is already being begged against her position, she needs to recognize just how dramatic her position is. It seems to find no room in the world for people or states of mind. In that case, it is hard to see how anyone could coherently maintain it. I count myself as already being committed to the existence in the world of people who think and feel and act, and will proceed on that basis.

How can we make sense of the idea that someone is the doer of her deeds? I think we need the idea of a course of things *pivoting* on people. Some things have to be seen as terminating with a person; others as originating at or with a person. A person is influenced, and under the influence, she acts or reacts. Unless we can make sense of this, all we will have will be *things happening*: there will be no idea of anything being *done*. There is nothing really unfamiliar in the idea: it even has its echoes in scientific descriptions in talk of 'inputs' and 'outputs'. And this idea of things pivoting on people seems required just for the most minimal sense of people really being agents.

But although it is quite familiar, and although we seem to be committed to it just by thinking of *people*, the idea is not insignificant. What we have to think of is a different kind of causal order from that with which natural science is concerned: we might call it a *person-pivoting* causal order. (Note that I am *not* talking just about what is often called 'agent causation': the reason will become clear by the end of the section.) Describing things in the terms of the person-pivoting causal order, we talk of people being influenced, doing things, reacting, affecting other people. This is not naturally thought of as just a matter of things happening.

If person-pivoting descriptions are not just descriptions of things happening, then the person-pivoting causal order will not be reducible to the order of *events* (outcomes, happenings, occurrences), and will not be capturable in terms of event causation. And so indeed it seems. Recall this:

(3) He made me raise my hand.

This is already a person-pivoting description, but we might try to make the poles on which things pivot more explicit by rewriting it like this:

(5) He affected me in some way or other, and I, being so affected, raised my hand.

If we try to force this into the mould of event causation, the best we can do is something like this:

(6) His doing something or other caused my raising of my hand.

That phrase following 'caused' must sound awkward to any grammatically sensitive ear. There is a reason for the awkwardness: the analysis is a fudge, an attempt to blur the distinction between the conception of things which is amenable to analysis in terms of event causation, and that which is not.

The important thing about the idea of person-pivoting descriptions—or, about the idea of agency—is that some things are seen as terminating with a person, and some things are seen as originating with a person. An action is essentially something which originates with a person. This distinction is reflected in the 'and' in (5): what is to the left of it terminates with me; what is to the right originates with me. (5) portrays my action, correctly, as originating with me: that is, I am portrayed as its agent. (It does not, of course, portray me as acting in a vacuum, uninfluenced: the influence appears in the phrase 'being so affected'.)

Now consider the grammatical awkwardness of (6). This arises because (6) appears to haver between two grammatically felicitous resolutions:

(7) His doing something or other caused my hand to rise.
(8) His doing something or other caused me to raise my hand.

(7) is an account of something properly portrayed in terms of event causation (at least if we do not worry about the idea of *his doing something*). But it is an inadequate analysis of (3), since it is consistent with (4), which is inconsistent with (3). (8), on the other hand, is a satisfactory rewriting of (3), but only because it simply incorporates, without analysis, the idea that my action originates with me. The sense of 'origin' involved in the idea that actions originate with their agents seems not to be capturable in terms of event causation.[16] This point will be reinforced by the rest of the argument.

It seems, then, that we are committed to there being two kinds of causal order, just in virtue of recognizing people as the doers of

[16] Davidson accepts this; see 'Agency', in his *Essays on Actions and Events*, 49. But he hopes (without argument) that he can preserve the event-causation account of the special relationship.

their deeds. One is an order of happenings, and the notion of origin proper to it is captured by event causation. The other is an order of doings, and being affected (not merely altered), and the notion of origin proper to it seems not to be captured by event causation. But they are both properly *causal* orders, and the notion of origin proper to each is a notion of *causal* origin. (I am the cause of things which I bring about by acting.) This is reflected in the fact that (NAP*) characterizes the notion of causation involved in each of them, although to accommodate that we will have to let '*a*' and '*b*' be capable of being schematic for names of people as well as names of events.

These, then, are the crucial points I need for the argument that follows. First, we are committed to a person-pivoting causal order; secondly, all forms of causation are subject to (NAP*).

Now for the first of the claims which I said I wanted to establish. Here it is again:

(I) If anything is the cause of behaviour in a way that is relevant to the special relationship, then the person is.

If anything is the cause of my behaviour in the auction room, it must be something whose name could replace '*x*' in one of these two:

(9) *x* caused me to raise my hand;
(10) *x* caused my hand to rise.

I think it is clear from the attempt to analyse (3) in terms of event causation that these are the only alternatives.

There is an extremely swift intuitive argument from here to (I). The gap in (9) is ruled out, because the special relationship is all on the *right* of 'caused' in (9): compare (5) and (8) above. And the gap in (10) is ruled out, if it is not filled by a name for *me*, because then I will not be responsible for the fact that my hand rose.

That argument seems to me completely sound, but it may not convince everyone. So let us take things more slowly. If anything other than me was the cause of my behaviour, in a way which is relevant to the special relationship, then my belief was. (The belief was that raising my hand would be a good way to attract the auctioneer's attention.) That means that we can establish (I) by showing that my belief was not the cause of my behaviour.

If my belief was the cause of my behaviour, then one of these two must be true:

(11)　My belief caused me to raise my hand.

(12)　My belief caused my hand to rise.

Again there is a very simple argument. In (11) my belief seems somehow to act on me; but in (12) it seems somehow to act without me. And, again, I think these simple thoughts are quite right. But, again, they may not convince everyone. So let us take each of (11) and (12) in turn.

We can begin with a slightly more sophisticated version of the simple thought about (11). Within the person-pivoting causal order, we recognize two kinds of cause: things which affect people, and people. In (11) my belief is cast in the role of something which affects me; so it cannot be part of the special relationship, which holds between my being somehow affected and my behaviour. ('Among the notable influences on my performance, I would like to pay special tribute to my beliefs.')

Let us move up another level of sophistication. The *explanandum* in (11) is an action, something for which someone is responsible, from which it follows a priori that it has a belief as *explanans*—in the special relationship, at least. So if the special relationship is causal, my belief cannot figure in (11) as part of the special relationship, given (NAP*).

There seem to be just two ways of trying to resist that:

(*a*)　We could deny that it is part of the nature of my raising my hand that it was someone doing something.

(*b*)　We could deny that it is part of the nature of what is in fact my belief that it is a belief.

But (*a*) seems tantamount to denying the reality of the person-pivoting causal order, which in turn leaves no room for belief. And (*b*) seems unintelligible without (*a*). For if it is not part of the nature of my belief that it is a belief, then it is hard to see how it can be part of the nature of what is explained by citing my belief that it is apt for explanation by citing a belief. Either way, there seems no room for belief at all.

So much for (11); now for (12). The simple thought was that, if my belief caused my hand to rise, I am somehow supplanted as the doer of my deeds.[17] The problem can be reformulated in terms of a threat of over-determination. If my belief caused my hand to rise,

---

[17] Strawson anticipates this argument at *Freedom and Belief*, 39. But he simply insists that it cannot be right if my belief explains my action. See also 12.4, below.

then, even if I am the one who raised my hand, my appearance seems somehow unnecessary, since it seems that my belief would have got my hand to rise even without me. The problem seems absurd, but it is real enough. There seem to be just three ways in which the rise of my hand might not be over-determined if my belief caused my hand to rise:

(c) My belief might have affected me, and so be an indirect cause of my behaviour.

(d) My belief might be a state of some part of me, which is involved in my raising my hand.

(e) My belief might be something I use to get my hand up.

(c) has already been ruled out by the argument against (11). (e) is absurd. Part of its absurdity rests on the fact that it seems to generate a regress, because my use of the belief would itself be something which is apt for exactly similar explanation in terms of belief.

We seem left with (d), as the only way in which my belief could have caused my hand to rise without supplanting me as the doer of my deeds. Under this treatment, the explanation provided by (11) becomes analogous to that provided by something like this:

(13) That bit of neuron activity caused my hand to rise.

But if (12) is true in virtue of (d) being true, it seems irrelevant to the explanatory power of my belief that it is *mine*—that is, that it is a state of a *person* at all (except perhaps in the irrelevant sense that a person's body is its location). What matters is the causal capacity of some *part* of me, and it is hard to see how that could be dependent on its being part of something which is a proper subject of responsibility. But then it must be purely incidental to what is in fact my belief that what it causes is something for which someone is responsible. That means that it must be incidental to what is in fact my belief that what it explains is something which is apt for explanation in terms of belief. Once again, we have lost the person-pivoting causal order; and without that there is no room for belief either.

What has happened here is that, in (d), we have been forced to place talk of beliefs in a level of description *below* that to which talk of people belongs—a level upon whose facts the facts about people might be thought to supervene. But the core of the idea of this level of description's being *below* that to which talk of people belongs is just this: we do not need to mention people to explain what goes on in these terms. And that means that the problem raised for (*d*)—that we end up losing the person-pivoting causal order, and therefore beliefs too—is independent of precisely how we think of the causal powers of parts of people. It will be *natural* to think in mechanical terms—which is why the comparison with (13) is apt—but the point does not depend on that. All that matters is that it is irrelevant to the causal power of a belief that a belief is a state of a *person*.[18]

It seems then that there is no way of stopping me being unnecessary for the performance of my own actions, if (12) is true. The original simple thought seems to have been vindicated. There seems no way in which beliefs can be causes of behaviour, if we are to remain even minimally responsible for what we do.

If I am responsible for the fact that my hand rose, the only thing that could have been the cause of my behaviour seems to be me. That gives us (I). I wanted next to argue for this:

(II) If the person is the *cause* of her behaviour, then there is no more to the person than a Cartesian mind.

I shall proceed as before. If I was the cause of my behaviour in the auction room, one of these two must be true:

(14) I caused myself to raise my hand.
(15) I caused my hand to rise.

There might be circumstances when we might be tempted to say something like (14), but the 'I' in (14) cannot be the basis of the initial attribution of responsibility to me. If the *explanandum* is my raising of my hand, one can infer a priori that I did it, which means, by (NAP*), that I am not the doer of the deed in virtue of being its *cause* in the way that (14) suggests.

So we are left with (15). This is, of course, the result reached immediately by the first intuitive argument. But the position we end up with is not entirely satisfactory. It should already be possible to hear Descartes's ghost clanking its chains. Let us turn up the sound.

We should recall an important feature of my action, which I drew attention to in the beginning. I did not use peculiar mechanical devices to get my hand up, and nobody else lifted it for me on my instructions: I just raised my hand. Now consider the effect of (15)

---

[18] This seems to be one source of the difficulties with Hume's conception of the self; see Hume, *Treatise*, I. iv. 6, and the Appendix, at Selby-Bigge, 633–6.

on this. Given (NAP*), if I am the cause of my hand's rise even here, then it cannot be part of the intrinsic nature even of this behaviour that it is mine. In fact, the point is quite general. The whole strategy of (15) is to account for my responsibility for my behaviour by taking me to be its cause. And then, by (NAP*), it cannot be intrinsic to *any* of my behaviour, however intimate to me it may seem, that it is *mine*.

All of my behaviour, if I see it right, will seem foreign to me. I may find myself treating some movements of some objects in the environment as if they were intrinsically mine. But this must be a misconception: on the account which leads to (15), it can only really be mine by not being intrinsically mine.

Worse, the world, including my own behaviour, is complete without me. Nothing which ever happens could strictly require one to posit an *agent* as the cause of anything. For if it were strictly required, we could derive the existence of such causes a priori from a full knowledge of the intrinsic nature of things which happen; and that is ruled out by (NAP*). The world must make sense without agents. Even the activity of what I like to think of as my own body makes sense without me, since I am only ever the cause of what it does. But if the world makes sense without agents, it is hard to see how agents, strictly so-called, could be part of the world. The limits of the world are drawn with all of us on the outside.

And, in any case, I could not really intervene. Everything I do is analysed as my causing something to happen. But my causing something to happen is itself something I do, and so is subject to the same analysis. My contribution is always of infinitely short duration, and makes an infinitely small impression.

This relates to a recurrence of the problem of over-determination. Its guise is different this time. Recall this:

(13) That bit of neuron activity caused my hand to rise.

How is the rise of my hand not over-determined by (13) and (15)? Once again there are three possible solutions, which correspond to the three that were considered in the previous over-determination problem:

(f) That bit of neuron activity caused me to raise my hand.

(g) That neuron activity's causing my hand to rise is partially constitutive of something I do as responsible subject.

(h) I caused that bit of neuron activity.

(*f*) simply postpones the problem: we will still have to consider how I got my hand up sometime. (*g*) is what we all would like to believe. Unfortunately, we cannot make sense of it on the picture which leads to (15): if my contribution is always of infinitely short duration and makes an infinitely small impression, it cannot be partially constituted by something as gross as a bit of neuron activity. That leaves us with the fantastic (*h*). But the way I cause neuronal activity will have to be other-worldly, since it cannot be even partially constituted by any events in the world of even minimal significance.

Finally, for good measure, there seems no more to me than a disembodied mind. For if no causal sequence involving my body, however small, can ever be even partially constitutive of the contribution *I* make, as a responsible subject, what reason could there be for thinking that my existence depends on that of my body? What more can I be than a mind? At last the ghost stands on the stage, in person as it were, ready to take its bow. In other words, we have just argued for (II).

The moral of all this is that, if we are to avoid being trapped in a Cartesian limbo, we must acknowledge that there is *some* behaviour whose intrinsic nature includes the fact that it is something someone is responsible for. But that means that beliefs and desires cannot figure in the special relationship as *causes* of such behaviour—which is just the behaviour they are cited in the standard way to explain.

But what *does* cause the behaviour? Nothing. The relevant kind of behaviour is not caused; it is just done. This does not violate such principles as that every event has a cause. People's deeds are not events: that is the point of the difference between event causation and the person-pivoting causal order. Events happen; they occur; they are caused. Deeds are just done. Being uncaused does not make deeds random: to think that it does is just to assimilate deeds to events again. The fact that their deeds are uncaused does not mean that people act uninfluenced: the deeds will always reveal the influences on the doer. But the influences affect the doer; they do not cause the deed. And being uncaused does not cut deeds adrift from the order of event causation. There is no problem, for example, with thinking that that bit of neuron activity's causing my hand to rise is partially constitutive of my action when I raise my hand.

All this will horrify those who have thought of actions as events.[19] But I cannot see any good reason for maintaining their view. Actions do not *seem* like happenings: what could make us think they must be?

8.7. Conclusion

The argument of the last section was meant to deal with the uncritical assumption that the onus of proof must always lie on someone who opposes the causal conception of the special relationship. It deals with the assumption in two ways. First, it actually shoulders the burden and provides the proof, as requested. Secondly, it suggests a diagnosis of the uncritical assumption itself.

The diagnosis is that the causal conception is often motivated by the secret operation of the spirit of the Cartesian conception of the self. That motivation might manifest itself like this. It seems to us that we must suppose that our beliefs and desires *cause* our behaviour, because otherwise it seems that we could make no intervention in the world. What use would all our careful deliberation be if it could make no difference? (This might account for some of the passion in the statement I quoted from Fodor in 8.4, although, of course, I hesitate to ascribe a Cartesian view to him.)

This would make sense of two features of the causal conception which might seem to require explanation. The insistence on the predictive direction of talk of beliefs and desires would be natural, if this diagnosis were right. We would want our states of mind to have predictively determining consequences: how else could making up our minds help? How could our decisions ever get anything done? And it would explain why attention is almost exclusively focused on *action*, and on the kinds of contentful states of mind which may be cited to explain action. Why is there so little mention of smiles and winces, of fond or anxious looks, of a sudden stutter in our speech when we rise to speak from the floor in a conference hall? These all demand explanation and understanding in terms of a person's state of mind just as much as action: why are they so seldom mentioned? If our concern is with the question of how we can affect things at all, the omission is natural: the question of how

[19] That is, notably, Davidson and his followers. For something from the other side, see K. Bach, 'Actions are not Events', *Mind*, 89 (1980), 114–20.

we can make a difference is especially piquant when we *want* to make a difference, when we are *trying* to make a difference.

But to think that we can only affect the world if our beliefs and desires cause our behaviour (move our bodies), and our state of mind can, all being well ('other things being equal'), make it predictively certain that action will result, is to be committed to a Cartesian conception of the person. This kind of causal connection is only necessary for *us* to affect the world, if there is no more to what is strictly *us* than those states of mind which we here hope we can line up right to get things moving.

On the alternative conception, on which there is no strict distinction between thinking and behaving, we are already altering things in making up our minds. We were never outside the world to need to intervene. That we can think at all is all the proof we need, or can have, that we can make a difference.

I suggested in 8.4 that one motivation for the causal conception might be a scientistic insistence that all explanations conform to the model of explanations to be found in natural science. We have now found what seems to be another: that we are still haunted by Descartes's ghost. On reflection, however, it is not clear that these motivations are entirely distinct. Scientism and the Cartesian picture are alike in conceiving of the world in such a way that mind has no place in it. Both find no more in behaviour than non-mentalistic descriptions could report. They may differ in that Cartesianism seems to have to inject spirit mysteriously into an essentially inanimate world, whereas scientism mysteriously spreads or projects it on the top; but this difference does not seem to be of decisive importance.

However this may be, it seems clear that the causal conception of the special relationship should be rejected. Learning the lessons of its rejection, the task of fitting a theory of content into a plausible conception of the explanation of behaviour must be more demanding. A proper conception of the understanding of others which we get when we learn what they think and feel will have to represent a range of classical philosophical 'problems' as being tightly intertwined. The 'mind–body problem', the 'problem' of the relation between the self and the world, and the 'problem of free will' must all be treated together. All were involved in the links between the causal conception of the explanation of behaviour and Descartes's ghost.

In short, we can confidently reaffirm the anodyne constraint:

(C10) A theory of content must be harmonious with a plausible account of the way in which contentful states of mind are properly cited to explain behaviour.

But we cannot be sure that it can be met without labour.

PART III
An Evaluative Theory of Content

9

The Core of a Theory

9.1. The Theory in Outline

We have an idea from Part I of the kind of thing a theory of content should do: it should describe the facts of content from another perspective. There is, however, no generally privileged perspective: the requirement is just that one should describe the facts of content using concepts other than the concepts of content.

Part II has imposed some more specific restrictions upon an adequate theory of content. Selective reflection on these suggests a way ahead. Consider these four constraints:

(C9) A theory of content should explain why there can be no natural-scientific reduction of content (the anti-scientism condition: see 7.4).

(C8) A theory of content must be consistent with unified externalism (the externalist constraint: see Chapter 7).

(C7) A theory of content must be extensional at base (the extensionality constraint: see 6.3).

(C10) A theory of content must be harmonious with a plausible account of the way in which contentful states of mind are properly cited to explain behaviour (the explanation condition: see 8.1).

It is not easy to exaggerate the significance of the anti-scientism condition. First, it means that a theory of content must be fundamentally different from what custom might lead one to expect. The initial presumption of almost all recent theories of content is that a theory must be 'naturalistic': that is, content must be explained within the concepts of natural science. That presumption almost exhausts the explanatory ambitions of most proposed theories: the idea seems to be just to make content fit natural science. There seems little in the way of a larger attempt to make one at home with the facts of content. Since the crucial assumption of 'naturalism' is denied here at the outset, we should expect a theory of content to look quite different from those within the 'naturalistic' tradition.

Secondly, an account of what makes a natural-scientific theory of content impossible must be a source of hope that some kind of reduction *can* be given. If we can identify their omission of some particular factor as the reason for the failure of natural-scientific reductions, we must hope that a theory which included explicitly what natural science must leave out might work.

That said, let us leave the anti-scientism condition on one side for a moment, and turn to conditions (C8) and (C7), the externalist and extensionality constraints.

A theory which explained content in terms of the attribution of truth might be extensionalist at base. We also have a special interest in truth in a theory of content, if our interest in content is animated by an interest in metaphysical theories in the sense of Part I—that is, theories which explain what makes true thoughts of any given category true. Explaining content in terms of the attribution of truth seems a promising idea.

A truth-conditional account would also meet the externalism condition. Amidst the controversy surrounding various other features of Davidson's philosophy of language, it is easy to forget the beauty of one of its leading ideas: by describing the world in a certain way one can give the meaning—the content—of utterances of sentences. This is an expression of a form of unified externalism.[1]

An account of content in terms of the attribution of truth looks attractive, then. Can we tie that thought up to some account of the impossibility of any natural-scientific reduction of content?

A diagnosis of the inadequacy of natural-scientific reductions of content is suggested by Kripke in a well-known passage. He is discussing a dispositionalist account of what it is to mean *plus* rather than *quus* by '+'—to be doing *addition* rather than *quaddition*. *Quus* is defined as follows:

$$x \text{ quus } y = x \text{ plus } y, \text{ if } x, y < 57$$
$$= 5 \text{ otherwise.}[2]$$

The dispositionalist says that, if I mean addition by '+', I will be disposed to respond to the question 'What is $68 + 57$?' with the

---

[1] For a view of Davidson's project which brings this out, see J. McDowell, 'On the Sense and Reference of a Proper Name', *Mind*, 86 (1977), 159–85.

[2] S. Kripke, *Wittgenstein on Rules and Private Language* (Oxford: Blackwell, 1982), 9.

answer '125'. Kripke replies: 'The point is *not* that, if I meant addition by "+", I *will* answer "125", but that, if I intend to accord with my past meaning of "+", I *should* answer "125" '.[3] The moral generally drawn from this is that meaning and content are 'normative' notions. Whatever other resonances the word 'normative' might have, the point here seems simple: normativity has something to do with value, and no causal (dispositional) account can capture that.

Here then is the suggested diagnosis of the impossibility of any natural-scientific reduction of content. A version of the 'is'–'ought' distinction is true: there can be no non-evaluative reduction of the evaluative. There is something evaluative about content. There is nothing evaluative about natural science. So there can be no natural-scientific reduction of content.

This diagnosis can be linked with the suggestion of a truth-conditional theory of content with brutal simplicity: truth itself, we might suppose, is a value. This would mean that it was not just a coincidence that having a true belief is a matter of getting things right. It would also have venerable support; here is Frege: 'Just as "beautiful" points the way for aesthetics and "good" for ethics, so do words like "true" for logic.'[4] With such support, the attractiveness of the idea of explaining content in terms of the attribution of truth is enhanced still further.

But something is being fudged here: what is truth to be attributed *to* in the theory? The problem is that truth is only uncontroversially a property of conceptual content, or of things which have conceptual content. (That is the heart of one of the classic arguments against eliminativism: see 6.1.) Talk of truth seems already to have imported the whole framework of conceptual content.

Let us now turn to (C10), the explanation condition. In Chapter 8 I argued that a proper conception of the way in which reports of belief and desire are explanatory of behaviour could not regard the explanatory relation as causal. Summarizing savagely, a principal point was this: mentality must be regarded as being *in* behaviour, not behind it (as a property of its cause).

---

[3] S. Kripke, *Wittgenstein on Rules and Private Language* 37.

[4] G. Frege, 'Thoughts', trans. P. Geach and R. Stoothoff, in Frege, *Collected Papers on Mathematics, Logic, and Philosophy*, ed. B. McGuinness (Oxford: Blackwell, 1984), 351.

That view can seem like behaviourism, but it does not have behaviourism's objectionable features. In behaviourism, properly so-called, the behaviour to which mentality is reduced is behaviour which has no mentality in it. (That is why behaviourism looks like a dismissal of the mind, rather than an explanation of it.) But the conclusions of Chapter 8 are similar enough to behaviourism for it not to be absurd to think of content as a property or feature of behaviour. That can now be used to get us out of the circularity which appeal to truth to explain content seemed to have left us with.

Let us just call the kind of behaviour which can be explained by citing a belief *reactions*. Obviously reactions will include actions, but much more too. Winces and involuntary cries can be explained by appeal to a person's beliefs. So can decisions and periods of havering indecision. All of these I am now counting as *reactions*.

The problem with the appeal to truth was that truth is naturally taken to be a property of conceptual content. Suppose then that we try to explain content in terms of the attribution of some property to the relevant kind of behaviour, reactions. To do the right work, this property of reactions will have to be truth-*like*, in having the right links with metaphysical explanations (in the sense of Part I); and it will have to be a *value*. Let us call it the value T.

We have moved, then, from the attribution of truth to conceptual content to the assessment of reactions in terms of the value *T*. We now need to impose some conditions upon the basis of that assessment. Recall the minimal condition on theories of content:

(C1) Being describable as registering or processing information is not sufficient for possessing concepts, and having propositional attitudes.

Clearly something does not count as possessing a concept just because its behaviour *can* be assessed in a certain way. That would mean that something could count as a concept-possessor just in virtue of its being convenient to treat it as if it were a concept-possessor. That view is not only false: it is self-undermining. 'Treating' something in any way at all is something only a concept-possessor can do; so the statement of the view presupposes some kind of concept-possession which is not just a matter of the ascriber's convenience. And 'treating something as if it were a concept-possessor' presupposes a class of real concept-possessors with which this thing is being compared when it is treated as if it were one.[5]

Let us say, then, that something can only count as a concept-possessor in virtue of making reactions which are *non-arbitrarily* assessable with respect to the value T. This is to mean just that the assessment is not merely a matter of connvenience: there is something as it were *already right* about this way of treating the thing.

But by this definition of non-arbitrary assessability, even very simple computers do things which are non-arbitrarily assessable. When we say that an adding machine, say, has produced the right answer, this means that what is presented as the sum of the numbers entered really is the sum of those numbers. And that presupposes that it is already right to say that the final display on the screen is meant to represent the sum of the previously entered numbers; and hence that it is already fixed that that final display is correct just in case *that* (what the display represents on a standard interpretation) is the sum of those numbers.

Simple computers and adding machines do not have concepts. What is it about them which rules this out? A natural thought is this: in the case of a simple device like this, it is only already right to interpret its displays ('behaviour') in some particular way because that is what the thing was designed for. This kind of direct dependence on the intentions and competence of a designer seems to prevent these simple devices from counting as concept-posses-sors.

Let us say, then, that to count as a concept-possessor one must react in ways which are not only non-arbitrarily but *intrinsically* assessable with respect to the value T. Being intrinsically assessable just means being non-arbitrarily assessable for some reason which is not a matter of too direct dependence upon a designer's intention.

At this point it might seem that talk of *assessability* is being evasive or covertly fictionalist about value: why not just say that it is intrinsic to the reactions that they are good in the value T way if certain conditions obtain? There is no reason not to say that. The point of the complex locution in terms of assessability was just to mark certain points of comparison—between mere convenience, whatever is true of computers, and whatever is true of real concept-possessors, like us. Those comparisons will be helpful when it comes to the explanation of the theory.

[5] These points are made more laboriously in M. Morris, 'Why there are no Mental Representations', *Minds and Machines* 1 (1991), 1–30.

We began with the idea of explaining content in terms of the attribution of truth. We are now talking of the intrinsic assessability of reactions with respect to the value T. Someone might wonder whether any progress has been made. We moved from direct appeal to the notion of truth because that seemed to presuppose the whole bristling panoply of the concepts of conceptual content. But we have replaced talk of content being true with talk of reactions; and were not reactions just defined as the kind of thing which is properly explained by appeal to contentful states of mind?

They were; but they need be no longer. We can cross over to what I shall regard as the more general notion of a response, which we can characterize aseptically enough for our present concerns. We can allow anything at all to respond. A flat stone responds to water in that particular sliding see-saw way. Let us stipulate: there is to be nothing in the notion of a response which presupposes conceptual content. We can now say that a reaction is simply a response which is intrinsically assessable with respect to the value T.

Possessing a concept and believing something are not just a matter of responding. I can possess a concept now (this minute) even if nothing I am doing now is a display or exercise of that concept. Similarly for belief: not all of my current beliefs are on show in my current behaviour.

Traditionally the notion of a disposition is used to plug this gap: possessing a concept and believing something are said to be dispositions.[6] But disposition-talk seems to me too theoretically loaded to accept uncritically. Let us use a different term, so that at least we will start different hares. We might say that having a concept is a matter of being *liable* to respond in a certain kind of way. But it is to be understood that 'liable' here is meant for just this role: it is meant to describe how a concept-possessor stands to appropriately assessable behaviour even when she is not actually responding appropriately.

Putting it all together we get this: possessing a concept is being *liable* to respond in ways which are *intrinsically assessable* with respect to *the value T*—in whatever way is appropriate for that concept in particular.

[6] See, e.g., G. Ryle, *The Concept of Mind* (London: Hutchinson, 1949), ch. V.

That is the skeleton of a theory. So far all that is in its favour is its response to the four conditions I began with, together with some promise of a treatment of the minimal condition. It offers a diagnosis of the irreducibility of content to natural science that has some initial plausibility; it gives us some hope of extensionality and externalism; and it involves a conception of the behaviour which is explained in terms of content which at least is rich enough to embarrass most causal theorists.

What still needs to be done is obvious: all the italicized expressions in the rough definition I gave need to be explained. So far, they have only been defined in terms of the concepts of content. In addition to that, we need to make some intuitive sense of the theory so that the shift from truth to a truth-like value of behaviour does not seem like just an arbitrary theoretical manœuvre.

Those tasks will be tackled in later chapters. But there is still some preliminary work to be done. We can already do something to justify the claims that truth is a kind of value, and that what makes it impossible to give a natural-scientific reduction of content is the impossibility of catching value in the specimen net of science. Those tasks will occupy the next three sections.

We also need some more precise statement of the theory, if only to provide a clear target for others to shoot at. That will be done in 9.5.

9.2. Is Truth a Value?

Is truth a value?[7] Too sudden a reliance on Kripke's formulation in introducing the idea of value here might lead to doubts. Here again is what he said: 'The point is *not* that, if I meant addition by "+", I *will* answer "125", but that, if I intend to accord with my past meaning of "+", I *should* answer "125".'[8] There are two problems with this. First, there is the curious suggestion that meaning is a matter of being deliberately faithful to one's own past usage. Let us deal just with present meaning. The claim will then be that, if I mean addition by '+', I should answer '125'.

[7] Many of the objections considered in this section are inspired by J. Heal, 'The Disinterested Search for Truth', *Proceedings of the Aristotelian Society*, 88 (1987–8), 97–108.

[8] Kripke, *Wittgenstein on Rules and Private Language*, 37.

This now faces the second problem: why *should* I say that? Perhaps it is not my turn to answer. Perhaps something awful will happen if I speak at all. The problem is that in effect truth is being counted as a value because it is supposed that one should speak the truth. But it is not obvious that one should always speak the truth. So the idea of truth being a value seems under threat.

A small qualification will deal with this. The revised Kripkean claim should read: if I mean addition by '+', I should answer '125', if I am to say what I believe. And that is just to say that truth is a value because one should believe the truth.

There are two kinds of worry that this may provoke. It may seem, on the one hand, that truth is not motivation enough for anything. And, on the other hand, it may seem that there is not enough gap between realizing that something is true and believing it for truth to count as motivating at all.

If I say that one should believe the truth, am I committed to endorsing the grotesquely encyclopaedic project of gobbling up all the truths I can lay my hands on? I do not think so. The statement that one should believe the truth seems to me to be interpretable in two different ways:

(1) It should be the case that, if something is true, one believes it.
(2) It should be the case that, if one believes something, it is true.

(1) is what encourages the image of the fact-sucker; but (2) looks enough to sustain the claim that truth is a value. If (2) is true, then one would expect some filling of the blanks in the following to yield a truth:

(3) It should be the case that, if something is true, and . . . one believes it.

Something like 'relevant to one's concerns' might fill the blanks. However this may be, it seems clear that, given a choice between a truth and a falsehood, one should believe the truth.

'Seems clear', I said; but someone might doubt even this. Might someone not be better off believing some falsehood than having to cope with the unpalatable truth? I think there are two related things wrong with this.

First, the suggestion seems to be based on the idea that truth is only of instrumental value, useful in furthering our desires. And then, of course, one can imagine those desires being more efficiently furthered if one had certain false beliefs. (Dogmatists get a lot done.) Against this, first, we do not merely share the meta-desire that our desires be satisfied. It matters to us that we know what we are doing when we act; and that requires that the beliefs on which we act be true. So an easy life based on false belief will be a life in which an important desire is not satisfied. The second point against the idea that truth is only of instrumental value is swifter: it does not seem possible to make sense of having desires at all without having some true beliefs. How could our desires relate to anything if we had no knowledge of anything?

The other problem with the objection that someone might be better off believing a falsehood is just that it does not undermine the claim that one should believe the truth. Suppose we grant that someone might be better off believing a falsehood, and that it is on balance right to keep her in the dark. That does not stop that person's life being flawed. A mark of this might be that, if the person in question is not a child, or in some relevant way childlike, it shows disrespect to her as a person to keep her in the dark. If being based on a falsehood is enough to make a person's life flawed, it seems safe to say that it should be the case that, if one believes something, it is true.

All this suggests that truth matters, and in its own right. So far the claim that truth is a value seems plausible. But is there enough of a gap between realizing that something is true and believing it?

Let us lay out the reasoning here a bit more carefully. The property of being F is an evaluative property just in case realizing that something is F *ipso facto* provides one with reason to do something with it (choose it, reject it, or whatever). This is a rough statement of a thesis known as *internalism* in ethics. Alternatively, one might say that being F is an evaluative property just in case it is a priori that if something is F there is reason to do something or other (choose, reject, or whatever) with it. We do not need to worry here over the details of the formulation.[9]

One can only speak of reason, in the relevant sense, where there is room for choice. And there is only room for choice where one could have chosen otherwise. But in our case, the argument goes, the property of being true is held to be an evaluative property because realizing that something is true *ipso facto* provides one

---

[9] For a thorough examination of the detail, see D. Brink, *Moral Realism and the Foundations of Ethics* (Cambridge: Cambridge University Press, 1989), 37–45. (Brink himself is not an internalist about value.)

with reason to believe it. But realizing that something is true *is* believing that it is true, and believing that it is true *is* believing it. So it is impossible to choose not to believe the truth once one has realized that it is the truth; so one cannot speak of reasons here in the right way for truth to be counted as a value.

This argument goes wrong in the rush through the alleged equivalences at the end. One crucial equivalence is assumed, but the assumption gets suppressed in informal exposition. The important equivalences are these:

(4) Believing that something is true is, for some '*p*', believing that it is true that *p*.

(5) Believing that it is true that *p* is believing that *p*.

(5) is plausible enough for any subject who has the concept of truth. But (4), as it is intended, is not in the least plausible. Believing that what Hawking says about physics is true is not generally believing that *p* for any relevant '*p*' at all: many of us just do not know what Hawking says about physics. So (4) is false, and the argument fails.

When one sees why (4) is false one can see how truth can be motivating. If I know that someone is an expert on something, while I am not, I have reason to believe what she says before I know what she says. The reason is, of course, that I have reason to think that what she says is true. Acting on that reason, I go and listen to what she says—assuming the topic is relevant to my concerns—and I listen trustingly. In this way I bring it about that I believe something which I was *already* convinced was true. And of course I could have chosen otherwise: I could have avoided speaking with the expert; or I could have refused to listen to what she said, determined not to let my prejudices be threatened.

It appears from this that the motivating power of truth can emerge only when one thinks that something is true without knowing what it is. This fact, I think, counts in favour of the view that truth is a value. This is because it coincides with the classic problem with a redundancy theory of truth.

Let '=' express a strong biconditional: an a priori and necessary equivalence. Given that, we can formulate the redundancy theory of truth as holding these two theses:

(R1) The use of the *operator* 'it is true that' is redundant, in virtue of this schema:

[It is true that *p*] = *p*.

(R2) All uses of 'true' as a *predicate* can be reduced to uses of the operator 'it is true that'.

The classic objection to the redundancy theory attacks (R2). The problem is with statements which attribute truth to what someone says or believes without saying what she says or believes. Here is an example:

(6) Fermat's last theorem is true.

To interpret that predicative use of 'true' as (R2) requires, the redundancy theorist will need to appeal to something like this:

(7) For some p, Fermat's last theorem says that p, and it is true that p.

Classically the objector will now insist that the quantifier here must be read substitutionally, so that (7) really means just this:

(8) There is some sentence whose insertion in the gaps marked by 'p' in the schema 'Fermat's last theorem says that p and it is true that p' yields a *true* sentence.

And that last, italicized, use of 'true' is predicative.[10]

The general tenor of this objection seems right to me, but I doubt if the problem really rests on the technical question of how these particular quantifiers ought to be read. This is partly because I am not convinced that the difference between substitutional and 'objectual' quantification is a deep one. But it is also partly that I suspect the issue is more fundamental than this kind of objection acknowledges.

Here is one way of sowing the seeds of such a suspicion. If the redundancy theory were really right, should it not be possible to teach a child to speak without ever suggesting, even implicitly, that an utterance was correct—that some value *predicate* applied to it? Should it not be possible to turn the trick by just describing the world—repeating what the child says when she says something right, and just saying the relevant right thing when she does not, without any indication that one kind of saying is right? The suggestion does not appear even to make sense, since we would hardly be able to count the result of such a process as knowledge.

Bearing that in mind, we can suggest that the problem with (7) is not specific to quantification into *sentence* position, but affects

---

[10] This account of the redundancy theory and the classic objection to it is indebted to S. Haack, *Philosophy of Logics* (Cambridge: Cambridge University Press, 1978), 127–34.

quantification in general. How can a redundancy theorist explain quantification without appeal to a *predicative* conception of truth? We might try to explain quantification directly, by means of a specification of the truth conditions of quantified sentences. But that seems to force us to explain the quantifiers in terms of the truth of instances of quantified claims. And that involves appeal to a predicative use of 'true'.

Thus consider the two leading accounts of the truth condition of a claim of this form:

(9) For some x, x is F.

On one, semi-substitutional account, this just means: there is some meaningful singular term whose insertion into the 'x' position in the open sentence 'x is F' yields a true sentence.[11] On the other, more nearly Tarskian account, it means: the open sentence 'x is F' is true *of* some object. But what is it to say that an open sentence is *true of* an object? It seems to mean just this: there is some object such that, if we take the variable as a temporary name for that object, the open sentence is (temporarily) true.[12]

Alternatively, we might try a proof-theoretical approach, explaining the meaning of quantifiers in terms of the supports for and consequences of quantified claims. But such an approach requires one to appeal to some notion of a correct proof: how is that to be explained? We might say that, if a form of proof is correct, then, given the first line, one *may* write the last. But how are we to explain that 'may'? It seems unintelligible without appeal to some such idea as that writing that line is *all right*; and that again seems to involve some use of a value *predicate*.

If this argument is anything like right, then it provides helpful confirmation of the view that truth is a value. It is in the stubbornly predicative uses of 'true' that the concept has some work to do. The stubbornly predicative uses are those in which truth is attributed to what someone says or believes without saying what is said or believed. But those are the cases where there is the right kind of gap between realizing that something is true and believing it, for the thing's truth to provide one with reason to believe it.

Someone might say: certainly something's being true is a reason for believing it, *given* that we have an interest in knowledge. But

---

[11] For such an account, see G. Evans, 'Pronouns, Quantifiers and Relative Clauses', *Canadian Journal of Philosophy*, 7 (1977), 467–536.

[12] See Field, 'Tarski's Theory of Truth', 349.

take away that interest, and truth is of no concern to us.[13]

We need not suppose that the concern for truth is separable from the concern for knowledge, but this response seems to imagine that we could step aside from both: we could have noted the existence of truth and knowledge quite dispassionately, as one might note the position of the stars at night.

This suggestion is fantastic. Suppose we know that what someone thinks on a certain subject is false. Could we (unprejudiced by any interest in knowledge) take that fact as a reason for believing what she says? We might not be as critical as we should be; we might be foolishly tolerant. We might be interested in recording her views for anthropological reasons. But could we seek her out, become her disciple, listen to what she says with unwavering trust, believe her, just because her views are false? This seems precisely as intelligible as the perverse determination famously expressed in the vow, 'Evil be thou my good'. And if it is precisely as intelligible as that, then truth is a value.

9.3. Values and Reduction

Does the presence of value in content explain the impossibility of natural-scientific reduction? The fundamental worry about a natural-scientific reduction of content, traced back to Chapter 4, is that a natural-scientific reduction of content would require a natural-scientific reduction of everything. But a natural-scientific reduction of everything would rule out a priori knowledge, which in turn would leave all reduction—indeed all theories—unconstrained. So one way of reformulating the question is this: is it in not engaging with questions of *value* that a general natural-scientific reductionism is prevented from allowing a priori knowledge?

In response to this I shall simply record a number of coincidences, though they seem striking enough. Having done that I shall suggest a reason for being cautious about making grander claims.

Consider first Kripke's target, a causal dispositional account of meaning. If we took such a theory seriously, it would become an

---

[13] A hint of this appears in D. Papineau, *Reality and Representation* (Oxford: Blackwell, 1988), p. xi.

empirical question whether the sum of 68 and 57 is 125. That would become a matter of what someone was, as a matter of empirical fact, disposed to say (if they said what they believed). And, as Kripke says, that involves losing the idea of the answer being right.

That is reminiscent of a certain caricature of ordinary language philosophy (which is not altogether unlike the position which Kripke puts forward as 'Wittgenstein's' solution to the problem of what determines meaning). We imagine such a caricatured philosopher dismissing scepticism, for example, on the basis of a claim about how the word *know* is usually used. The issue has turned empirical: one could do a survey to test the usual application of the word. And, at the same time, the question has obviously been begged against scepticism, since the issue was precisely whether those everyday applications are *right*.

Or take the notion of the inconsistency of beliefs. If two beliefs are inconsistent, it seems that that inconsistency will in the end be explicable in terms of an evidently a priori discernible inconsistency between some pair of beliefs (though perhaps not those from which we began). This is the assumption behind the idea of *demonstrating* inconsistency, which is a matter of trying to make the a priori uncotenability of the relevant beliefs as blatant as possible. If we try to treat inconsistency in an a posteriori manner, it has to be characterized in terms of psychological tension, or in terms of the dispositions of subjects who have inconsistent beliefs to alter their beliefs. But if we do this we lose the heart of the notion of inconsistency: the idea that there is something *wrong* with having inconsistent beliefs.

In all of these examples, the attempt to treat a priori relations as if they were a posteriori marches with a failure to take account of right and wrong.

Another aspect of the difficulty that scientism faces is the paradoxical nature of such claims as 'There are only scientific facts'. This seems to be connected with its inability to accommodate the a priori. I suspect that the exclusion of value will itself lead to paradoxes which are at least analogous to that. The case of Hume is instructive here. In the *Treatise*, philosophy is presented as 'the science of MAN',[14] and the fundamental empiricist principle is accordingly established, it seems, on the basis of the meticulous

---

[14] Hume, *Treatise*, ed. Selby-Bigge, p. xv.

experimentation of introspection. In this light the principle seems nothing more than empirical psychology, untainted by value. But the principle must nevertheless support the fairly striking claims of *legitimacy* which are made on its basis: concerning the well foundedness of such and such a view, or the emptiness of this or that concept.

The problem with this is that value is now involved. And according to Hume's own 'is'–'ought' distinction, any principle which can support such evaluative claims should itself be evaluative. But if it were evaluative, the principle could not, according to Hume, make any claim on reason. Under this pressure the principle seems to hop from one foot to the other, putting weight on the empirical credentials of introspection when its rational basis is challenged, but quickly transferring the load when philosophical conclusions are to be drawn.

The difficulty seems to be a deep one: Hume could not easily have given up his 'is'–'ought' distinction. It is tempting to think that both the principle and its suppression are essential to a natural-scientific reductionism. On the one hand, the distinction needs to be maintained to preserve the natural-scientific conception of objectivity; but, on the other hand, it needs to be suppressed, and the evaluative reduced to the non-evaluative, if the questions of legitimacy and right that are essential to philosophy are to be treatable within the framework of natural science.

These points are all suggestive. It seems that the problems created by disallowing a priori knowledge are matched repeatedly by problems created by ignoring questions of value. It would seem to be at least a good explanation of this persistent correspondence, if the source of the impossibility of a natural-scientific reduction of content were the presence of value in content, and the inability of natural science to deal with value.

But I think it would be wise to be cautious about this. I have concentrated on the problems for scientism that relate specifically to its inability to admit the a priori. But these problems might be felt to be just one manifestation of what might be a more general kind of difficulty: the fact that the theory is prevented by itself from applying to itself. And the moment that kind of formulation is used, rather different associations for the paradoxes of scientism suggest themselves. We think of the whole network of paradoxes and counter-paradoxes that dominated logical thinking in the first half of the century: specifically, the liar paradox and Godel's proof. If the explanation of the problems of scientism, which is provided by the idea that truth is a value, is really to be as sweet as I have been suggesting, one might wonder whether it should not also extend to these other areas too.

What this would require would be something like this. Both the liar paradox and the incompleteness of arithmetic—to name but two—would have in the end to be explicable by its being impossible to capture value by non-evaluative means.[15] Some of the language in which issues connected with Godel's proof are discussed is suggestive: talk, for example, of there being no 'mechanical' method of demonstrating every truth. But it is unclear that the sense of 'mechanical' in such talk is properly to be contrasted with the evaluative.

In the light of the difficulty of the issues in this area, it seems best to leave the question open. It has not been proved that the presence of value in content ultimately *explains* the impossibility of scientistic reduction. But the parallels which I have noted between difficulties over the a priori and difficulties over value suggest that there is at least this in favour of an evaluative theory of content: value is something whose omission from a theory of content will ensure that theory's failure.

9.4. The 'Is'–'Ought' Distinction

The strategy of the evaluative theory of content requires that we be able to maintain some version of the 'is'–'ought' distinction while counting truth as a value. But *is* this possible?

The problem can be raised sharply by noting that the evaluative theory needs both of these claims:

(1) For some 'p', saying that p is non-evaluative, while saying that it is true that p is evaluative.

(2) For all 'p', [it is true that p] = p.

(Once again, '=' expresses an a priori necessary equivalence. One might restrict the range of 'p', if that is the best way of dealing with the threat of semantic paradox from (2).)

---

[15] McDowell comes close to this kind of suggestion in 'Functionalism and Anomalous Monism', 388.

We need (1), or else we will lose the contrast between the evaluative and the non-evaluative. And we need (2), or else we will lose the right to claim that it is really truth we are talking about.

But we need to deal with two difficulties:

(i) Given (2), it is always possible to infer 'it is true that *p*' a priori from '*p*'; but, given (1), this will at least sometimes be inferring something evaluative a priori from something non-evaluative: but is that not just what the 'is'–'ought' distinction prohibits?

(ii) The 'is'–'ought' distinction requires at least that there be a *difference* between evaluative and non-evaluative claims; but does not (2) subvert even that, given that truth is a value?

In order to be able to answer these questions, we need to be clear about exactly what kind of 'is'–'ought' distinction the evaluative theory of content requires. Here is Hume, introducing the issue:

I cannot forbear adding to these reasonings an observation, which may, perhaps, be found of some importance. In every system of morality, which I have hitherto met with, I have always remark'd, that the author proceeds for some time in the ordinary way of reasoning, and establishes the being of a God, or makes observations concerning human affairs; when of a sudden I am surpriz'd to find, that instead of the usual copulation of propositions, *is*, and *is not*, I meet with no proposition that is not connected with an *ought*, or an *ought not*. This change is imperceptible but is, however, of the last consequence. For as this *ought*, or *ought not*, expresses some new relation or affirmation, 'tis necessary that it shou'd be observ'd and explain'd; and at the same time that a reason should be given, for what seems altogether inconceivable, how this new relation can be a deduction from others, which are entirely different from it. But as authors do not commonly use this precaution, I shall presume to recommend it to the readers; and am persuaded, that this small attention wou'd subvert all the vulgar systems of morality, and let us see, that the distinction of vice and virtue is not founded merely on the relations of objects, nor is perceiv'd by reason.[16]

Hume appears to be making three distinguishable points here:

(*a*) 'Ought' and 'ought not' (or value terms in general) introduce a 'new relation or affirmation', which is 'entirely different' from that involved in 'is' (non-evaluative) propositions.

(*b*) The 'new relation' cannot be a 'deduction' from the old.

[16] Hume, *Treatise*, III. i. 1; Selby-Bigge, 469–70.

(c) The 'is'–'ought' distinction confirms what we know as 'the fact–value distinction' (that values cannot be 'perceiv'd by reason').

And it seems that (b) and (c) are supposed both to be consequences of (a).

Attention to that last point might seem to subvert the standard interpretation of the 'is'–'ought' distinction. The standard interpretation takes the distinction to be just point (b), which in turn is read as saying that it is impossible to infer something evaluative a priori from something non-evaluative.[17] The sense in which the new and the old are 'entirely different' is then itself read in those terms, so that point (a) becomes something like the claim that no evaluative term can be synonymous with any non-evaluative term. From which point some philosophers seem inclined to draw the controversial 'consequence' that evaluative and non-evaluative properties are distinct, if indeed there are any evaluative properties at all.

But this seems to get Hume back to front. Hume seems to think that it is obvious that the new 'relation' and the old are 'entirely different', from which it appears to *follow* that it is impossible to 'deduce' the one from the other.

I shall therefore propose a different reading of Hume, which we might call the *irreducibility* interpretation of the 'is'–'ought' distinction. On this reading the 'is'–'ought' distinction states simply that no evaluative concept is *reducible* to non-evaluative concepts. This, then, is Hume's claim (a). Given the links between the notion of reduction and the notion of property identity which I proposed in 1.2, claim (a) is already the claim that evaluative and non-evaluative properties are distinct, if indeed there are any evaluative properties at all. And this is how (a) implies (c) on Hume's view, since he is committed to the claim that what cannot be reduced to natural science does not relate to 'matter of fact and existence'.[18]

This might seem to be taking Hume to be simply assuming something which is too controversial to be simply assumed. I doubt both that it is too controversial to be assumed, and the idea that Hume cannot be portrayed as simply assuming something controversial. Here is something on the first point.

[17] For such an interpretation, see, e.g., J. Mackie, *Hume's Moral Theory* (London: Routledge and Kegan Paul, 1980), 61–3.

[18] Hume, *Enquiry Concerning Human Understanding*, ed. Selby-Bigge, 165.

What is at issue in reductions, as reductions were characterized by the knowledge constraint in Part I (see especially 5.1), is what kinds of perspective are authoritative for any given subject-matter. Thus, if 'H₂O' really does provide a reduction of 'water', the perspective of chemistry is authoritative on whether something counts as water. Now consider that point in the area of value. Could it ever be *right* to count a non-evaluative perspective as authoritative about questions of value? One might as well set up the blind as authorities on colour. In fact the point is stronger than that, since here the suggestion seems immoral, not merely absurd.

If we give this reading of (*a*), can we derive (*b*)? I think we can derive at least a plausible, and textually supported, version of (*b*). The standard interpretation of (*b*) takes it to be a thesis about deducing evaluative *statements* from non-evaluative *statements*. Let us connive at that for a moment, and explain what (*b*) is saying in terms of a special sense of 'deduction' of one statement from others. Consider *this* conception of a 'deduction' of an evaluative claim from non-evaluative premises: if such a deduction were possible, knowledge of those non-evaluative premises would make one authoritative in the application of some value, in these particular circumstances—*quite independently of any general competence one might have in evaluating things*. That final rider is what makes the sense of 'deduction' here distinctive. If deduction of value from the non-evaluative, in *this* sense, were possible, we would then be able to define a new, genuinely evaluative, expression, whose extension was restricted to just the circumstances specified by the non-evaluative premises. We would then have some evaluative expression for whose application knowledge of those non-evaluative facts was absolutely decisive, quite independently of any other considerations to do with value. And that looks enough to ensure that this (restricted) value concept would be *reducible* to the non-evaluative; which conflicts with the irreducibility reading of (*a*). So (*a*) does seem to imply that evaluative statements cannot be deduced from non-evaluative premises, in the special sense of 'deduction' I have introduced.

This interpretation represents Hume as claiming in (*b*) that it is impossible to *ground* value in the non-evaluative. This is the point we might put by saying that the only authority for an evaluative claim is an evaluative perspective. The attribution of this view to Hume seems exactly right. For the claim that we might express (supposing we believed it) by saying that there are no moral facts, Hume expresses by saying that 'morals . . . cannot be deriv'd from reason':[19] that is, value cannot be legitimated from a perspective which is authoritative just about the non-evaluative (which Hume takes to be the same as: a perspective from which one can see the facts and nothing but the facts).

That general harmony with Hume's views would be support enough for this interpretation of (*b*). But the detail of this text is decisive anyway. For (*b*) does *not* in fact claim, as is usually assumed, that evaluative *statements* cannot be deduced from non-evaluative premises. What he claims is that the 'new *relation*' cannot be deduced from the old. That is *value*—not evaluative claims—cannot be deduced from (that is, legitimated by) what is non-evaluative—that is, non-evaluative properties, not non-evaluative statements. His words are: 'the *distinction* of vice and virtue is not founded merely on the *relations* of objects' (my emphasis added).

This reading of (*b*) does not make it equivalent to the view that no evaluative statement can be inferred a priori from non-evaluative premises. On the reading I have suggested, (*b*) leaves it open whether some thoroughly *evaluative* perspective might legitimate an inference from something non-evaluative to something evaluative. The point is simply that such an inference cannot be legitimated in any *other* way than from a thorough and general evaluative pespective.

So much for scholarship. What understanding of the 'is'–'ought' distinction does the evaluative theory of content require? Obviously, it simply requires the irreducibility reading which I have just provided: what is important for the explanation of the failure of natural-scientific reductions of content is just that the evaluative should not be reducible to the non-evaluative. But that means, as I have argued, that the evaluative theory of content is not committed to the view that it is impossible to infer something evaluative a priori from non-evaluative premises. So problem (i) need not concern us.

Now for problem (ii). What we need to do to be able to deal with problem (ii) is to define quite carefully what is required for a claim or a statement to count as evaluative. Suppose we had said that a claim is evaluative if it cannot be understood except in the light of

<hr />

[19] Hume, *Treatise*, III. i. 1; Selby-Bigge, 457.

some value. Then it would seem that all claims run the risk of being evaluative, if truth is a value, since to be a *claim* at all it must be evaluable in terms of truth; and presumably one could only count as understanding a claim if one took it *as* a claim, and hence as evaluable in terms of truth.

And we cannot just amend this in the obvious way by saying this: a claim is evaluative if, in order to understand it, one must bring to bear considerations of value beyond those involved in counting the claim as a claim. For that would seem to prevent *truth* being a value. And we cannot just amend that in turn to reach this: a claim is evaluative if, in order to understand it, one must bring considerations of value to bear on more than just the question of whether it is a claim. For if I was right in thinking, in 9.2, that an understanding of the notion of truth is required in order to understand quantification, then all quantified statements would count as evaluative, including, fatally, those in natural science.

What these points show is that, if truth is a value, every claim is in a sense implicitly evaluative. What we need then is the idea of an *explicitly* evaluative claim. Let a claim or belief count as explicitly evaluative if it expresses or involves an evaluative concept. And let an evaluative concept be one which is expressible by means of an evaluative word or phrase.

An evaluative word or phrase may belong to a range of parts of speech, but it cannot be a whole sentence. For each kind of evaluative expression, I shall want to be able to talk about what the expression is *applied to* when it is used. The idea is quite intuitive, but it is best captured by example. If the evaluative expression is a common noun ('hero', 'thug'), then the expression is *applied to* whatever is called by that noun (called a hero, or called a thug). If it is an adjective, it is *applied to* whatever is referred to by the grammatical subject of the attribution (with suitable adjustments for quantified claims). If it is an operator ('it would be good if'), it is applied to the state of affairs described by the sentence governed by the operator. If it is a *general* evaluative verb ('ought to', 'should'), it is applied to whatever it is, property or activity, whose description is governed by the verb. If it is a more specific evaluative verb ('violate', 'boast'), it will be applied to the activity described.

This description is fairly rough, but it will be enough for our purposes. It provides us with the idea that, whenever any evaluative expression is used, it is *applied to* something, and gives a conception of what different kinds of evaluative expression will be applied to when they are used. What an evaluative expression is applied to is what is thereby evaluated. We can now say what an evaluative word or phrase is. It is a word or phrase with this property: to count as understanding it in any use, one must recognize that the thing to which it is applied is thereby being favoured, or disfavoured, as the case may be. And that will mean, I take it, that *accepting* an evaluative claim is a matter of counting oneself as having a reason to do something or other (choose, or reject, say) in relation to the thing to which the evaluative expression is applied.

By this definition, 'it is true that p' will count as an explicitly evaluative claim, even if 'p' itself is not explicitly evaluative, provided that 'true' is an evaluative word. But note that it must be 'true' which is the evaluative word: 'it is true that' cannot count as an evaluative operator, on the definition I have just given. For if it were, then it would be *applied to* the state of affairs described by 'p'; and to say that it is true that p is not to favour its being the case that p. (It is too easy to lament the state of the world.)

We can deal with this by saying that, in a sentence of the form 'it is true that p', the word 'true' applies to the *belief* that p. That is, 'it is true that p' just means 'the belief that p is a true belief'. That expression, 'the belief that . . . is a true belief' is an operator; but the word 'true' figures as an *adjective*, and so applies to what is referred to by the grammatical subject—the belief in question. The operator is extensional, in the sense that sentences with the same truth value may be swapped within its scope, *salva veritate*.

This makes good sense of a point which I insisted on in Part I. Metaphysical explanations were characterized as explanations of that in virtue of which truths are true. They offer replacements for 'q' in this schema:

(T) It is true that p, because q.

The point I insisted on was just that, if one replaces 'p' in any instance of this schema with a sentence which is not *conceptually equivalent* to the one from which we began, one will be explaining the truth of a *different truth*. That is why it is natural to call a truth a *true thought* in Frege's sense of 'thought'. Clearly if 'it is true that p' means the same as 'the belief that p is a true belief', this will not be surprising.

It also makes sense of another feature of conceptualism, as that view was developed in Part I. A fact is that in virtue of which some truth is true. If a truth is just a true belief, then the existence of any fact will require the existence of the corresponding belief. This is exactly analogous to the second tenet of conceptualism:

(B) The nature of the objects, properties, and facts to which our concepts correspond is not fixed independently of the concepts which correspond to them.

And the apparent threat of idealism will be removed in an exactly similar way, by insisting on the timeless (atemporal) existence of beliefs, in the relevant sense of 'belief' (see 1.3).

In fact, the view that 'it is true that p' means the same as 'the belief that p is a true belief' seems generally plausible, except that it will not be welcomed by one who believes in the redundancy theory of truth. For on this reading, even the redundancy theorist's preferred operator construction turns out to involve an implicit use of 'true' as a predicate. But, given the argument against the redundancy theory in 9.2, this should be neither surprising nor worrying.

We seem able to count 'it is true that p' as an explicitly evaluative claim even when 'p' is not explicitly evaluative. This does not threaten, and is not threatened by the a priori and necessary equivalence of 'it is true that p' and 'p'. A theory of content which aims to explain belief in terms of truth will hold that understanding the notion of belief requires understanding the notion of beliefs being true. If 'it is true that p' means the same as 'the belief that p is a true belief', then one might expect the a priori and necessary equivalence to be confirmed rather than threatened. Nor is the thesis that evaluative concepts are not reducible to the non-evaluative threatened by the equivalence between 'it is true that p' and 'p'. Provided the redundancy theory of truth is false, that equivalence does not form the basis of a *reduction* of the notion of truth. In short, problem (ii) can be dismissed.

All this is in tune with a Humean conception of the 'is'–'ought' distinction. But we now need to part company with Hume. I noted earlier a third point which Hume made in introducing the distinction:

(c) The 'is'–'ought' distinction confirms what we know as 'the fact–value distinction' (that values cannot be 'perceiv'd by reason').

If truth is a value, this cannot be right. Here is some laboriously impeccable reasoning to prove it. Suppose:

(3) It is true that p.

By (2) (our redundancy equivalence) we derive:

(4) It is true that it is true that p.

Given that it is a fact that p if and only if it is true that p, we can derive:

(5) It is a fact that it is true that p.

And if truth is a value, (5) commits us to evaluative facts. The 'is'–'ought' distinction becomes not a distinction between fact and value, but a distinction between two kinds of fact.

This is connected with another feature of Hume's insistence on a distinction between fact and value: his conception of a certain perspective which is itself value-neutral—the perspective of 'reason'. Here is what he says (in a passage also quoted in the Introduction):

> Thus the distinct boundaries and offices of *reason* and of *taste* are easily ascertained. The former conveys the knowledge of truth and falsehood: the latter gives the sentiment of beauty and deformity, vice and virtue. The one discovers objects as they really stand in nature, without addition or diminution: the other has a productive faculty, and gilding or staining all natural objects with the colours, borrowed from internal sentiment, raises in a manner a new creation.[20]

Hume here imagines, in effect, that reason *could* operate alone, that there could be a value-free picture of the world. It appears to be an accident of evolution, or a thoughtful dispensation of creation, that the same creatures have both reason and taste.

But if truth is a value, this is not easy to understand. If it is true that one ought to believe the truth, that says something about belief as much as it does about truth: it is not just an accident that it is *beliefs* which ought to be true—as if the requirement might have applied to desires, but happens not to. It is hard to make sense of this without concluding that, if truth is a value, then to be a believer one must be someone *for whom* truth is a value, to whom it matters that one gets things right. If it is as much essential to the notion of belief that one's beliefs ought to be true, as it is to the notion of truth that one should believe the truth, then if one attributes beliefs to someone, one must regard her as concerned to get things right.

---

[20] Hume, *Enquiry Concerning the Principles of Morals*, ed. Selby-Bigge, 294.

Otherwise, one would be forced to count her as failing in something which she never aimed to do, if her beliefs are false.

That means that there can be no such thing as a value-free perspective on the world. There are perspectives, which are shot through with value, and there are whatever stones have—colours, weight, and the rest, but no value and no perspective. There may also be various uncertain gradations in between. But the 'is'–'ought' distinction marks a distinction within a concerned perspective, not one between perspectives.

These points all contribute to a larger metaphysical picture which does not seem easy to grasp. Its three central features are these:

(I)   The evaluative is not reducible to the non-evaluative.
(II) Values are part of the world (there is no 'fact–value' distinction).
(III) Valuing things is constitutive of having a perspective.

Despite the formal consistency of (I) and (II), it is still these two which create the difficulty in comprehension: the easier picture seems always to be one which accepts (I) but denies (II). That, for example, seems to be what is in common between Hume and the early Wittgenstein, though they differ, I think, over (III).[21]

Wittgenstein and Hume both appear to think that it is essential to value that it is not reducible to the non-evaluative; and this seems to both to require that values are not part of the world, among the facts. For Hume they become a subjective addition to the world, an overlay or gilding—or, to vary the figure, they are (the result of) the tint in spectacles which in principle we need not have worn. For the early Wittgenstein, values seem to be not part of the world because they *shape* the world; hence, 'The world of the happy man is a different one from that of the unhappy man.'[22] I take it that Wittgenstein accepts (III), which Hume denies. This is a very radical difference, but this fundamental disagreement (what, I presume, the Vienna Circle missed) itself appears to be the product just of their different responses to what they both agree on—the difficulty of making sense of (I) and (II).

What causes the difficulty? The problem seems to arise from a certain conception of what it is to make sense of the world, and of how the world must be if it is to be made sense of. The guiding thought (which was also expressed in 5.3) is that the world must be

---

[21] I have been helped to see the *Tractatus* like this by Leo Cheung.
[22] Wittgenstein, *Tractatus*, 6.43.

somehow unified: all the different kinds of fact must somehow fit together. And embracing (I) and (II) seems to make that difficult to understand.

The demand for unity is, admittedly, not a very clear demand, not least because it is not quite clear what requires it; but it seems to me powerful enough for all that, and to be a demand whose spirit we should try to respect. But even if we take the demand seriously, it is not obvious that we should find (I) and (II) as difficult as Hume and Wittgenstein seem to. This is because there are at least *two* ways in which one can think that the demand might be met.

The first insists that a unified conception of the world requires that, in some very large sense, all the facts must be of the same kind. This view faces the threat that, however large the sense of 'same kind' we use, if the requirement that the facts be all of the same kind is to impose any constraint at all, it seems likely that the requirement itself is not going to be a fact of the right kind. I take it that both Hume and the early Wittgenstein adopt something like this conception of a unified world (though in Wittgenstein's case the threat is embraced too).

The second way of thinking of the world as unified is holistic rather than foundationalist. On a holistic view, the unity of the world is constituted by its being impossible to understand any particular kind of fact except in terms of its relations with all the other kinds of fact. This is as much a conception of a unified world as the first; but on this conception there is no problem in principle with there being irreducibly different kinds of fact.

If we adopt a holistic conception of the unity of the world, there ought to be no difficulty in principle with (I) and (II). Some might object that a holistic view makes it impossible to understand any particular kind of fact without understanding every kind of fact. I am not sure why this is an objection: is it so obvious that we *can* understand a particular kind of fact without understanding every kind? Understanding need not be thought of as an all-or-nothing affair. It seems entirely natural to think that we have a partial understanding of a particular kind of fact in virtue of understanding some of its relations to some other kinds of fact. This may be enough for such certifications of merit as 'She's got the idea'. But it still leaves plenty of room for further questions, further assimilations, and further contrasts. I see no reason to deny that these further things to be done enhance our understanding of each particular kind of fact involved.

Even so, I doubt if anyone who was disturbed by (I) and (II) will yet have felt their worries laid to rest. Let us see if we can manage a little more. Evaluation appears to be governed by a principle whose specifically moral version is one of the things known as 'the principle of universalizability' in ethics. Here is a more general formulation:

(U) Where '*E*' is an evaluative term, if something is *E*, then anything else which resembles it in evaluatively relevant non-evaluative respects is *E* as well.

Consider this first from a broadly Humean point of view. We can only strictly see something if it is really there in the world. Hume's world is non-evaluative, so all that can be seen is non-evaluative. Indeed, perception itself is a non-evaluative, empirically describable process.

On this view, the facts available to us are non-evaluative, so the basis of all our judgements—in so far as they are well founded at all—must be non-evaluative. In this light, (U) seems to say something which must seem just common sense to the Humean: value judgements are constructions on the basis of what we are strictly aware of—the non-evaluative empirical world.

In so far as value judgements are reasonable ('deriv'd from reason', as one might put it), we should expect similarities of value to match non-evaluative similarities. An evaluative similarity might correspond to some disjunction of non-evaluative similarities; but if value judgements are reasonable, we should expect the disjunction to be finite, and the boundaries of evaluative similarities to be no less determinate than those of the underlying non-evaluative similarities, so that the evaluative can be properly guided by the non-evaluative facts.

In short, if our values are reasonable, we should expect value judgements to be based on *principles*, where a principle is some modal claim of the form,

All *N* are *E*,

where '*N*' is a non-evaluative term, and '*E*' an evaluative term. ('Thou shalt not kill'; 'Human beings should be respected'; 'All of Bach's music is great'.) As it happens, such rigid principles tend to turn out either to be unacceptable, or else to cheat by covertly importing value into the purportedly non-evaluative replacement for '*N*'. This is not altogether unexpected. The Humean expects the business to be a fudge; it was anticipated in what the Humean will regard as the fudging phrase 'evaluatively relevant' in (U).

This is how (U) seems to a Humean. But now consider it from the point of view of someone who holds that truth is a value, and hence that there are evaluative facts.

Such a person does not need to think of perception as a non-evaluatively describable process. She accepts that there are evaluative facts. So there is no reason of principle to deny that one can, quite literally, see value in the world.[23] If someone objects that 'see' must be metaphorical here, that what must be meant is either some mysterious special faculty, or else the combined exercise of several senses together with some non-sensory theoretical principle, she can reply: no, what is meant is just seeing with the eyes. Once one has abandoned natural-scientific reductionism, there is no clear need to insist that what is seen with the eyes must be explicable by appeal to a scientifically describable process occurring in the visual organs.

From this perspective, the reference in (U) to non-evaluative similarities cannot be there to point to the objective ground of value judgements; the objective ground of value judgements, on this view, is just the evaluative facts. So why do we appeal to non-evaluative similarities? Why, indeed, should we believe that (U) is true at all?

A bold move is open to the non-Humean at this point. We can say that (U) is true because it follows from *this* (roughly-speaking, its contrapositive):

(U*) Where '*E*' is an evaluative term, if one thing is *E* and another is not *E*, there must be some evaluatively relevant non-evaluative difference between them.

This is just the thesis of the *supervenience* of the evaluative upon the non-evaluative: no evaluative difference without some non-evaluative difference.

We can argue for supervenience as follows. Suppose that *a* is good and *b* is not good. That is, there is at least one evaluative difference. If *a* is good and *b* is not good, we must be able to make sense of thinking that *a* is good and that *b* is not good. This follows from conceptualism, as that was characterized in Part I. If those two thoughts are to make sense, we must be able to make sense of

---

[23] This kind of use of literal perception is encouraged by McDowell; see, e.g., 'On "The Reality of the Past"', in C. Hookway and P. Pettit (eds.), *Action and Interpretation* (Cambridge: Cambridge University Press, 1978), 136.

having false beliefs about *a* and *b*. That is, we must be able to make sense of thinking mistakenly that *a* is not good, and that *b* is good. That means that we must be able to think of *a* in some other way than just as 'the good one', and of *b* in some other way than just as 'the one which is not good'. And if those other ways of thinking of *a* and *b* are really to be ways of thinking of *a* and *b*, they must reflect properties which *a* and *b* actually have. That means that *a* and *b* must have some other properties, apart from just being good and not good.

What if they coincided in those other properties? Then one could not make sense of thinking truly that *a* is good and mistakenly that *b* is good too. There would be nothing to make the one thought about *a* and the other thought about *b*. So *a* and *b* must differ in some way other than just goodness.

That other difference might be either an evaluative difference or a non-evaluative difference. If it is a non-evaluative difference, we now have a non-evaluative difference to match our original evaluative difference, as (U*) requires. If it is an evaluative difference, it cannot be just a difference in the utterly general evaluative respect of goodness or not goodness, for that is the difference we began with. It must, therefore, be a difference in respect of some more specific value property, something like bravery, kindness, or whatever. But these more specific value properties are only more specific in that they incorporate non-evaluative differences themselves. So, again, we must have a non-evaluative difference to match our original evaluative difference.

Moreover, the evaluative difference we began with must in a sense *depend* on the matching non-evaluative difference. Otherwise, it would seem to be entirely arbitrary that it was *a* which was good and *b* which was not good. And if it was entirely arbitrary, it would be hard to see why the thought that *a* is good is really a thought about *a* rather than about *b*: we would lose any sense in which the thought that *a* is not good could be really mistaken. So it seems that it must somehow be *in virtue of* their non-evaluative difference that *a* and *b* differ in value. We end up with a fairly standard form of supervenience.

There is one premiss in this argument which might seem controversial: the assumption that the other ways of thinking of *a* and *b* (other than as 'the good one' and 'the one which is not good') must reflect properties which *a* and *b* actually have, if they are to be ways of thinking of *a* and *b*. This might seem to presuppose a descriptional theory of names. But I do not think it does. All that it is required is that, in order to think of something as *F*, one must know something about it other than that it is *F*. This something more need not amount to a uniquely identifying description. And if one is to think that one thing is *F* and another is not *F*, one must know something which is different between them, other than the fact that one is *F* and the other is not. This need not be a uniquely discriminating factor. It might just be something like 'is called *Sam*', or 'which I was thinking about just now'. Nor is it supposed that any such way of thinking of *a* or *b* gives the sense of the names '*a*' and '*b*'.

Suppose, even, that the imagined thinker just thinks of *a* as 'that one' and of *b* as '*that* one' (slightly different emphasis). This is enough. If it is to be intelligible to the thinker that she is thinking about different things, these two demonstratives must present themselves to her as being made in different circumstances of ostension; and if they are to count as demonstrating the right objects, she must know enough about those circumstances for her ostensions to be ostensions of different things.

We seem, then, to have an argument for the supervenience of the evaluative on the non-evaluative, and hence for (U), which does not rest on any Humean conception of the objective ground of value judgements. There are two striking features about the argument. The first is that it can be used to argue for the dependence of the non-evaluative upon the evaluative. The second is that its form suggests that it is not restricted to just the evaluative/non-evaluative distinction.

The first point can be made out like this. The argument for supervenience I have given shows that evaluative differences *require* supporting non-evaluative differences. To someone who thinks that the non-evaluative is basic, and that the evaluative is parasitic upon or derivative from it, this will seem just a further confirmation of her view. But that is the Humean position. We are now trying to convey a picture of a unified world that might be held by someone who does *not* think that the non-evaluative is basic, and who does *not* think that if the evaluative is to count as 'deriv'd from reason' it must follow the outlines drawn by the non-evaluative.

If we adopt this non-Humean line, we will not think that the argument for supervenience displays the roots of the legitimacy of the evaluative in the non-evaluative. What *should* we think, from within *this* perspective, is the significance of the fact that evaluative differences require non-evaluative differences? The natural response is obvious: it is the *evaluative* differences which legitimate the *non-evaluative* differences. That is, once we abandon the Humean conception of the non-evaluative being the true description of 'objects as they stand in nature', the obvious thing to do is to invert the significance of supervenience, just as we inverted the 'universalizability' thesis (U) to get (U*).

I think this position has been held before. Recall the Platonic claim (which again I quoted in the introduction): 'The good is the source not only of the intelligibility of what can be understood, but also of its being and essence.'[24]

This suggests the following bold claim: the fundamental rationale for *non-evaluative* differences is that they are needed to make sense of *evaluative* differences. That claim is too bold, since it suggests a form of evaluative foundationalism, which we ought to be as suspicious of as we are of any form of foundationalism. So we might say, slightly less extravagantly: there would not have been those non-evaluative differences if there had not been those evaluative differences.

This is something which we would seem to be committed to anyway, in virtue of conceptualism and the evaluative theory of content. Conceptualism requires that there would not have been those objects, properties, and facts, if there had not been the corresponding concepts. Suppose the objects, properties, and facts in question are non-evaluatively individuated. Their existence then depends on the existence of the concepts, whose individuation is evaluative.

But the point seems more general than just a reaffirmation of conceptualism combined with the evaluative theory of content. It seems quite generally intuitive that a difference of any kind is only real in so far as we can make sense of some project, some concern, something which might matter to someone, whose success or worth might depend upon that difference. The appeal of that thought might be taken to be a confirmation of the combination of conceptualism with the evaluative theory of content, rather than just a restatement of the views.

[24] Plato, *Republic*, 509 B6–8.

The picture that we are here presented with is one of a strong mutual interdependence between the evaluative and the non-evaluative. Evaluative differences require non-evaluative differences. If we are already committed to value, we are committed to the non-evaluative. On the other hand, the picture encourages us to say that being committed to the non-evaluative, we are already committed to the evaluative. What is attractive about this is that it produces a conception of the world as unified which, so far from encouraging reduction, actually seems to require irreducibility: we need the differences to be different *kinds* of differences. In consequence, there is nothing odd about its being difficult to produce plausible evaluative *principles*. The evaluative domain does not need to be kept on the rails of the non-evaluative. Indeed, we should *expect* the two domains not to match, since each requires that the vocabulary of the other be run on different lines.

The other feature of the argument for supervenience is that its basic structure seems applicable more broadly than just to the distinction between the evaluative and the non-evaluative. Indeed, for any particular difference, it seems that there must be some other difference on which that difference depends. This will apply even to physical differences. For every particular physical difference, there will be some other difference.

Not only do we see supervenience relations all around us: the significance of supervenience in general is changed. Within the non-Humean picture, we do not see the supervened upon as basic, a level of unquestioned objectivity and legitimacy, and the supervening as secondary and parasitic. On the contrary, the supervened upon is legitimate only in virtue of what supervenes upon it.

The point is general, but it has a particular and revolutionary application to our conception of *physics*. Physics is (by stipulation) that upon which *everything* supervenes. There can be no difference of any kind without there being some difference which physics can describe. Here is Quine, putting the point as well as it could be put:

nothing happens in the world, not the flutter of an eyelid, not the flicker of a thought, without some redistribution of microphysical states. It is usually hopeless and pointless to determine just what microphysical states lapsed and what ones supervened in the event, but some reshuffling at that level there had to be; physics can settle for no less. If the physicist suspected that there was an event that did not consist in a redistribution of the elementary states allowed for by his physical theory, he would seek a way of supplementing his theory. Full coverage in this sense is the very business of physics, and only of physics.[25]

In a scientistic age we are inclined to suppose that physics has the vocabulary which really touches the world where the current flows, and is therefore in a position to prescribe the proper course of every other kind of talk. But this is an unmotivated kind of Platonism (in the sense of 'Platonism' defined in 1.3). The moment we abandon it, the significance of the supervenience of everything upon physics is hugely altered. It is not physics which validates everything else, but everything else which validates physics. If there had not been those kinds of *non-physical* difference, there would not have been those *physical* differences.

This might seem to be a merely epistemological claim: it is just that we would have no reason to believe in those physical differences if there had not been those non-physical differences. But the point is not merely evidential. There really would not have been those physical differences if there had not been those kinds of non-physical difference. It is essential to the physical differences there are that they explain the kinds of non-physical difference they do. Otherwise, it would seem a kind of accident, a wonderful and miraculous coincidence, that those physical differences actually do explain those non-physical differences.

But could there not have been a different universe, which could be described in the vocabulary of our physics, but in which there were not (many of) the kinds of non-physical property which we find in the actual world. Of course there could. But that other universe would have to have been one from whose point of view, so to speak, the actual world is possible. It is a fundamental essential property of any real physical difference that it is *apt* for explaining a difference there might be in a world which includes all the kinds of non-physical difference which there actually are. (And, of course, there could have been a different universe in which there were many of the actual non-physical differences there are, and few of the actual physical differences.)

Sometimes the significance of the supervenience of everything on physics is expressed like this: when God created the world, all he needed to do was fix the physics; that was enough to fix everything

[25] W. V. Quine, 'Goodman's *Ways of Worldmaking*', in his *Theories and Things* (Cambridge, Mass.: Harvard University Press, 1981), 98.

else as well. This is true, of course; but it is highly misleading. God could only have fixed the physics *by* fixing everything else as well. There are no short cuts in creation.

If we pursue this kind of thought into every kind of super-venience, we get a very general conception of the world as being unified in virtue of the distinctions there are to be drawn being interdependent with one another. This is an anti-foundationalist conception of unity: it requires no sense in which all the facts must be of the same kind. And the attraction of the general picture takes some of the pressure off the irreducibility of value to the non-evaluative. That irreducibility can be seen as one among many, and need not be thought to threaten the reality of value any more than the irreducibility of other distinctions threatens their reality.

This has been a response to a Humean exclusion of value from the world. What of the early Wittgenstein? Wittgenstein (in that frame of mind) might be happy to accept that there would have been no non-evaluative distinctions without distinctions of value, and hence that there is a sense in which the evaluative determines the non-evaluative. The world of fact, he might have agreed, is dependent upon value and content; but value and content are always in a sense *external* determinants, never determining from within the world. He wrote: 'What the solipsist means is quite correct, only it cannot be said.'[26]

But this position now looks both unnecessary and impossible. The impossibility is the impossibility of Descartes's ghost, which we tried to exorcize in Chapter 8. The position is unnecessary, since, with the tight interdependence between the evaluative and the non-evaluative that has been proposed, we have a conception of a unified world. It may have seemed important to view the world as a 'limited whole',[27] but if we set the limit that Wittgenstein proposed, we do not get a whole. There is no world of facts, if 'facts' are taken to exclude value. What is left is always only part of a world.

Will everyone who was worried by the joint acceptance of (I) and (II) now feel satisfied? I doubt it. All that has been done is that we have met a formal objection with an abstract description of an alternative kind of picture of the world. To do more we will need to develop the evaluative theory of content, and add some living detail. If the evaluative theory of content is properly developed, it

---

[26] Wittgenstein, *Tractatus*, 5.62.
[27] Ibid. 6.45.

should seem so attractive that a Humean or Wittgensteinian exclusion of value from the world will seem untenable.

That will be the concern of the rest of this chapter and the next four. In the meantime, we might pause to note the irony that the kind of transcendental realism known—with some justice—as Platonism, should thereby bear the name of the philosopher who first saw how one might resist the Platonistic relegation of value to the margins of reality.

9.5. A More Precise Formulation of the Theory

We reached *this* rather schematic evaluative definition of concept-possession in 9.1: possessing a concept is being liable to respond in ways which are intrinsically assessable with respect to the value T—in whatever way is appropriate to *that* concept in particular.

Later chapters will attempt to supply the necessary fuller explanation of the so far merely dummy notions of liability, intrinsic assessability, and the value T. But more needs to be said immediately about the idea of a way of assessing a response being appropriate to a particular concept.

The fundamental difficulty here is the requirement that the theory construct intensionality from an extensional base. The idea of the proposal I will put forward is this: even to fix extensionally specifiable assessability we have to appeal to a background which could have provided quite exigent constraints on substitution. In fixing extensional assessability we must already have done enough to generate intensionality.

The problem is complicated by the fact that different kinds of demand are imposed by different concepts. And there is a difference, I think, even in what is meant by 'different concept'. When we think of different concepts, we think first of the concepts expressed by different words. Different words, and different kinds of word, create different kinds of difficulty for a theory of content beginning from an extensional base. For expressions other than singular terms and predicates, there is a technical problem dealing with the grammar. And then there are other differences too. Sentences involving some expressions can have their *truth conditions* specified extensionally—at least on a thin reading of 'truth condition'—although there are obvious problems with capturing the expressed *concepts* extensionally. Expressions with implicit structure are obvious examples here: I take it that the adjective *renate* involves some implicit reference to kidneys, although it is familiarly co-extensive with *cordate*. But it is impossible to specify extensionally even the *truth conditions* of sentences involving some other expressions: so-called 'intensional attributive adjectives', like *good*, seem to fall into this class.

That might seem variety enough. But I think the constraints on substitution in belief contexts can vary even for the same word (with the same reference). This is what I called *flexible opacity* in 6.3. I wanted there to be two readings of this pair of sentences:

(1) Pierre believes that London is pretty;
(2) Pierre does not believe that London is pretty.[28]

On one reading, they come out inconsistent; on the other they do not.

With this kind of variety, there seems no possibility of producing an absolutely general definition of concept-possession, of the form: someone possesses the concept C if and only if p—at least if we are to be able to say something explanatory.

In the face of this, what is proposed is a theory of particular very simple cases—perhaps they are even fictional cases—from which one can imagine the materials for dealing with more complicated cases being constructed. We might call these the *core* cases, round which we hope to be able to wind enough layers to account for any concept.

I shall present definitions for possessing concepts of just two types: certain kinds of singular-term concepts, and certain kinds of one-place-predicate concepts. (These are concepts expressed by singular terms and one-place predicates, respectively.) By 'singular term' and 'predicate' I am referring to categories of expression defined by the syntax of standard first-order predicate calculus. This saves me having to worry about complications of grammar.

There are two further kinds of simplification. First, the definitions deal only with what I call *simple* singular terms and *simple* one-place predicates. A *simple* expression of either category is one which is semantically unstructured, and is such that there is no single referentially unambiguous semantically structured expression which can be substituted for it whenever it occurs in belief

---

[28] See Kripke, 'A Puzzle about Belief'.

contexts. This *identifies* simple expressions in conceptual terms. But there is no circularity, since the fundamental account of what it is for such an expression to be simple is just this: an expression is simple just in case an account of what it is to possess the concept it expresses is provided by an appropriate definition in the theory.

The other kind of simplification I shall introduce in the definitions is not strictly necessary, but will help to make them intelligible. The definitions provide only the most minimal level of opacity for such simple expressions. Call this *level-one* opacity. A belief report imposes level-one opacity with respect to a singular-term position if and only if it is possible to intersubstitute co-referring *simple* singular terms in that position, *salva veritate*. And a belief report imposes level-one opacity with respect to a predicate position if and only of it is possible to intersubstitute co-extensive *simple* predicates at that position, *salva veritate*.

Two things should be noted about level-one opacity. First, it only concerns the intersubstitutability of *simple* expressions. Complex (that is, not simple) expressions will not be so easily substituted for simple expressions, or for one another. Secondly, whether a real word can be subject to level-one opacity is a property of that word. So not all simple expressions need be capable of being subject to level-one opacity. The definitions that follow deal only with the imagined case of those words which can be used in the way imagined. (The details of these points will be clarified in Chapter 13; and in 13.6 I shall explain how to do without level-one opacity.)

Now for the definitions. I use the term *concept* to refer to both singular-term concepts and predicate concepts, the difference being marked by the style of expression filling the gap in a phrase of the form 'the concept " . . . " '. I shall use '*a*' as schematic for simple singular terms, and '*F*' for simple one-place predicates. '*E*' is used for any expression of an appropriate category to form a whole sentence when combined with a singular term or one-place predicate, as the case may be. I shall always write '*E*' first, taking this to cover also the cases where the completing expression surrounds or follows the singular term or predicate. Quantifiers with quoted schematic letters are to be read substitutionally, as usual.

Here, then, are two complementary definitions:

(S) A subject *s* has the level-one concept "*a*" at a time *t* if and only if

s is liable at *t* to make responses each of which would be an *r* such that, for some '*E*', *r* is intrinsically assessable with respect to the value T as: good if and only if *Ea*;

(P) A subject *s* has the level-one concept *F* at a time *t* if and only if

s is liable at *t* to make responses, each of which would be an *r* such that, for some '*E*', *r* is intrinsically assessable with respect to the value T as: good if and only if *EF*.

In both of these definitions, the final biconditional is to be read as a material biconditional. Intersubstitutivity on the right side of that biconditional is the condition for sameness of simple level-one concept. (It should be emphasized once again that it is not a condition for sameness of concept generally.)

If those final biconditionals are to be read as material biconditionals, some constraint is already imposed upon how we are to understand the notion of liability: it cannot be understood in counterfactual terms. If the notion of liability were understood in counterfactual terms, the weakest imposable constraint on substitution on the right-hand side of the final biconditionals would be this: terms which are co-extensive *in the world in which* r *is made* are intersubstitutable.

The intention, however, is that terms should be intersubstitutable in that position which are co-extensive *in the actual world*. The import of the possession of a liability for the making of responses cannot, then, be understood in standard dispositional terms. We must instead take it as something like this: someone who is liable to respond in a certain way *will*, for all we know, respond in that way. The subjunctive 'would' in both definitions must be read as an economical way of dealing with responses in the actual world which we do not know will be made.

There might be some technical way of avoiding this, but I am not myself distressed at the consequences of this formulation. What it means, in effect, is that we must not think of concept-possession as determinative of the occurrence of future behaviour. But that seems in tune with a conclusion reached in 8.3, that talk of beliefs and desires is not directed towards prediction.

But there is something odd about (S) and (P). Why are *they* used at all? Why have we not begun with a definition of *belief*?

A corresponding definition of belief might look like this:

(!) A subject *s* has the level one belief that *p* at a time *t* if and only if

s is liable at *t* to make responses, each of which would be an *r* such that *r* is intrinsically assessable with respect to the value T as: good if and only if *p*.

This would seem to give us just two level-one beliefs—the true one and the false one (unless we also allowed a not precisely either true or false one). And it is not clear that we can make sense of a notion which cuts as coarsely as this being a notion of *belief* at all.

In fact we are under no obligation even to make sense of the idea of level-one beliefs. Level-one opacity was defined only for simple content: that is, for content expressed by expressions which are themselves semantically unstructured, and for which no referentially unambiguous semantically structured expression can be substituted within belief contexts. But there are no simple beliefs: thoughts are essentially structured.

Am I not cheating, though, in simply presuming this, and taking structure for granted? Yes, but only temporarily. It will need to emerge from the theory of content itself that thoughts are essentially structured. The point simply adds to the debts of the theory. This one will be paid back in 10.6.

The other debts were incurred in the stipulative introduction of key notions to meet certain theoretical demands, and these key notions now need fuller explanation if the theory is not to be circular. Chapter 10 will attempt to provide such a fuller explanation of the notion of intrinsic assessability. Chapter 11 will deal with the value T. Chapter 12 will attempt to explain the notion of liability in the context of a larger account of the explanation of behaviour. The question of opacity will be examined in Chapter 13, when I hope it will be clear how the account of the simple cases provided by the two definitions given here can be extended to provide as rich a conception of the intensionality of belief as anyone could want.

So far, though, we have a treatment just of certain core cases, and that treatment itself is no more than the core of a theory.

10

Intrinsic Assessability

10.1. The Basic Requirements of Intrinsic Assessability

We can, if we like, count something as going right or wrong just because it is convenient or pleasant for us to think of it in those terms. That would be the pathetic fallacy turned simply frivolous. The notion of intrinsic assessability was introduced to get us two steps beyond that frivolity. In the first step we move beyond mere convenenience: we have a sense in which a particular mode of assessment is *already right*. I called this the step to *non-arbitrary* assessability, assuming that simple computers and things like calculators can be non-arbitrarily assessed.

The machines I am thinking of here are certainly not concept-possessors. Why not? The obvious, natural, intuitive answer is: because these machines only do what they do because they have been designed to. There is, in some sense, too close a dependence upon the intentions of their designers for these machines to count as thinkers. In a certain sense of 'only because', these machines are non-arbitarily assessable only because of their designers' intentions. That thought takes us the second step away from merely convenient assessment. The notion of intrinsic assessability was introduced just to take that step; something is intrinsically assessable just in case it is non-arbitrarily assessable for some other reason than 'only because' of a designer's intentions. It might be tempting to think of certain organs in animals as intrinsically assessable: it is certainly not in virtue of some designer's intentions that parts of the visual system, say, are treated as registering or processing such and such information. I shall argue later, however, that we should not in the end succumb to this temptation (see 11.4).

What I want, then, is an account of non-arbitrary assessability to which some feature can be added to provide us with an account of intrinsic assessability. And that added feature must somehow explain what is wrong with counting something as a thinker when its responses are too closely dependent upon a designer.

But I shall hope for more than this from an account of intrinsic assessability. It is clear that it is in virtue of being intrinsically assessable in a certain way that a response is genuinely a response *to* something. Intrinsic assessability is where aboutness comes in, on an evaluative theory of content. It is notable, though unsurprising, that whatever a theory puts forward as its account of aboutness it also proposes as its account of knowledge. (Those who like causal theories of reference, for example, also tend to adopt causal theories of knowledge.) This unsurprising correspondence is what I exploited in proposing the knowledge constraint in 5.1.

We should, therefore, expect our account of intrinsic assessability to yield an account of knowledge. This is helpful, since it enables us to meet what I called the *analysis of knowledge requirement*:

(C4) A theory of content must be capable of generating a theory of knowledge (see 6.2).

This was required because, according to the version of conceptualism developed in Part I, the nature of a fact is determined by what it would be to have knowledge of it, and the nature of reality is determined by the nature of concepts.

We have two constraints on an account of intrinsic assessability, then: it must get us the required two steps beyond merely convenient assessment; and it must yield an account of knowledge.

With that in mind, let us react to some intuitions. Suppose I am sitting in the garden, reading a book. It is a funny book: I smile. At the very moment when my lips begin to twitch, the first drop of a rain-storm falls on my mother's house thirty miles away. Is my smile a response to the rain on my mother's roof? Would it be reasonable to assess my smile as correct (appropriate?) if and only if a drop of rain falls simultaneously on my mother's house?

No. Why not? Because these two things just happen to occur at the same time. If we count my smile as correct if and only if a drop of rain falls simultaneously on my mother's house, it is, and could only be, a fluke that I am right. We would want at least some regular correlation between my smiling and rain at my mother's even to begin to make it plausible that my smile is a response to that apparently unrelated event.

Now consider an extremely unfanciful case. I have a piece of chalk in my hand. I let go of it. It falls to the ground. There is clearly some sense in which the descent of my piece of chalk is a response to gravity. But is the movement of the chalk correct if and only if the laws of gravity are as they actually are? Here the correlation seems too *tight*: how could the chalk have gone wrong? And if we cannot make sense of its having gone wrong, it is hard to see how we can make sense of its now being right.

These two childish examples suggest two conditions for non-arbitrary assessability. If a response is to be non-arbitrarily assessed in a certain way, it must be possible to make sense, first, of that response being somehow non-accidentally right, and, secondly, of its being wrong.

But that is too quick: we cannot have to make sense of the same response being, on the one hand, non-accidentally right, and, on the other, wrong. Suppose the response is in fact wrong: how could *it* have been non-accidentally right? Only if the world had been conveniently different. And, again, if this response is non-accidentally right, *it* could only have been wrong if the world had been disobligingly otherwise. But this is not what we want when we want to make sense of non-accidental correctness or error. We want to be able to say, when we are wrong, that we could have been right *in the world as it is*; and, when we are right, that we could have been wrong *in the world as it is*. It is, as it were, the possibility of actual world failure that makes success worth having, and it is the possibility of actual world success that makes failure failure.

What we want, then, is not to make sense of *this* response being both non-accidentally correct, and incorrect. We want to say that this response belongs to a type, and this type can have both non-accidentally correct tokens, and incorrect tokens.

What conditions must two tokens meet to belong to the same type, in the relevant sense of type? They must be similar enough to be similarly assessable. A proponent of the evaluative theory should resist pressure for further definition at this point, since that would amount to defining an evaluative similarity in non-evaluative terms, which the whole strategy of the theory requires to be impossible.

It is being suggested, then, that a response's being non-arbitrarily assessable is a matter of its belonging to a certain kind of (evaluatively conceived) type. Of course, we must not allow it to be counted as belonging to such a type just because it is convenient or pleasant for us to treat it so. It is tempting then to insist that it must be *essential* to this response that it belongs to the type it does. Succumbing to the temptation, that is what I shall propose.

We have here the basis of a definition of *non-arbitrary* assessability: it must be essential to a response that it belongs to a type which may include both non-accidentally right, and also incorrect responses. What else is needed for *intrinsic* assessability?

If a simple computer produces the right answer, and it is no accident—in an intuitive, if rough, sense—that it does, then this will be because the designer or programmer, who must herself be competent, has so adjusted things that a correct answer is guaranteed unless there is a malfunction. This is just the kind of dependence upon a designer that seemed to prevent simple computers from counting as having concepts. So to get intrinsic assessability we just need to rule out non-accidentally right responses being non-accidentally right for this sort of reason. Let us postpone the detail of what this requires (until 10.5), and just insist on *this* for the moment: non-accidentally correct tokens of the type must be non-accidentally correct for the right sort of reason.

These points can be summarized in a provisional but semi-formal definition of intrinsic assessability:

(IA) *a*'s response *r* is intrinsically assessable (as good if and only if *p*, say) if and only if

(a) It is essential to *r* that:
   (i) There is something which it would be for some response, sufficiently similar to *r* in relevant respects to be similarly assessable, to be *non-accidentally right*.
   (ii) There is something which it would be for some response, sufficiently similar to *r* in relevant respects to be similarly assessable, to be *wrong*;
(b) Any relevantly similar response which was non-accidentally right would be non-accidentally right *for the right sort of reason*.

Clause (*a*) here is the hurdle for non-arbitrary assessability; clause (b) is a gesture towards intrinsic assessability. It might be noted that clause (i) does not require that there must actually have been some appropriate non-accidentally correct response. This allows us to accept that a computer could go wrong on its first trial.

This definition of intrinsic assessability, laborious though it seems, does little more than sketch out the shape of the full explanation of the notion which is required if it is to be used in a theory of content. The notion of non-accidental correctness has been floated on no more than the breath of an intuition, and has not been properly explained. And clause (*b*) could never pretend to be more than a gesture.

10.2. An Analysis of Knowledge

We need to generate an account of knowledge out of the notion of intrinsic assessability. We also need to explain what is involved in a response's being non-accidentally correct. Some sort of no-accident theory of knowledge seems called for.

In this section I will present an analysis of knowledge which is a kind of no-accident theory. In 10.3 I shall develop an account of non-accidental correctness which mirrors the analysis of knowledge. I do not pretend that the account of non-accidental correctness was developed with no eye to the analysis of knowledge, but I think it could also have been reached just from thinking about computers. In 10.4 I shall respond to a certain kind of objection to my kind of analysis of knowledge.

Anyone who presents an analysis of knowledge must know that it is certain to fail. The birds are lined up along the fence-wires, ready to transfix any analysis with their counter-examples at the first sign of a faltering step. My aim is not to produce an analysis which is immune to objection. The idea is just to present an analysis of knowledge which is initially plausible, and an account of non-accidental correctness which is initially plausible, and to link the two together tightly enough for it to be clear that any fault in the one will be matched by a corresponding fault in the other. If I can do that, it will be plausible that a correct account of intrinsic assessability will generate a correct analysis of knowledge. And *that*, rather than any particular analysis of knowledge, is what matters to the evaluative theory of content.

Since my aim is relatively modest, I shall not survey the vast literature of and on analyses of knowledge. Nor do I claim that the analysis I offer is wholly original. I shall just try to address the issues directly, in a fairly elementary way, beginning at the beginning.

Someone who knows something must be right. That is what makes knowledge worth having and experts worth consulting. And that deceptively simple truth is what every analysis of knowledge aims to capture.

Suppose one took the important point about this to be just that knowledge involves true belief. True belief is not enough for knowledge, since one can be right by accident. (Imagine that you believed something on the basis of what you had heard; what the person you heard said was false, but you misheard it, as something which happened to be true.) We have not got enough of the idea that a person who knows *must* be right. What we want is for it to be true of someone who knows that it is no accident that she is right. The attraction of all no-accident theories of knowledge is that they bring that simple guiding thought out into the open.

Our task, then, is to capture the sense in which the knower is non-accidentally right. But in doing this we need to beware of what is called 'the threat of scepticism'. Classical scepticism begins from the (sometimes hidden) assumption that knowledge requires *infallibility*. That assumption is always tempting, not least because it provides an apparently solid sense in which someone who knows can count as non-accidentally right. But it quickly leads to disaster, since, even if we are prepared to *countenance* infallible knowledge, it seems that one could not know anything infallibly unless one could also know something fallibly. (For example, you cannot know that you are in pain—supposing, for the sake of argument, that this is infallible knowledge—unless you can also know that someone else is in pain.)

The conclusion that knowledge is impossible is comparatively trivial on its own. What is really unbearable is the consequence of combining that with two theses which are central to the conceptualism I developed in Part I: that one can only think about things which one knows something about, and that one cannot think without thinking about something. When these two theses are added, the assumption that knowledge requires infallibility wipes out the mind.

We need, then, to find a middle course for knowledge, between luck and infallibility. The now standard response to this difficulty is to accept that knowledge requires true belief, and then to add a clause requiring some appropriate grounding for the belief. The result is a 'tripartite' account of knowledge, whose classic form is this:

(1) *a* knows that *p* if and only if

(i) it is true that p;
(ii) a believes that p;
(iii) a's belief that p is justified.

We ought to know immediately that there is something wrong here. We want some sense in which someone who knows could not have been wrong. Clause (iii) is supposed to ensure that. Well, if it does ensure it, clause (i) ought to be unnecessary. So if we need clause (i), clause (iii) must fail to capture what is crucial for knowledge. In fact, there seems to be a dilemma here. If we need clause (i), clause (iii) cannot be enough. On the other hand, if we do not need clause (i), and this simple clause (iii), with its unanalysed notion of justification, *is* enough, this can only be because the notion of justification in clause (iii) incorporates unanalysed exactly what we wanted to understand about the notion of knowledge.

The fact that clause (iii) must be inadequate if clause (i) is necessary is what Gettier's counter-examples make vivid.[1] Gettier cases can be modified to provide recurrent problems for attempts to rule out merely lucky true belief, while remaining on the liberal side of infallibilism. I shall take Gettier cases and their direct descendants to provide the hardest challenge for an analysis of knowledge. It will be helpful if we have an example to focus on, which can be modified to counter refinements in proposed analyses. Here is a simple schoolroom example, derived from one of Gettier's own.

If clause (iii) is not just to reproduce the problems and virtues of the notion of knowledge, 'justified' must mean something like *reasonable*. Well then: Susan leans out of a window, and sees Jim driving past below. She assumes, quite reasonably (who would not?), that Jim is driving his own car. The car is quite evidently a Ford (it has 'Ford' written in huge letters on the back). She concludes—impeccably, given her quite reasonable assumption—that Jim owns a Ford. He does indeed; so she has a reasonable true belief. But this car is not his own, but Brenda's. It is just a fluke that Susan ended up right.

That problem was anticipated. Why not address directly the intuition that knowledge requires non-accidentally true belief? We might get this:

(2) a knows that p if and only if
    (i) a believes that p;

---

[1] E. Gettier, 'Is Justified True Belief Knowledge?', *Analysis*, 23 (1963), 121–3.

(ii) *a* would not have believed that *p* if it had not been true that *p*.

This has the advantage of needing no separate truth clause, but, if it is not to be read charitably, it is familiarly vulnerable to a slight modification of Gettier cases. To construct Gettier cases to get round this kind of analysis in general, all one needs to imagine is one of the original Gettier cases set up on purpose, precisely in order to be a Gettier case. Here is a slightly different modification of our original example. Suppose Brenda is very nervous about her car being properly treated, so that she will lend it only to Ford-owners. In this situation, Jim would not have been driving her Ford if he had not owned one himself. So Susan would not have ended up believing that Jim owns a Ford if it had not been true. But it is still a fluke that she is right.

If we recall the use of the notion of knowledge in the conceptualist conception of metaphysical explanation in Chapter 5, it should be obvious what this kind of account is missing. The idea there was that one could use a conception of what it would be to have knowledge of a fact to reveal the nature of that fact. This rests on the thought that different modes of knowledge are required for different kinds of fact. To put the point crudely, blindness need not inhibit one's ability to tell if someone is playing out of tune, though it is likely to make colour discrimination more difficult.

Along with this point comes a conception of different circumstances being safe or unsafe for making different kinds of judgement. The notion of 'circumstances' here includes the state of the judge's own body, her situation, her frame of mind, background assumptions, and perhaps more. Let us call all of this the *condition* the person is in when she makes a judgement. We can now introduce a refinement of that notion: the idea of an *absolutely safe* condition. An absolutely safe condition will satisfy this requirement: whatever anyone judged in that condition would be true.

It is clear that there cannot be any condition which is absolutely safe for every kind of judgement, on this definition of absolute safety. Consequently, there will only be a limited range of judgements which can be made *in* any given condition, in the sense of 'in' which is relevant to the characterization of absolute safety (whatever anyone judged *in* such a condition would be true). This in turn intuitively expands the notion of a condition to include any method on the basis of which the judgement might be made, and the assumptions which are used in any inference whose conclusion the judgement is. This all seems unobjectionable. The notion of a condition was introduced to reflect the different kinds of things that need to be in order for different kinds of judgement to count as knowledge. One would expect considerations of method or assumptions in reasoning to be relevant.

Someone might fear that the idea of an absolutely safe condition is infallibilist. It is a good thing that the idea should *sound* infallibilist, provided it can be shown that in fact it is not: this suggests that we are getting to the heart of the thought that one who knows must be non-accidentally right. But there is nothing infallibilist about the idea of absolute safety, if it is possible to be in an absolutely safe condition with respect to a certain kind of judgement without knowing infallibly that one is. But this surely is possible. If I am competent with colour concepts, in good light, at a reasonable distance, judging on the basis of the way things look, not mentally unhinged, and so on—then the thing I am looking at will be the colour I think it is. This does not stop it being conceivable that each of the crucial features of this absolutely safe condition might fail to obtain without my noticing.

So let us suggest *this* analysis of knowledge:

(3) *a* knows that *p* if and only if

   a believes that *p* in some condition of which this is true: whatever anyone believed in that condition would be true.

It might be tempting to deal with our latest Gettier case (involving the cautious Brenda) using this definition, in the following way. We take Susan's condition to be: generally sound in mind and body, presented with a clear view of the make of car Jim is driving. In that condition, we suggest, she makes a judgement about the make of car Jim *owns*. If she can make that judgement in that condition, the condition cannot be absolutely safe. This is because it is just luck that Jim happens to be driving a car of the same make as the one he owns. He could easily have hired one of a different make, instead of borrowing Brenda's.

But this is inadequate, for two reasons. First, even if we maintain this intuitive way of thinking of Susan's condition, we can once again modify our Gettier case to meet the requirement, without ensuring knowledge. All we need to imagine is that, unbeknownst to Susan, *every* car-owner is as cautious as Brenda (even car-hire firms), and car thieves are all so timid that even they only steal cars of the same make as their own, for fear of mechanical difficulties which they cannot deal with. In this peculiar world, forming beliefs about the types of cars people own on the basis of beliefs about the kinds of car they are driving will be absolutely safe. But it will still be just luck that Susan is right.

The other problem is that, although this conception of the 'condition' which Susan is in is intuitive, it is quite uncompulsory. There is no reason not to include in the condition the whole scenario of the case, including the fact that Jim really does own a Ford. But if we include all that in the condition, it will certainly be absolutely safe for believing that Jim owns a Ford.

The natural way of dealing with both problems is the same. We insist simply that absolute safety must play some role in explaining why Susan believes what she does.[2] We can incorporate that by moving on to this definition:

(4) *a* knows that *p* if and only if

    a believes that *p* in some condition of which this is true:
- (i) whatever anyone believed in that condition would be true;
- (ii) *a* would not have believed anything in that condition if (i) had not been true.

This certainly seems to deal with the last two problems. There is no condition, in any example yet described, in which Susan believes that Jim owns a Ford, which meets these two conditions.

But is there not something infallibilist about clause (ii) here? Surely, someone might say, the reason why we get into an absolutely safe condition is just that it *looks* absolutely safe. Does this clause not insist that *looking* safe is a guarantee of *being* safe? No. The idea is merely this. Suppose that the reason one gets into an absolutely safe condition is, as suggested, just that it looks absolutely safe. But the reason why an absolutely safe condition *looks* absolutely safe can be just that it *is* absolutely safe. And that is enough to sustain the subjunctive conditional in clause (ii).

There is nothing infallibilist about clause (ii) if there is nothing infallibilist about clause (i). If we cannot tell infallibly whether a condition is absolutely safe, we cannot tell infallibly that the reason

---

[2] For such a suggestion, see C. Peacocke, *Thoughts: An Essay on Content* (Oxford: Blackwell, 1986), 141.

it looks absolutely safe is that it is absolutely safe. Even so, it seems appropriate to say that what we are responding to, when things run properly, is in fact just the absolute safety of the condition, not merely the appearance of absolute safety. If we cannot say that, we seem to be opening the floodgates to the full tide of the argument from illusion. I cannot be infallibly certain that what I see out of the window is a car. It looks like a car, and that is, no doubt, why I think it is a car. But, I assume, the reason it looks like a car is just that it is a car. And that is how I can now be responding to a car, and not just to the appearance of a car.

There is, however, a kind of counter-example even to this definition, although it is not of the Gettier family.[3] Can we not imagine a subject being carefully monitored by expert supervisors, who twiddle her beliefs in whatever way is necessary for her to be always right? I am not sure that this really is imaginable, since I am not sure that the result of such interventions could count as beliefs. But it will do no harm to rule it out anyway.

What does seem clear is that a person under such careful monitoring has become just like a simple computer in the hands of a designer or programmer. The intervention seems too direct for the person to count as knowing, just as, in the case of the computer, the intervention was too direct for the computer to count as possessing concepts. (This is why it should not be obvious that what are engendered in the imagined subject here are beliefs.) Since the two cases belong together, I shall postpone discussion of both together (until 10.5). We end up with this definition ('NAK' for '*no-accident theory of knowledge*'):

(NAK) *a* knows that *p* if and only if

> *a* believes that *p* in some condition of which this is true:
> (i)   whatever anyone believed in that condition would be true;
> (ii) *a* would not have believed anything in that condition if (i) had not been true;
> (iii) (ii) is true *for the right sort of reason*.

In addition to whatever plausibility this definition has so far collected, it also has the advantage that it fits well with an intuitive diagnosis of what goes wrong in the simple Gettier cases. The diagnosis is that the justification is incomplete because the belief in

---

[3] This example is due to Peacocke, *Thoughts*, 138.

question rests on a false intermediate belief.[4] Thus, in our case, Susan concludes that Jim owns a Ford on the basis of the false belief that Jim is driving his own car. We should clearly insist that no belief can count as knowledge which rests on false lemmas.

The no-false-lemmas approach is not finally satisfying. Its appeal seems in the end to depend upon the idea of a no-accident theory. Why should we not count beliefs based on false beliefs as knowledge? Because no false belief has only true consequences, so it will always be lucky that the subject ended up with a true one.

Nevertheless, appeal to a no-false-lemmas requirement is natural and easily manageable: it is a handy diagnostic tool. Could (NAK) certify something as knowledge which the no-false-lemmas approach would bar?

Imagine an engineer who believes that a certain bridge will not collapse within five years, under normal environmental conditions and with the projected traffic load. She reaches that belief on the basis of a complex calculation, an important premiss of which is a law of Newtonian mechanics. The engineer believes the law to be true. In fact, it is false, but the results it delivers are so near to the consequences of the true physical laws for the cases which the engineer has to consider that using the Newtonian law will always be safe in reaching beliefs like the one the engineer in fact reaches here. That gives us something like clause (i) of (NAK).

Imagine, too, that, although the engineer believes the Newtonian law to be true, she remains an extremely cautious practical engineer: she never actually uses that law in the exercise of her profession, except in the kind of case where she knows from experience that the results it delivers are safe. This seems to be meeting clause (ii), and in a way which ought to satisfy clause (iii).

Does the engineer *know* that the bridge will not collapse within five years, under normal environmental conditions and with the projected traffic load? (NAK) seems to say that she does. What does the no-false-lemmas approach say?

It is not clear. The problem is that, because the engineer is cautious, it is not clear that her final judgement really *depends* upon the false Newtonian law, rather than upon some more cautious claim to the effect that the law holds in certain circumstances to a certain degree of tolerance.

[4] See G. Harman, 'Inference to the Best Explanation', *Philosophical Review*, 74 (1965), 88–95.

The uncertainty seems quite general, and it rests upon the simple fact I mentioned before, that no false belief can have only true consequences. That means that no piece of reasoning involving a false belief can appear as part of a condition meeting clauses (i) and (ii) unless something prevents the false consequences of the belief being drawn. But then it will always be hard to claim that the final resulting belief really depends upon the false belief, rather than upon some suitably related, but more cautious, true belief.

It seems to me that (NAK) emerges as at least an initially plausible account of knowledge. That is enough for my purposes.

10.3. Non-Accidental Correctness

I want now to see if by thinking about simple mechanical devices we can motivate a definition of non-accidental correctness which mirrors the analysis of knowledge which has just been offered.

Consider an electronic gadget of a familiar kind. It has a small keyboard, on whose keys are marks which we naturally take to be numerals and signs for arithmetical functions. It has a small liquid-crystal display screen, on which may appear shapes which are also naturally taken to be numerals and signs for arithmetical functions. What has to be true for this to be a calculator—or, to simplify things, an adding-machine?

Would it be enough if, after we had pressed the keys marked '5', '+', '1', and '2', in an appropriate order, the shape '17' appeared on the screen? Obviously not: the machine might have been badly designed, so that '17' only appeared on the screen because of a short circuit.

The problem here does not depend upon this being an isolated example. Suppose that the machine always, but miraculously, produced what is naturally taken to be the sum of the previously entered numbers—but always, miraculously, as a result of some unforeseen short-circuit. If we saw this for long, we would find it hard to believe that this was really a coincidence, but for all that it could be. It seems to me that there is no sense in which this device, wonderful though it might be as a natural object, is an adding-machine.

The problem seems obviously to be that we have no right to rely on this machine. So far all has gone 'well', but at any moment the sequences of coincidences might cease. And while they remain coincidences, we also have no right to regard the machine as *adding* the entered numbers. An indication of this is that we would be quite wrong to complain that the machine had gone wrong, or made an error, if it happened not to produce a coinciding kind of display. It would just have done what it had always been doing—throwing up what we might as well regard as random responses to the depression of its keys. There is no basis for talking of right or wrong here.

What one wants of an adding-machine is something one can trust to produce the sum of any two numbers one enters. The whole point is that one does not want to check every result. One wants the machine to be so constituted that whatever appears on the screen will, on the natural interpretation, be the sum of the previously entered numbers. If this is to say that we want every response of the machine to be non-accidentally right, we might be tempted to offer this definition:

(1) *a*'s response *r* is non-accidentally correct if and only if

a makes response *r* in a condition of which this is true: whatever response anything made in that condition would be right.

This seems to me not to be enough. The previous problem was, in effect, that good intentions are not enough to make something an adding-machine: the designer must also be competent. Something does not count as an adding-machine if it is mere luck that what it produces looks like the sum of the entered numbers. But (1) does not rule that luck out.

Suppose I build an electronic device, but I do it so badly that, every time a key on the keyboard is depressed, circuits are unexpectedly joined or cut out. But the miracle is that appropriate 'numerals' appear on the screen after appropriate entries. Not only that, but—more miraculous still—it is in fact, unanticipated by me, causally determined that the product of all these unforeseen electrical changes will always be a display of what looks like the sum of the entered numbers. If being luckily 'right' prevented the first device from counting as an adding-machine, being luckier still can hardly be what is needed.

The point can be put in another way. If the circuitry in my miraculous device decays after a time, with the result that the device no longer reliably generates what looks like the sum of the entered numbers, it would not be right to say that the device was malfunctioning, or going wrong. We have no right to speak of error here. The device was not functioning properly when it produced what looked like right answers, so it cannot be malfunctioning when it does that no longer. It has not become faulty; it is just doing something different. The device was never an adding-machine, although it could be used as one; just as the sky on a clear night is not a compass, although it can be used as one.

The amendment that is needed is obvious. The problem is dealt with if we move to this definition:

(NAC) *a*'s response *r* is non-accidentally correct if and only if

   a makes response *r* in a condition of which this is true:
   (i) whatever response anything made in that condition
        would be right;
   (ii) *a* would not have made any response in that
        condition if (i) had not been true.

In effect, what we want is for a designer or programmer to build the machine so that it does what it does (or to leave it so that it does what it does) just because it is reliable.

(NAC) in fact seems a fair general definition of the notion of a thing performing its function. We might note the difference between it and the provisional definition it replaced in relation to a very simple case. Suppose I have a wobbly table in my office. I am very untidy, so there are books and papers all over the floor. One of my students accidentally kicks a book under one of the legs of my wobbly table. The table no longer wobbles. At this stage, we have in effect satisfied the requirements of (1). It seems to me that, although the book is stopping my table wobbling, it is not its function to do so: it is not functioning as a stabilizer. But now suppose I notice that my table has stopped wobbling. I peer round the side, see the book under the leg, realize how the wobble has been stopped, and then deliberately leave the book where it is. Now the book *is* functioning as a stabilizer, and (NAC) has been satisfied.

In the light of that, it seems that, if a device met (NAC) in the relevant way, it would count as an adding-machine; a failure to generate the true sum of the entered numbers would count as a malfunction; and assessing its performance in terms of addition would not be arbitrary.

In the case of (NAC) there is obviously no need to insist on a further clause which will prevent clause (ii) being true in virtue of a designer's manipulation, since (NAC) is meant to apply precisely to the behaviour of the products of design. Otherwise, our definition of non-accidental correctness precisely matches the definition of knowledge.

That means that, provided the other aspects of the definitions of concept-possession given in 9.5 are satisfactory, a response which is non-accidentally correct under assessment with respect to the value T—and is non-accidentally correct for the right sort of reason (no too close dependence on a designer)—will be an expression of knowledge. And that means that the definition of intrinsic assessability does generate an analysis of knowledge, just as it was required to do; and, as a result, an evaluative theory of content seems well-placed to explain, in the way that conceptualism requires, how the nature of content determines the nature of reality.

10.4. Epistemological Internalism

In proposing (NAK) as an analysis of knowledge my aim was modest: it should at least be initially plausible. The general project of the evaluative theory of content can tolerate any particular analysis of knowledge being revised, provided that a corresponding revision is always required in the analysis of non-accidental correctness.

That proviso is not entirely empty. It is quite unclear, for example, how a revision of (NAK) in the direction of an internalist or justificationist epistemology could be matched in an account of non-accidental correctness which was motivated by consideration of such things as adding-machines.

I shall count as internalist any theory of knowledge which insists that for a belief to count as knowledge the subject must in some sense have (perhaps just have available) a justification of that belief—that is, something which a sufficiently articulate subject might produce as a reason, which would also be a good reason. The least demanding form of internalism would accept that sometimes beliefs are held without reasons, insisting merely that a justification should somehow be available. I shall take Peacocke's 'Model of Virtual Inference' as a paradigm of such an undemanding form of internalism. It holds that 'a belief held without reasons is knowledge only if a sound, and in the circumstances knowledge-yielding, inference to the best explanation *could* be made from the evidence available to the believer to the truth of his belief'.[5]

Those who are inclined towards an internalist epistemology bring quite different intuitions to the imaginary examples from those which are held by the advocates of 'externalist' theories, like no-accident theories. The issue is not just a matter of favouring different policies for achieving a commonly agreed end. In this section I will try to discredit the internalist's intuitions. I doubt if this will be decisive on its own, but I hope that, in the light of the sweetness of the match between (NAK) and (NAC), it will be enough to uphold the generally externalist character of the analysis of knowledge which an evaluative theory of content appears to require.

Peacocke has an example which serves as a good test of the intuitions.[6] In one of those routine lectures on the history of philosophy someone was told that Hume died in 1776. Now, thirty years later, she is asked (in a quiz, say) when Hume died, and answers, truly, '1776'.

We can imagine that (NAK), or some favoured externalist revision of it, is satisfied. It is actually her memory which is being exploited, and, as things are with her, she would not now have produced this answer (or any answer) if it had not been prompted by real memory. But those conditions can all be met while it is true, in Peacocke's words, that 'there is not a rational, sound abduction to be made from this belief to its truth'.[7] We can elaborate on that. Suppose that some of the things she heard in those lectures she now misremembers—even very similar sorts of things: she now thinks falsely, for example, that Voltaire died in 1779. And suppose she is not aware of any reason for believing any of them. From her point of view, '1776' just pops into her mind when she is asked when Hume died, and '1779' just pops into her mind when she is asked when Voltaire died.

Does she *know* that Hume died in 1776? Peacocke's intuition says 'no'; mine says 'yes'. I shall now try to discredit the internalist intuition.

---

[5] Peacocke, *Thoughts*, 163–4.
[6] Ibid. 165–6.
[7] Ibid. 165.

In the first place, it is unclear how Peacocke's judgement about the Hume answer can make a satisfactory contrast between this case and a reflective modification of it. Imagine everything the same, except that the person does not actually *say* '1776'. That answer occurs to her, but she hesitates. She wonders whether she has any reason to think this answer is right. She thinks Voltaire died in 1779, but perhaps she has got the two dates muddled. The year 1776 has some interest for her for other reasons; perhaps that has confused her here. She tries to visualize Hume's dates on a page, like a page of an encyclopaedia, but finds that '1771' and '1775' look equally good; and what about '1767'? She remembers her confusion over the dates of the plague and the fire in London in the seventeenth century. After a short while, five or six alternative dates for Hume's death all strike her as equally plausible. She cannot even remember which was the date she first thought of. She writes all the options down, shuts her eyes, and jabs with her pen. The pen lands on '1776', so she says '1776'.

Two things are clear about this new case. First, the person here does *not* know that Hume died in 1776—or, at least, her answer is not an expression of knowledge. Secondly, she is worse off in this case than in the first. The externalist has an easy description of the contrast between the two cases: in the first case she knew; in the second she does not. The internalist can see the difference, but cannot count it as a difference in knowledge. This seems to me both not to do justice to the difference, and to be hard to motivate.

Why should one think that the difference between these two cases is not a difference of knowledge? We can begin to get at what I think underlies this thought by supposing that the motivation is a belief in the power of reflection. We might express that as adherence to this:

(R) Reflection on any particular belief can never make one worse off with respect to knowledge.

We should not include under 'reflection' here just any foolish wondering: let us restrict the term just to sensible and serious questioning of the reasons for one's beliefs. And it should be noted that (R) does not encourage us to reflect on everything at once. It is tempting to think that (R), so understood, is at least close to the guiding thought behind epistemological internalism. After all, if one's counting as knowing depends on there being good reason for one's belief, proper reflection will reveal the reason if one knows, and if it reveals no good reason, and one's reflection was thorough, argumentatively imaginative, and so forth, that suggests merely that one never knew after all.

There is a faintly Cartesian flavour about this. That flavour can be enhanced by thinking further about what reflection seems to involve. It appears to require that, in reflecting whether something is true, one suspend one's belief in it, or distance oneself somehow from that belief. But once one has done that, it now seems irrational to re-adopt the belief without the reason for which reflection is searching—unless, of course, there was no need for a good reason in the first place.

Let us elaborate that more carefully. An internalist like Peacocke can accept that it is all right to believe something for no reason, in the first place. But once reflection on that belief has begun, and the belief has been suspended, it is only all right to *re-adopt* the belief without good reason being found, if one of these is true:

(i) It is all right to adopt a belief without caring whether it is knowledge.

(ii) One can know something even if there is no good reason (in the internalist's sense) for believing it.

Internalism is defined by its denial of (ii). And it is hard to see how anyone could care about knowledge at all and accept (i). But (i) is the attitude the internalist would herself have to adopt, if she thought it was all right to re-adopt a suspended belief without good reason. So it looks as if an internalist cannot think it is all right to re-adopt a suspended belief until a good reason has been found for it.

This position seems to face the two central problems that confront Descartes: it is in some difficulty when its principles are applied to itself; and it requires considerable optimism about the availability of good reasons. If these two problems are insuperable, the internalist will find herself in the terrible Humean position of having to believe things which she knows in a serious sense it is not all right for her to believe.

First, then, what happens when we reflect upon (R) itself? Is there any good reason for believing it? If it is part of the best explanation of the internalist intuitions we are now considering, then that fact would be a reason in its favour, *if* those intuitions were correct. But the intuitions themselves are now in question, so we cannot appeal to that reason. Good reason for (R) now looks hard to find. And the prospects will look worse if the internalist's general optimism about the availability of good reasons turns out to be ill founded.

I have been considering (R) as a particular motivation for internalist intuitions, and (R) seems to require one to be optimistic about the availability of good reasons. But *any* internalist must be optimistic in this way, if she is not to end up drastically reducing what we can count as knowing. Is that optimism well founded? Peacocke's undemanding internalism requires that a belief held without reasons can only count as knowledge if a sound inference to the best explanation could be made 'from the evidence available to the believer to the truth of his belief'. There seems to me to be something curious about the phrase I have just quoted, but for the moment I shall take it in what I think is the intended sense.

There is a blind across the window in my office—at least, I believe there is. Why do I believe it? Because I can see it—at least, I believe that I can see it. This last belief certainly seems to be a belief held without reasons. If it is to count as knowledge, it seems that we need to be able to argue that the best explanation of my believing that I can see a blind is that it is true that I can see a blind.

How could we meet that demand? I suppose we will be driven to the resources of classical empiricism. We will note first that the experience 'as of a blind' comes to me without my choosing it—or seems to—and that this experience is coherent with all my other experiences—or strikes me so. And we must then suppose that the best explanation of my experience having these properties is that it is veridical—that is, I *can* see a blind. But why should we believe that the best explanation of the experience having these properties is that it is veridical? What alternative explanations are there? Someone might have given me a peculiar drug of a kind that I have not heard of—although I certainly do not recall the drug being given to me. Is this less *likely* than that the experience is veridical? The difficulty is that we do not know what to make of our judgements of likelihood if we are prepared to question even such things as whether we are now really seeing something before us. The point is not that it is *impossible* to maintain our usual conception of likelihood while suspending belief in our current experience; it is just that we would have no *right* to trust our usual conception of likelihood under such conditions.

It might be objected that it is not the subject's own conception of likelihood which needs to be deployed in an abductive inference from the 'evidence available' to her: it is ours, the theorists'. If we are allowed to appeal to this, we may avoid the difficulties, but we get a peculiar form of internalism. If we are allowed to appeal to an external conception of likelihood, why can we not appeal to an external conception of the facts? And if we do that we can *know* that the reason the belief is held, in the circumstances, is that it is true—even in the first of the cases about the date of Hume's death. Only allowing one kind of external appeal seems to produce a strange hybrid form of internalism, whose philosophical motivation is hard to understand—unless it be just to accommodate various intuitions which, on inspection, we find ourselves to have.

It seems to me that the demands of a motivated internalism seal us off from the world. This does not seem to be an over-reading of the view: it fits with the curious phrase of Peacocke's which I drew attention to before. There is supposed to be an argument 'from the evidence available to the believer to the truth of his belief'. What can 'available' mean here?

Apparently, what I know without reason does not count as evidence available to me—at least when we are considering the reasonableness of the belief involved in this piece of knowledge. And that requires that for every belief, however immediate, there is something which counts as evidence for that belief—something, I presume, that we can properly take for granted without already being committed to the truth of the belief itself. But this already involves us in just the difficulty over our right to trust in other things, once certain beliefs are put in doubt, that I raised before.

Given that, the idea does not seem to be just an incidental adjunct of internalism, the result merely of an infelicitous use of the phrase 'evidence available'. It appears to be essential to the very idea of an internalist epistemology that there is something like a ground for every belief which can count as knowledge.

If this is right, the difference between internalism and the kind of epistemological externalism that might consort with the conceptualism of Part I seems to centre around their attitudes to very fundamental doubt. The internalist wants to tackle the doubt head-on, taking its threat seriously, and then argue in the face of it that it is unreasonable, and that the beliefs which are doubted are likely to be true. The opposing externalist, on the other hand, will hold something like this. If you take fundamental doubt literally and seriously, there is literally nothing to say: one's right to believe even in the meaningfulness of one's own words will be undermined. The fact that one is saying something shows that one is already committed to not admitting the doubt. This is not a demonstration that the doubt is ill grounded, and that common sense is safe. There are no demonstrations of this kind to be had. There are no grounds for confidence: there is only confidence.[8]

From this perspective, internalism seems to demand a kind of grounding that cannot be provided. And the intuitions which favour internalism—intuitions about particular imagined examples— appear to rest on a reluctance to accept as knowledge any belief which does not come wrapped with the materials for overcoming doubt of itself.

I have provided a diagnosis of internalist intuitions, and of what seem to be the central tenets of internalism. I cannot be sure that I have been fair to internalism. But at least *this* is true: I have provided an explanation of the internalist intuitions which in no way requires their truth. The internalist now faces the challenge of producing another, better explanation, whose truth does require the truth of the intuitions.

10.5. The Right Sort of Reason

The last clause of the definition of intrinsic assessability requires that an appropriate non-accidentally-right response must be non-accidentally right *for the right sort of reason*. The third clause of (NAK), the proposed analysis of knowledge, also required that the second clause be satisfied *for the right sort of reason*. In both cases, what is achieved is the kind of thing which careful design might achieve. And, in both cases, what is required for this to be achieved in the *right sort* of way is that the achievement must not be due to any unduly direct intervention by a designer, programmer, or supervisor.

We need some fuller account of this to avoid the charge of circularity. Where content is the result of the too direct intervention of a designer or supervisor, it is natural to think it is derivative from

---

[8] I take it that this approach to doubt echoes that favoured by Wittgenstein in *On Certainty*, trans. D. Paul and G. E. M. Auscombe (Oxford: Blackwell, 1969).

the content of the designer's or supervisor's beliefs and intentions. And, if we simply say that the assessability of something must not be too dependent upon a designer or supervisor, it is natural to read this as saying, in effect, that the assessability must not be derivative from the beliefs and intentions of a designer or supervisor. But that specification uses the very notions we are trying to explain in a theory of content.

For someone who hopes to provide a natural-scientific account of content, there is a very tempting solution to this difficulty. We are trying to explain the kind of thing which design might produce, but without appeal to a designer. Evolution is a theory precisely suited to explaining such effects without appeal to design. The definition of non-accidental correctness produces quite an intuitive account of the notion of a function. Evolution seems to underwrite the attribution of function to organs and other bodily parts. It is natural, sometimes compelling, to describe parts of animals as registering or transmitting or processing information. Such descriptions do not rest on the animals in question being concept-possessors: the descriptions seem to be legitimated by evolution. Indeed, to many people, certain parts or subsystems of animals will be natural examples of things whose behaviour is intrinsically assessable, given the definition I used to introduce that notion. The behaviour of these parts and subsystems will seem to be non-arbitrarily assessable, and it is clearly not non-arbitrarily assessable just in virtue of design. This behaviour seems just the kind of thing we might hope to be able to appeal to in order to give general credence to the notion of intrinsic assessability, before its specific application to the case of concept-possession. Moreover, the notion of *adaptation* seems to provide a natural model for an epistemologically externalist conception of the development of a competence. Evolution, in short, seems just right for the evaluative theory of content.

I think the blandishments of an evolutionary grounding for the notion of intrinsic assessability should be resisted. We should be suspicious of it immediately. After all, it seems to hold out the promise of a natural-scientific theory of content, and there are reasons of principle for thinking such a theory is impossible (see 7.4). I shall argue in 11.4 that these suspicions are well founded. (This does not stop us, if we are circumspect, using adaptation as a helpful metaphor for the development of a competence.)

For the moment, however, we can argue that an evolutionary account of intrinsic assessability is unsatisfactory just because it does not explain what has to be explained. There are two fundamental thoughts which I am concerned to respect:

(1) Something whose 'success' is too closely dependent upon the intervention of a designer or supervisor does not count as a thinker.

(2) It is not easy to say what counts as 'too closely dependent'.

The notion of 'the right sort of reason' for being non-accidentally correct was keyed precisely to (1), and therefore must take account of (2). A proper account of the right sort of reason should explain what it is about too close a dependence upon a designer or supervisor which prevents one counting something as a concept-possessor. And it should also explain why it is not easy to say what counts as 'too closely dependent'.

An evolutionary account can do neither of these things. It just provides an explanation of success (or perhaps 'success') which does not appeal at all to a designer or supervisor. It is therefore just not—or not yet—a response to the problem in hand. In fact, things look worse than that: it is unclear how an evolutionary account *could* do what we want.

What is the relation between evolution and design? There seem to be two fundamental points:

(i) Certain correspondences, which are so widespread, intricate, and multifarious that they had seemed to be explicable only as the product of design, are explained by evolution as the natural result of the long-term operation of naturalistically describable processes.

(ii) Certain features and correspondences, which seem so sweet and perfect that they strike us as *meant*, and indeed are counted as meant by a design theory, are explained by evolution as not being meant at all.

These points seem exactly wrong for dealing with (1) and (2). The intuition behind the difference between merely non-arbitrary and intrinsic assessability is that, in a sense, assessability engendered by design is not *real* assessability: it is imposed, as it were. But, in so far as evolution explains the same effects as would be explained by a design theory, it does not reveal the effects as any more real. And, so far from *grounding* the sense of the significance of things which a design theory exploits, evolution either denies or ignores all such significance. Fodor puts it well: '*Of course* Darwin has nothing to say to Brentano: the whole point of Darwin's enterprise was to get biology out of Brentano's line of work.'[9]

The conviction expressed in (1) also gets blurred and confused by representing the issue as one of 'derived intentionality' as opposed to 'original intentionality'.[10] Why should 'derived intentionality' be any less properly intentional than 'original intentionality'? If the thought behind (1) is represented in these terms, it sounds as if it is being claimed that a reproduction of a photograph in a book would be somehow less properly *about* the subject of the photograph than an original print from the negative.

Once the temptations of an evolutionary account have been suppressed (even if only temporarily), and the confusions of the talk of 'derived' and 'original' intentionality set aside, I think it should just strike one as obvious what guides the thought expressed in (1). It is an issue of responsibility. Something whose 'success' is too closely dependent upon the intervention of a designer or supervisor does not count as a thinker, because it is not *responsible* for what it does.

This fits precisely the point I insisted on in 8.6. Beliefs (and hence concepts) are used to explain behaviour for which the subject is responsible. Something which is not the sort of thing to be responsible for anything is not a thinker. The notion of responsibility used here (and in 8.6) is meant just to capture whatever is required to make sense of the idea that a person is the doer of her deeds. Someone who is responsible in this sense is not always to be praised or blamed for what is done—if praise or blame is due at all. But, where praise or blame is due, the doer of a deed should get it, unless there is some other person to whom it can be passed. And we cannot make sense of a person being a responsible subject in this sense, if she could never be properly praised or blamed.

That seems to fit with our attitude to simple computers and calculators. If a machine goes wrong, it is the designer or manufacturer we curse—unless we have got to the stage of kicking even tables and chairs for daring to obtrude their presence. Computers—simple ones at least (and 'simple' here includes very

---

[9] J. Fodor, 'A Theory of Content, I', in his *A Theory of Content* (Cambridge, Mass.: MIT Press, 1990), 79.

[10] See Dennett, 'Evolution, Error, and Intentionality', in his *The Intentional Stance*.

complicated machines indeed)—are not to be praised or blamed for their success or failure, because they are not responsible for it: it is not really *their* success or failure.

The suggestion that (1) is guided by considerations of responsibility also makes good sense of (2). It should be no surprise that we cannot say what precisely 'too closely dependent' means, if what counts as too close is determined by what counts as not responsible. Apart from anything else, responsibility is a moral notion, and therefore should not be reducible to the non-evaluative in the way that a precise specification would seem to require.

The definition of knowledge also included a clause insisting that the existence of the belief involved should be dependent upon its being held in a condition of absolute safety 'for the right sort of reason'. The clause was inserted to rule out someone who met the previous conditions in virtue of some monitoring engineer adjusting her beliefs—as it might be, with a screwdriver—to keep her on the right track. Is it a plausible diagnosis of this to say that what is wrong is that the person is no longer responsible for her beliefs?

I think it is. A useful case to contrast this one with is that of a person who is accompanied by an adviser, whom she consults whenever she is at a loss or uncertain what to do. We can make sense of criticizing such a person for gullibility. That criticism will not always be fair, but sometimes it will be. But the idea of criticizing someone for gullibility whose beliefs—if they can be called beliefs—are adjusted by screwdriver or electric shock is absurd. If that is right, the idea of responsibility does seem to mark what prevents the person who is literally manipulated from counting as knowing.[11]

But although responsibility seems the right kind of notion to appeal to in order to capture the idea of 'the right sort of reason', and we should not attempt to reduce the notion of responsibility to anything non-evaluative—even so, the notion of responsibility itself seems too close to the notion of content to be used neat in a theory. The notion of responsibility might seem, for example, to introduce immediately the notion of choice, and the notion of choice the ideas of belief, desire, and intention.

I suggest a simple solution to this difficulty, one which harks back to the intuitive thought I used in 8.6, that what is important

---

[11] This point seems to have been important for Augustine; see M. Burnyeat, 'Wittgenstein and Augustine *De Magistro*', *Aristotelian Society Supplementary Volume*, 61 (1987), 1–24.

about the idea of a responsible subject is that it is the idea of a doer of deeds. Here, then, is a definition, in a form suitable for explaining the notion of the 'right sort of reason' (RSR) in the definition of intrinsic assessability:

(RSR)   *a*'s response *r* is non-accidentally right for the right sort of
        reason only if, in virtue of *r* being right, *a* is right herself
        (/himself/itself).

The idea is extremely simple, but intuitive for all that. What happens on the display of a calculator, or on the print-out from a computer, may be literally and unproblematically correct. But the calculator itself is not right, nor is any existing computer—not literally, that is, although the pressure towards anthropomorphism is severe. Similarly, if I simply engender true beliefs (assuming they are beliefs) in someone, with a screwdriver or electrodes, what she says will be literally and unproblematically true, but *she* will not be right.

What is distinctive of being a concept-possessor, then, is that, in virtue of the correctness of one's responses, one is right oneself. And, of course, when one's responses are incorrect, one is wrong. That seems both natural in itself, and nicely in tune with the emphasis that was put on the notion of a person in trying to set constraints on a plausible conception of the explanation of behaviour.

This definition also confirms the suspicions I voiced about an evolutionary approach to intrinsic assessability. Suppose we want to count some behaviour of a part of an organism as somehow right. If that behaviour were intrinsically assessable, we ought to be able to find something which is counted as being right in virtue of the behaviour's being right. But when we think of the evolutionary history of this behaviour, there seems no natural choice: is it the *part* of the organism, or the organism itself, or the *species* perhaps, or just *nature*? We seem to be able to find no settled subject of responsibility for evolutionarily generated 'success'.

10.6. Non-Arbitrary Assessability Requires Structure

In the definition of concept-possession for the simple core cases, the requirement of an extensional base to the theory was met only by insisting on the structure of thoughts. This is only legitimate if thoughts are essentially structured,[12] and the evaluative theory of content can explain that fact.

Why should one believe that thoughts are essentially structured? What, indeed, does the claim mean? Here is a thin reading of the claim. We can make sense of unstructured sentences, linguistic items which have no semantically relevant components but which nevertheless count as whole sentences. But we can only make sense of a sentence being unstructured if it is conceptually equivalent to (expresses the same thought as) some structured sentence. Perhaps the structured sentence does not have to be in the same language as the unstructured sentence; perhaps it is not even required that there be a language which is actually spoken in which the relevant structured sentence can be constructed—I do not want to chase those issues here. But unless we can make some sense of the claim that there is some structured sentence which expresses the same thought as the unstructured sentence, we have no reason to think that the unstructured item is a whole sentence (expresses a whole thought) at all.

A corollary of this is that, where 'p' is an unstructured sentence, if we can describe someone as having the thought that p, there must be some other description of the same thought which is structurally revealing, in the sense that it uses a structured sentence in the relevant 'that'-clause. This is what I take to be the thesis that thoughts are essentially structured: for any thought, it must be possible to describe that thought using a 'that'-clause containing a structured sentence. The claim is very thin. It does not mean that an expression of a thought by means of an unstructured sentence is *wrong*: it is just not structurally revealing. Nor does it mean that only one kind of structure of sentence is appropriate for expressing a given thought in a structurally revealing way. The thinness of the claim seems to be due to the fact that it is not atomistic. If that is so, that is a virtue.

That is the claim, and I have presented an argument of sorts for it. The crucial premiss was the statement that we cannot make sense of an unstructured sentence which is not conceptually equivalent to some structured sentence. There is surely a sense in which this does

[12] The idea that thoughts are essentially structured is one of the main motivations for Evans's 'Generality Constraint'; see G. Evans, *The Varieties of Reference*, ed. J. McDowell (Oxford: Clarendon Press, 1982), 100–5.

not go deep enough. *Why* can we not make sense of an unstructured sentence which is not conceptually equivalent to some structured sentence? The evaluative theory of content can, I think, provide an explanation.

Non-arbitrary assessability requires that every properly assessable response must belong to a type which includes both a non-accidentally correct response and an incorrect response. Consider one of each of these, r_1 and r_2: one of them is correct, the other incorrect.

Suppose this is true:

(1) r_1 is good if and only if p.

Then this will be false:

(2) r_2 is good if and only if p.

For, if both (1) and (2) were true, the two responses would have to be made in different worlds. But what we wanted was the idea that, even if we are wrong now, we could have been right in the world as it is; and, if we are right, we could have been wrong in the world as it is. So, if (1) is true, there must be some 'q' which differs in truth value from 'p' such that:

(3) r_2 is good if and only if q.

So far we have got just the idea of a correct response and an incorrect response. We have not yet captured the idea that the responses must be of the same type. To count as belonging to the same type, two responses must be similar enough in relevant respects to be similarly assessable. If two responses are similarly assessable, there must be something similar about their conditions for correctness. If there is something similar about their conditions for correctness, it must be possible, at least when we are working within a material biconditional, to state the correctness conditions for both responses using sentences which share some common expression. That is, it must be possible to put in place of 'p' and 'q' two sentences which have some expression in common.

The common expression might be either subsentential or a whole sentence. If the common expression was subsentential, we might have, for example:

(4) r_1 is good if and only if Fa; and
(5) r_2 is good if and only if Fb,

where 'Fa' and 'Fb' differ in truth value.

If the common expression is a whole sentence, and the two responses differ in correctness, then the correctness condition of one will be, in effect, the negation of the correctness condition of the other. Within a material biconditional we can express it just as the negation of the other. We might then have:

(1) r_1 is good if and only if p; and
(2) r_2 is good if and only if not-p.

But it cannot be the case that this is the only difference between the correctness conditions of these two responses. For the difference between 'p' and 'not-p' is just that, where 'p' is true, 'not-p' is not true. But if truth is a value, that difference cannot be the only difference, because the thesis of the supervenience of the evaluative upon the non-evaluative requires that for every evaluative difference there must be a non-evaluative difference.

So there must be some other difference in the correctness conditions of these two responses. We should then be able to capture that difference using some different expression in the statement of each condition. We might mark it like this:

(7) r_1 is good if and only if ... a; and
(8) r_2 is good if and only if ... b.

But (7) and (8) now fail to reflect the fact that r_1 and r_2 are responses of the same type, and are therefore similarly assessable. So there must be some commonality about what fills the gaps. We will now find ourselves back once again with something like (4) and (5). In short, we have structure.

This has further implications. At the moment 'a' and 'b' in (4) and (5) mark a difference there might be between the correctness conditions of r_1 and r_2. But if they can mark a difference, they must also be able to mark a similarity. So we must be able to make sense of two responses whose correctness conditions share an 'a' feature, and two responses whose correctness conditions share a 'b' feature. So if we have (4) and (5), we must have at least something like these two as well:

(9) r_3 is good if and only if Ga;
(10) r_4 is good if and only if Gb.

And 'G' cannot be just 'not-F', for the same reason as (1) and (6) cannot express the only difference between the correctness conditions of r_1 and r_2.

It seems to me that we have here the basis of an argument for the claim that thoughts are essentially structured, of a kind which seems exactly right for the thin reading of the claim which I suggested. If any sentence can give the correctness condition of a response, then there must be some structured sentence which does.

In this exposition I have borrowed the grammar of standard first-order predicate calculus, for the sake of simplicity. Which grammar is actually appropriate will depend on the actual patterns of similarity across responses. And there are also ontological conditions which we might want to impose: say, that there can only be *names* for things which meet some condition of object-hood which is more than just grammatical. In that case, whether a name, say, may properly be used to express a response's correctness condition will also depend on factors which are determined by the way this particular type of response meets the condition of non-accidental correctness. This will fix the conditions of absolute safety which are relevant to that type of response, and hence, by the knowledge constraint of 5.1, it will also determine the nature of what the response is a response to.

It is true, of course, that it has not yet been shown that, for every sentence which expresses a thought, there is a structured sentence which expresses the same thought—that is, that there is a structured sentence which is *conceptually* equivalent to each unstructured sentence. But we have done enough to show how there can be a structured sentence whose components are all extensionally correct for representing the content of the thought. And the account of opacity in Chapter 13 will show how that can be the basis for constructing an intensionally adequate expression of the thought.

The aim of the argument here was just to discharge the explanatory debt incurred by the discernment of structure in the definitions of concept-possession offered in 9.5; so these questions do not need to be pursued in detail. But the fact that there seem to be the materials here for explaining why it is true that thoughts are essentially structured seems to me to provide further support for the evaluative theory of content, which supplies those materials.

There is a particular feature of the argument for structure which has some independent appeal. It works by showing that it cannot be the case that the only difference between two judgements is that one is the negation of the other. This would explain why languages in fact work with opposites—or, more generally, with notions of particular *ways* of not being thus and so—rather than just with negation: with notions of blue and green, for example, rather than just not-red, or not-yellow. That is something we ought to want to explain anyway.

11

Truth and Virtue

11.1. An Evaluative Theory of Desire

This chapter aims to explain the value T in contrast with other values, to show its inextricability from those other values, and, on the basis of that, to explain why there cannot be an evolutionary theory of content.

What are these 'other values'? The value T is a truth-like value which applies to responses. Truth itself I take to be a value of special importance to belief. The other values I shall be concerned with are also values which apply to responses, but they are not truth-like. They are rather the kin of the values which are special for desire, and other similar attitudes, in just the way in which truth is special for belief. This chapter therefore depends upon the idea that it is appropriate to give an evaluative theory of desire, just as it is to give an evaluative theory of belief.

When we talk of desire in this context, we should not think just of desires. We should also think of hopes and fears, of delight and distaste, of approval and disapproval, of pleasure and regret. I shall embrace all of these under the term 'orectic attitude'. The term itself preserves the bias towards desire in particular, and that bias is one I think we should be suspicious of (see 8.7); but I hope that conniving at it will not harm the points I want to make here.

What distinguishes the orectic attitudes is that they play roles which are combined and contrasted with the role of beliefs—most beliefs, that is—in the explanation of behaviour. The combination and contrast is most familiar in the case of desires. Here is a familiar schema of explanation:

She B'd because she desired that p and believed that B-ing would be a good way of bringing it about that p.

An explanation involving such beliefs and desires is only complete (in whatever sense it is complete), if both the belief and the desire are mentioned. And the roles of belief and desire are different; as witness the fact that one cannot replace the report of belief with the report of a second desire, or the report of the desire with the report of a second belief of the same kind. I shall assume that such a complementary combination with belief can be found for all orectic attitudes.

But having just included all orectic attitudes as relevant to our concerns, I shall return once again to consideration of desire in particular. Those who are likely to feel most uncomfortable about an evaluative theory of orectic attitudes in general will feel the worry first in relation to desire.

I shall put forward two reasons for favouring an evaluative theory of desire: first, that it is in tune with the general idea of an evaluative theory of content; secondly, that it actually best explains the links between desire and value which are exploited by Hume in the main argument he uses to question the reality of values. Since the principal worry about an evaluative theory of desire is that it involves a commitment to the reality of values in just the sense which Hume is there questioning, this should protect the theory from the principal source of objections to it.

The evaluative theory of content rests on two basic thoughts: first, that there are general reasons for thinking that there can be no natural-scientific account of content (see 7.4); and, secondly, that that fact is best explained by thinking of content as ineluctably evaluative. Desires are contentful states of mind (to desire is to desire something); so the point about the need to appeal to value should apply to the content of desires, and hence to desires themselves.

Indeed, it seems clear that a theory of content could as easily have *begun* with the content of desires. Certainly an evaluative theory could have done. Let us introduce a value D, which is to be a value applied to responses, which stands to the value proper to desire as the value T stands to truth, the value proper to belief. We might be tempted to say:

(D!) A subject *s* has the level-one desire that *p* at a time *t* if and only if

s is liable at *t* to make responses each of which would be an *r* such that *r* is intrinsically assessable with respect to the value D as: good if and only if it is desirable that *p*.

(I will return to the essential presence of some such phrase as 'it is desirable that' in 11.2.)

The temptation to offer something like (D!) should be resisted for the same reason that we could not accept the similar definition of belief ((!) in 9.5). If the context introduced by 'it is desirable that' is extensional—as it must be if we are to have level-one opacity—we would end up with too coarse a conception of desire to count as a conception of desire.

We should resort, then, to definitions of *concepts*. Here is the core case for singular terms:

> (SD)   A subject *s* has the level-one concept "*a*" at a time *t* if and only if
>
> *s* is liable at *t* to make responses, each of which would be an *r* such that, for some '*E*', *r* is intrinsically assessable with respect to the value D as: good if and only if it is desirable that *Ea*.

Provided that we understand 'it is desirable that' as introducing an extensional context—permitting intersubstitution *salvo bono*, as we might put it—this seems no worse, and no less fundamental, as a definition of possessing a simple singular-term concept than (S), the definition offered in terms of the value *T* in 9.5. And the general conception of intrinsic assessability, together with what will be said about liabilities in Chapter 12, could apply just as well to this too.

In fact, since we talk of the content of desires in the same sense of 'content' as that in which we speak of the content of beliefs, it would seem to be a requirement on any acceptable theory of content that it could equally well have begun with the content of either kind of attitude. And by the same token, it is hard to see how we could have reason to think of the content of beliefs in evaluative terms, without doing the same for the content of desires.

So much for the first reason for favouring an evaluative theory of desire—that it is needed for a general treatment of content which is harmonious with an evaluative theory of belief. The second reason in favour of an evaluative theory of desire will, in fact, provide further support for an evaluative treatment of content in general. Here is an argument derived from Hume:

(1) Nothing which plays the same kind of role in action as orectic attitudes can be true or false.

(2) Value judgements play the same kind of role in action as orectic attitudes.

(3) Value judgements cannot be true or false.[1]

Any theory which holds that truth is a value must deny (3), since it can be true or false that it is true that *p*. And any theory which holds that truth is a value will find it hard to deny (2). This is because (2) is a consequence of 'evaluative internalism'—to put it roughly, the thesis that something's having a value *ipso facto* provides one with reason for doing something with it. An example of what is at issue in (2) is the idea that the belief that it would be good if *p* can play the same kind of role as the desire that *p* in explaining attempts to bring it about that *p*. It is very hard to claim that truth is a value without accepting evaluative internalism, since without evaluative internalism one would be hard put to find a mark of the evaluative which was sufficiently topic-neutral. And I did in fact rely on evaluative internalism in defending the claim that truth is a value in 9.2.

This point does not require that *all* value judgements should play the same role in the explanation of action as orectic attitudes: a reason for questioning that will emerge later. But I take it that it is enough for a general Humean scepticism about value judgements being capable of truth and falsehood that at least *some* value judgements play that kind of role, and that that fact should depend upon their being *value* judgements. So I shall not quibble over premiss (2) on that score.

We cannot accept (3); we must accept (2); so the evaluative theory of content is committed to denying (1). Why might anyone believe (1)? The argument is surely simple: we are expected to derive (1) from these two assumptions:

(*a*) If orectic attitudes cannot be true or false, then nothing which plays the same kind of role in action as orectic attitudes can be true or false.

(*b*) Orectic attitudes cannot be true or false.

(*b*) is surely true. The special case of it which is relevant to a theory of desire is the claim that desires cannot be true or false, which seems undeniable. So the evaluative theory of content must deny (*a*). Now whether or not (*a*) is true must depend upon the reason why (*b*) is true. So we should ask: why can desires not be true or false?

The evaluative theory of content has a rather attractive answer to this question, which also makes it easy to deny (*a*). On the evaluative theory, truth is, in a sense, a value which is proper to belief. This requires that it is at least a necessary condition for a belief to count as a good belief that it be true. In other words:

(4) One only ought to believe that p if it is true that p.

It is natural for the evaluative theory of content to think that truth only applies to beliefs at all because it is a value which is in this sense proper to beliefs. If this is right, then it will seem natural to extend the point to any attitude of mind which can be assessed for truth. Taking 'A' as schematic either for an attitude verb, or for its cognate noun, as appropriate, the point could be put like this:

(5) If As can be true or false, then one only ought to A that p if it is true that p.

And, of course, we have, as always:

(6) It is true that p if and only if p.

These principles lead to grotesque results if we allow orectic attitudes to be assessed for truth and falsity. Here is one result of allowing hopes to be true or false:

(7) One only ought to hope that one's friends are healthy if they are healthy.

And here is one result of allowing desires to be true or false:

(8) One only ought to desire that famine be averted if famine is averted.

This combines the crippling restriction of one's projects to the mere acceptance of the status quo (which (7) has too), with simple impossibility. For while one can *hope* for something when one merely does not *know* whether it has occurred or will occur, one can only *desire* something which *has not* yet occurred. In short, (7) and (8) are obviously false. So orectic attitudes cannot be true or false.

This seems to me an appealing demonstration of what goes wrong if one thinks that desires—or orectic attitudes in general— can be true or false. But it means that we have no reason to accept (*a*), if we also hold (2). Holding (2), we can say that the belief that famine should be averted can play the same kind of role in action as the desire that famine be averted. Now suppose that this belief can be true or false. If we apply (5) and (6), we get this:

(9) One only ought to believe that famine should be averted if famine should be averted.

And that suffers from none of the absurdity of (8).

The point seems quite general. If one supposes that orectic attitudes can be true or false, one ends up with absurdities like (7) and (8). If one makes the same assumption about the most nearly corresponding evaluative beliefs, there is no absurdity. So we are under no pressure to accept (*a*).

What exactly is it that lies behind the absurdities of (7) and (8)? Is it the very idea of supposing that there is a necessary condition for a hope or desire to count as *good*? Or is it just that (7) and (8) give the wrong kind of necessary condition. An evaluative theory of desire chooses the second, of course: we have just given the wrong necessary conditions. Comparison of (8) and (9) suggests the right necessary condition for the goodness of the desire that famine be averted:

(10) One only ought to desire that famine be averted if famine should be averted.

And there is no absurdity about that. This suggests that the idea of an evaluative theory of desire is fine; but we had better not think the relevant value is truth.

Comparison of (9) and (10) in fact yields a further advantage of an evaluative theory of desire: it can *explain* the truth of the crucial evaluatively internalist premiss (2) in the Humean argument. For we seem to be able to say this:

(EI) For every orectic attitude, there is some evaluative belief the necessary condition for whose correctness is the same as that of the orectic attitude.

One might also be tempted by the converse of (EI):

(EI*) For every evaluative belief, there is an orectic attitude the necessary condition for whose correctness is the same as that of the evaluative belief.

But this is not so plausible. (The problem is finding orectic attitudes to correspond to such things as the belief that she is kind.) But we still have what we need to explain (2), just from (EI). The explanation of the fact that (the relevant) value judgements play the same kind of role in action as orectic attitudes is that orectic attitudes play the role of some value judgements.

To summarize this second reason for favouring an evaluative theory of desire, we can say this. An evaluative theory of content which incorporates an evaluative theory of desire has these three virtues: it can cope smoothly with the Humean argument; it can explain why desires cannot be true or false; and it can explain that feature of evaluative internalism which is incorporated in premiss (2) of the Humean argument. That seems to me to be a respectable tally.

It certainly seems more than any other theory of desire can match. Take, for example, the suggestion that desires are to be explained in terms of their satisfaction. The idea is that satisfaction is to desire what truth is to belief. If we take this line, we need make no appeal to values like desirability. The idea will be that we give the content of desires in terms of their satisfaction conditions, just as we might give the content of beliefs in terms of their truth conditions. The crucial schema will be this:

(D) The desire that p is satisfied if and only if p.

It is certainly true that the specification of satisfaction conditions is just as good at distinguishing between desires as the specification of truth conditions is at distinguishing between beliefs. (That is: not bad, although the conditions on intersubstitution are not quite right to capture the rich intensionality of conceptual content.) It does not follow, however, that satisfaction can form the basis of a theory of desire in the way that truth can form the basis of a theory of belief.

The difficulty for a satisfaction theory of desire is just that satisfaction does not stand to desire as truth stands to belief. Someone might say that desires aim at their own satisfaction just as beliefs aim at their truth. But this is false. Truth is a virtue of belief, a necessary condition of a belief's being good. Satisfaction is not a virtue of desire; that view would lead to absurdities like (8). The only thing which aims at a desire's satisfaction is the person whose desire it is. And this fact is hardly explanatory of the nature of desire. In desiring something, what I aim at is what I desire; what I desire is that whose obtaining would satisfy my desire; so it is hardly surprising that I should aim at the satisfaction of my desires. These are just trivial truths about the meaning of 'aim', 'desire', and 'satisfaction': they tell us nothing we did not already know in knowing that we are talking about desire. That is, they provide no *explanation* of the nature of desire.

If an evaluative theory of desire is right, the fact that satisfaction is not a virtue of desire should mean that a satisfaction theory of desire just *cannot* get to the heart of the nature of desire. This indeed seems plausible.

First, a satisfaction account does not extend very naturally to other orectic attitudes. This, for example, is almost nonsense:

(11) The delight that *p* is satisfied if and only if *p*.

The problem here seems to be that satisfaction is only appropriate for a state with ambitions, as it were: that is, its applicability to desire depends on the fact that a desire is always for what has yet to come about. There are other such states: wishes, for example. And hopes are prospective at least in that when one hopes one does not *know* whether what is hoped for obtains.

Satisfaction is an odd notion to use to talk about wishes and hopes: fulfilment seems better. Keen to produce redundancy schemata wherever possible, we might suggest a fulfilment theory of wishes, based on this principle:

(12) The wish that *p* is fulfilled if and only if *p*.

We still ought to be reluctant to propose a fulfilment theory of *delight*, but at least fulfilment seems more general than satisfaction. We can perhaps propose the notion of fulfilment as the basis of a general account of at least the *forward-looking* orectic attitudes.

Unfortunately, predictions can be fulfilled too. And predictions are fulfilled just in case they are true. Expectations can also be fulfilled, and, while it may sound odd to talk about expectations being *true*, expectations can be correct or right in a sense which is quite different from that in which a desire may be right or correct.

All of this looks just like superficial linguistic manœuvring. It is enough, however, to reveal a basic problem with any satisfaction theory of desire. If the notion of satisfaction is not to be specific just to desires—if it is even to cover just the *forward-looking* orectic attitudes as well—then differences of nuance between satisfaction and fulfilment will have to be ignored. We will want a single general notion for all of the forward-looking orectic attitudes; fulfilment just seems a nicer candidate. But once we ignore those nuances, we seem to have a notion so general that it is hard to see how it can fail to apply to attitudes like expectation, which are not orectic at all. We seem to face a dilemma: is our theory of desire to be extendable to other forward-looking orectic attitudes, or not? If it is not, it is hard to believe that we have captured what is distinctive of the orectic, what contrasts with the truth-assessable, and indeed what set us looking to desires in this context in the first place. But if a satisfaction theory is extended to the other forward-looking orectic attitudes, it appears that *all* we capture is the forward-lookingness: once again, we lose what is distinctive of the orectic, what contrasts with the truth-assessable, what set us looking to desire in the first place. In short, we can only understand satisfaction or fulfilment as being distinctive of the orectic, if we make it explicitly clear that we are concerned just with the satisfaction or fulfilment of orectic attitudes; and that presupposes the notion of the orectic, rather than explaining it.

Faults of a similar kind, and some others, affect the idea of distinguishing between desires and non-evaluative beliefs in terms of the notion of 'direction of fit'. Platts (who is no friend of a contrast in 'direction of fit') in fact links the notion of direction of fit with that of satisfaction ('realization' in his version) in this characterization:

Beliefs aim at the true, and their being true is their fitting the world; falsity is a decisive failing in a belief, and false beliefs should be discarded; beliefs should be changed to fit the world, not vice versa. Desires aim at realisation, and their realisation is the world fitting with them; the fact that the indicative content of a desire is not realised in the world is not yet a failing *in the desire*, and not yet a reason to discard the desire; the world, crudely, should be changed to fit with our desires, not vice versa.[2]

I have already remarked on the falsity of the claim that desires aim at realization. We should add that it is also false that 'the world . . . should be changed to fit with our desires'; it just depends whether our desires are good desires.

A direction-of-fit theory is in fact an evaluative theory. It characterizes belief, for example, in terms of what is required of a *good* belief. But it is an incomplete evaluative theory. It says that its not being the case that *p* is not a failing of the desire that *p*. (That much is obvious: it is *required* of the desire that *p* that it should not yet be the case that *p*.) But it does not say what *would* be a failing of the desire that *p*. And although it does not *say* what would be a failing of the desire that *p*, the whole style of the theory requires that *something* might count as a failing—indeed a decisive failing— of the desire that *p*.

Let me make a simple suggestion. It would be a failing of the desire that *p* if it would be a bad thing if *p*. No good desire can be a desire for something bad. Whether or not something is bad might

---

[2] M. Platts, *Ways of Meaning* (London: Routledge and Kegan Paul, 1979), 256–7.

seem to be a fact about the world. If it is, then it would seem that desires must fit the world just as much as beliefs.

To summarize these points, let us try to take a direction-of-fit theory at face value. In exactly the same sense of 'direction of fit', the direction of fit of beliefs is said to be of beliefs to world, whereas that of desires is of world to desires. That is:

(i) Beliefs must fit the world.

(ii) It is not the case that desires must fit the world.

(iii) The world must fit desires.

(iv) It is not the case that the world must fit beliefs.

Let us grant (i) and (iv). (iii) is false: if the desires are bad, the world must *not* fit them. And (ii) is false if there are value facts. And if there are no value facts, then neither (i) nor (iii) could have been true anyway.

This completes the survey of alternatives to an evaluative theory of desire. The evaluative theory is sweet and good in every way; the alternatives are non-starters. We should adopt an evaluative theory of desire.

But is there not another option? Could we not characterize desires as *goal-directed* attitudes? This is not another option: it is just a disguised evaluative theory. To be directed towards a goal is to be directed towards some as yet not obtaining state of affairs. That captures the forward-lookingness of desires.

But this is not all that is involved in having something as a goal: one only has something as a goal, if one regards the thing as good. But regarding something as good seems to be a matter of having a belief which is true if and only if the thing *is* good. At least, that must be how it seems unless the Humean argument to the conclusion that value judgements cannot be true or false goes through. But that argument has already been neutralized. The view that desires are goal-directed attitudes seems just a version of an evaluative theory.

I am sure that it is disquiet about value facts—more specifically, facts about values like desirability—which lies behind attempts to find an alternative to a straightforwardly evaluative theory of desire. That disquiet should be addressed directly.

I shall consider three kinds of worry about the idea that there might be facts about values of the kind which an evaluative theory of desire would introduce. Two of them have in fact been dealt with

already, but it will do no harm to have them aired again, so that it is
clear that they are not being ignored.

First, and most basic, is what Mackie calls the 'argument from
queerness', which is directed against the idea of facts about *moral*
value. Here is how Mackie puts it:

If there were objective values, then they would be entities or qualities or
relations of a very strange sort, utterly different from anything else in the
universe. Correspondingly, if we were aware of them, it would have to be
by some special faculty of moral perception or intuition, utterly different
from our ordinary ways of knowing everything else.[3]

This kind of argument is inevitably question-begging. It is assumed
that the world is in general value-free, and that perception is in
general a non-evaluatively describable process. But it is not clear
what could have entitled us to those assumptions. It is tempting to
suppose that they are motivated by the thought that there are only
natural-scientific facts, and that perception is a natural-scientifically
describable process. But we have independent reason to reject that
idea (see Chapter 4).

The argument from queerness also seems to rest on the thought
that the very irreducibility of the evaluative to the non-evaluative
makes it impossible for values to belong to the same world as the
non-evaluative. But that thought was explicitly addressed in 9.4. It
rests on an uncompulsorily foundationalist conception of how the
world can be a unified world.

Secondly, there is the common thought that what is part of the
objective fabric of the world cannot be intrinsically action-guiding;
but the evaluative is intrinsically action-guiding. This is precisely
the Humean argument which has just been considered ('action-
guiding' *means*: recognition of it plays the same kind of role in
action as orectic attitudes). We have shown how it can be resisted.

The key to resisting the Humean argument is in fact the same as
the key to resisting the first worry—the one expressed in the
argument from queerness. We are under no obligation to accept the
proffered conception of the objective world. Here the limiting
conception of the world is conveyed in the word 'fabric': as if the
fabric was all that could be objective. In the quotation from
Mackie, the trick was turned with the word 'universe': it is as if to

---

[3] J. Mackie, *Ethics: Inventing Right and Wrong* (Harmondsworth: Penguin,
1977), 38.

believe in objective values is to imagine that, if we could magnify a photograph of the night sky enough, we would find values lurking somewhere in some distant galaxy, peeping out from behind a cloud of gas. But this conception of the world is not required just by the notion of objectivity. To think it is seems to be precisely to accept a scientistic metaphysics. The world which we are interested in when we speak of objectivity is just 'the totality of facts'.

These first two worries affect the suggestion that *truth* is a value, as much as the commitment to the objectivity of the kind of values we will need to appeal to in an evaluative theory of orectic attitudes. But the third worry is specific to the idea that facts about such things as desirability are part of the objective world. These kinds of value seem to be subject to no decision procedure which could be agreed between people who differ over the values themselves.[4]

It is not exactly clear why this should seem to suggest that there are no real facts about this kind of value. But here is an argument which might seem tempting to some. Suppose we accept, as a first premiss, that, for there to be facts of a certain kind, there must be something which it would be to have knowledge of those facts. Let it also be insisted, as a second premiss, that one can only count as knowing if one has available a justification which would convince anyone who disagreed, provided only that she is rational. It then seems to follow that, if there are indeed no neutral decision procedures for judgements about values of this kind, there can be no real facts about such values.

The first premiss we are committed to, in virtue of the version of conceptualism which was developed in Part I. The second premiss, however, is just an assertion of the epistemological internalism which we found independent reason to distrust in 10.4. If this is the reason why a lack of a suitable decision procedure seems to threaten the possibility of facts about the rich values we are concerned with here, it can therefore be resisted.

This may sound unattractive. Is it not an argument in favour of moral dogmatism? I do not think so. First, dogmatism involves a refusal to accept that one might be wrong; but no such refusal is being recommended here. (Indeed, a thorough objectivism about these values seems to be needed even to make sense of the idea that

---

[4] For this kind of worry, see S. Lovibond, *Realism and Imagination in Ethics* (Oxford: Blackwell, 1983), 81.

one might be wrong.) And, secondly, it is not being suggested that one might not reasonably be swayed by what is called moral argument. But moral argument will generally have to be a process whose function is to change and develop *sensibilities*: it will not generally be a matter of providing one with a reason for accepting something, which would have been compelling even from our initial perspective. Being susceptible to change in one's sensibilities is not just a matter of being rational: one also needs to be sensitive.

It should be emphasized here that the distinction between what mere rationality requires and what an appropriate sensibility would recognize does not commit us to a Humean distinction between 'reason' and 'taste', one (and only one) of which produces knowledge, while the other supplies no more than 'sentiment'. If I am blind, I cannot see colours, and no grinding application of rationality can make me acknowledge their existence on the basis of my knowledge of sounds and tastes and textures. This does not threaten the idea that someone who can see can have knowledge of colours just by looking. In the same way, someone who is morally defective may not be open to conviction just on the basis of an appeal to her rationality; but this does not threaten the idea that there are moral facts to be known, which a defect in moral vision can make one blind to.

The accusation of moral dogmatism provides no decisive objection to the claim that there are facts about such things as desirability. But it is interesting in itself. It is a moral accusation— an accusation of moral defect—which is nevertheless felt to be an appropriate argument against the claim that a certain metaphysical-cum-epistemological position is *true*. (This is not uncommon: crude forms of conventionalism about morality are false because they are immoral.) It is unclear how one can hold that a position in the metaphysics of morality is false because it is immoral, unless one accepts the view that there can be facts about rich values.

I do not pretend to have considered every possible objection to an evaluative theory of desire, and of orectic attitudes more generally. These three objections, however, seem both central and recurrent. An evaluative theory of desire looks quite strong if it can stand up to them. Given the other things in its favour, it hardly seems rash to adopt it.

11.2. Alethic and Orectic Values

If we are to give an evaluative theory of desire, we must recognize that desires are to be assessed in terms of a different kind of value from the values appropriate to beliefs. Otherwise we will be stuck with the absurdities I considered in the last section: finding ourselves committed to thinking that one should desire only what is actually the case, for example. Let us call the general kind of value appropriate to the assessment of orectic attitudes *orectic* value. We may contrast it with a general kind of value to which truth belongs, which we might call *alethic* value. At the moment our only conception of the value T is that it is truth-like. That means that our conception of it rests on the concept of belief, since the idea of truth as a value has only been explained in terms of belief. But we cannot leave it at that in a theory of content. There is now a way ahead, however. Once we have accepted the idea of an evaluative theory of desire, we can explain the value T, as a particular example of a truth-like value, by means of a contrast with orectic values.

If we count truth as the proper value of beliefs, then, according to an evaluative theory of desire, there will be something which is analogously the proper value of desires. Suppose that the value D stands to that proper value of desires as the value T stands to truth. Then we will be able to make analogous claims about responses in terms of each value, following schemata like these:

(1) *r* is good with respect to the value T if and only if *p*;
(2) *r* is good with respect to the value D if and only if *p*.

Let us describe the function of replacements for '*p*' in instances of such schemata as being to give the *conditions of application of the value*. If these are really conditions of application of *value*, we might expect to be able to state them using sentences which involve evaluative concepts explicitly. And if there are distinctive kinds of value to be appealed to in such schemata, we might expect there to be something distinctive about the explicitly evaluative formulations of the conditions of application of each kind of value.

What I propose is that we distinguish between orectic and alethic values by distinguishing between the explicitly evaluative formulations of the conditions of their application.

First, an explicitly evaluative formulation of a condition of application can always be expressed by means of an operator which incorporates an appropriate explicitly evaluative expression. If we use '$E(\ldots)$' as schematic for such an operator, we could have written, instead of (1) and (2), statements of this form:

(3) r is good with respect to the value T if and only if $E(q)$;
(4) r is good with respect to the value D if and only if $E(q)$.

The appropriate sentence of the form '$E(q)$', as it figures in statements of assessability of the form of (3) and (4), must be necessarily and a priori equivalent to the replacement for 'p' in statements of the form of (1) and (2), respectively. This captures the idea that we are providing an explicitly evaluative formulation of what is, in a sense, the same condition of application that we began with.

We now need to ensure that the explicitly evaluative operator is distinctively appropriate to the kind of value whose condition of application is being expressed. We want, for example, 'it is desirable that' to be a distinctively appropriate replacement for 'E' in statements of the form of (4), and 'it is true that' to be an appropriate replacement for 'E' in statements of the form of (3). Let us describe this as the task of defining a *matchingly evaluative* replacement for 'E', for each kind of value.

First, we need to prevent 'it is false' being used as a matchingly evaluative replacement for 'E' in (3), if we are aiming to permit 'it is true' being so used. Let us then insist that the *polarity* of the value in a matchingly evaluative replacement must match the polarity of the statement of assessability. Thus, if we say that something is *good* if and only if some condition obtains, we will want the evaluative replacement for 'E' to have *positive* value; whereas if we say that something is *bad* if and only if something or other holds, we will want the replacement for 'E' to have *negative* value. An expression has positive value if what it is applied to is thereby favoured, and negative value if it is thereby disfavoured. Having said that, let us just concentrate on statements of assessability whose polarity is positive. Matchingly evaluative replacements for 'E' must then have positive polarity too. Call this the *polarity condition*.

If we want the matchingly evaluative replacement for 'E' to be distinctive of each type of value of responses (like D and T), we will need to insist that the *same* evaluative replacement for 'E' must be appropriate for every explicitly evaluative reformulation of a condition of application of the same value.

Thus it will only be appropriate to say that a particular response is good with respect to the value D if and only if it is desirable that *q*, if the phrase 'it is desirable that' can be similarly used in every statement of assessability with respect to the value D. Call this the *uniformity* condition.

The next thing we want is for the matchingly evaluative replacement for 'E' to capture any value of an appropriate kind which is implicit in the condition of application. What we need to do here is to distinguish between two kinds of evaluative statement: those which are a priori and necessarily reformulable in terms of an evaluative *operator* construction, and those which are not. Thus,

(5) One should help the poor,

seems equivalent to this:

(6) It should be the case that one helps the poor.

But there seems no such reformulation available for this:

(7) She is kind.

Let us call the first kind of statement one which incorporates an *operator* value, and the second kind one which incorporates a *predicative* value. What we want of our matchingly evaluative replacement for 'E' is that it should capture all the relevant operator values in the condition of application. Let us say, then, that there must be no relevant operator value expressed in the replacement for '*q*' in an explicitly evaluative formulation of a condition of application of the form 'E that *q*'. Call this the *value-capturing* condition.

What are the *relevant* operator values? Those which, intuitively, are distinctive of the kind of value whose conditions of application we are dealing with. We want a distinctive type of operator value for the value D, for example, which is different from any operator value associated with the value T. Let us then imagine a *comprehensive* distribution of operator values, which assigns each operator value to a particular value of responses, like D and T. Such a comprehensive distribution of operator values must yield correct explicitly evaluative reformulations of conditions of application, under the polarity condition, the uniformity condition, and the value-capturing condition so-construed. And no operator value may remain unassigned. Then an operator value is *relevant* to a particular value of responses if it is assigned to that value of responses under such a comprehensive distribution.

Let us summarize these points. I am suggesting that for every statement of the form,

(V) *r* is good with respect to *V* if and only if *p*,

there is a necessarily and a priori equivalent statement of the form,

(EV) *r* is good with respect to *V* if and only if *E*(*q*),

where '*E*' is a matchingly evaluative phrase appropriate for *V*. And to count as matchingly evaluative, it must meet the polarity condition, the uniformity condition, and the value-capturing condition.

Our task now is to use the notion of a matchingly evaluative phrase to distinguish between alethic and orectic values. This schema is suggestive:

(EE) *E*(*p*) if and only if *p*.

If an evaluative replacement for '*E*' satisfies this schema, for every replacement for '*p*', let us say that it is *eliminable*. We can now define alethic and orectic values as follows:

(AV) A value is *alethic* if and only if the matchingly evaluative phrase is eliminable from the conditions of its application.

(OV) A value is *orectic* if and only if the matchingly evaluative phrase is *not* eliminable from the conditions of its application.

It is worth pointing out that the definitions provided by (AV) and (OV) have a certain kind of robustness. The explanation which I gave of the idea of a *matchingly evaluative* phrase is fairly technical, and therefore vulnerable to counter-example as a result of some oversight. But the notion is reasonably intuitive itself, and ought to be able to be satisfactorily characterized somehow, even if my characterization turns out not to be quite right. And (AV) and (OV) could then exploit any improvement in the definition of matchingly evaluative phrases.

The value T can now be defined as an alethic value of responses, without appeal to the idea that it is truth-like; so we avoid the circularity which such an appeal might seem to introduce in a theory of content.

We can now define the general class of orectic attitudes as comprising those attitudes which are properly assessed in terms of an orectic value. That will block absurdities like those which we were concerned with in the last section. But we can count certain evaluative *beliefs* (those like the belief that it would be good if *p*, for example) as *orectic* attitudes, without threatening their status as *alethic* attitudes, and hence as being properly assessable for truth. This is because the *truth* conditions of such beliefs can only be stated in terms which include ineliminable evaluative expressions.

But this might all seem a terrible cheat. I seem to have made the distinction between alethic and orectic values appear almost grammatical. Surely (someone might say) this is disingenuous: is not the reason why mention of truth is eliminable just that to talk of truth is not to introduce a value at all? And is not the reason why mention of desirability (for example) is *not* eliminable just that it *does* introduce a value?

I will not rehearse the reasons for thinking that truth really is a value. But there is an independent challenge here: to provide some explanation of the eliminability of mention of truth which does not undermine its evaluative status. This challenge can be met. The reason why talk of truth is eliminable from the relevant contexts is just that (EE), and indeed (V) and (EV) too, are forms of *statement*, and can themselves only be understood in terms of truth. Indeed, if these schemata were intelligible without appeal to the notion of truth, it would be a kind of accident that 'it is true that' can replace '*E*' in (EE).

Here is another way of putting the point: truth is what does not need to be mentioned when a concern for truth is taken for granted. Or again: to understand truth is to understand what is distinctively at stake in *saying* something, or, more generally perhaps, in an *enquiry*. If that is true, two things follow. First, there is nothing in the least superficial about the characterizations offered in (AV) and (OV): truth and desirability are there explained in terms of their distinctive relations to a very general kind of project. It is not that there is almost nothing to truth; there is just nothing more than we have already understood in recognizing that something is being *said*. Secondly, the idea that truth is a value seems in fact to be *required* for the explanation of the eliminability of mention of truth in certain contexts: it is no accident that we talk in terms of *projects* here. The eliminability of mention of truth only seems to show that truth is not a value when we forget that our values are engaged the moment we say something, or try to find out how things work.

11.3. The Holism of Assessability

Although alethic and orectic values contrast with one another, they are inextricable from one another: no response can be assessable in terms of one without being assessable in terms of the other. That is the thesis I shall call the *holism of assessability*.

That name reflects the link between this thesis and a more familiar thesis, which is, in fact, just a special case of it: the holism of the mental.[5] The holism of the mental is a problem for behaviourism. One cannot define a belief in terms of a link with a certain (non-mentally conceived) kind of behaviour, because how someone acts on a given belief depends on what she wants. And you cannot define a desire in terms of a link with a certain (non-mentally conceived) kind of behaviour, because how someone acts on a given desire depends on what she thinks.

This case is special even in the area of attitudes—even in the mental. The focus is once again just on action. And, as a result, desire is once again singled out as the paradigmatic orectic attitude. There is a much more general thesis of the holism of the mental. In fact, it has two parts. First, no response can be an expression or a manifestation of a belief, without also being an expression of some orectic attitude—and vice versa. Secondly, no response could be an expression of the particular belief(s) which it *is* an expression of, without also being an expression of the particular orectic attitude(s) which it is an expression of—and vice versa.

Here are a couple of examples. My smile is only an expression of pleasure at my wife's return from work, if it is also an expression of my belief (or realization) that my wife *has* returned from work. Note that the smile must be an *expression* of my belief: it is not just enough that I should *have* the belief. Conversely, my anxious look up at the sky is only an expression of my belief that something I care about will be impossible if it rains, if it is also an expression of my fear that it is going to rain. Again, my smile could not have been a smile if it had not been a smile at something; and to be a smile *at*

[5] Championed by, e.g., Davidson in 'Mental Events'.

something, it must be an expression of some belief about the something. And my anxious look could not have been an anxious look if it had not been both an expression of fear and an expression of some non-evaluative belief about what I fear.

Once we release ourselves from the fixation with intentional action, the general thesis of the holism of assessability looks very plausible, if the idea of an evaluative theory of content was right in the first place. And something like it seems to extend to responses made by things other than concept-possessors.

Consider some part of the visual system of an animal, for example, which we might want to say is registering the information that there is light of a certain wavelength at some location. In line with the evaluative theory of content, this would require us to say that something about the way it is responding is correct if and only if there is light of that wavelength in that place. We can only treat this part of a visual system like this if we think that, if the response is correct, under this interpretation, some goal of the system, or of the organism, is thereby furthered.

It seems, then, that this kind of attribution of informational content requires one to attribute some goal to the system or organism concerned. But the possession of goals by *thinkers* is a matter of their having certain kinds of orectic attitude. On the evaluative theory of content, this is a matter of their being liable to respond in ways which are assessable with respect to orectic values. If we adopt the evaluative theory of content, the same general analysis must apply to the idea of the possession of goals by organisms or parts of organisms. Some outcome is a goal of an organism if that outcome is somehow a good for the organism; and its being a good for the organism must be a matter of some responses made by the organism being good if and only if the outcome is somehow good.

The case of calculators, and other such simple devices, is more complicated, because it is not clear whose goals are important: the designer's (or the manufacturer's), or the user's. No doubt different cases will require appropriately different analyses. But it is still hard to see how we could count the display on a calculator as giving a correct answer unless there was *some* goal which was thereby furthered.

There ought to be an explanation of the holism of assessability. Let us take each half of the thesis in turn.

Why must every response which is assessable in terms of an alethic value also be assessable in terms of an orectic value? Consider a response (a hug, say) which is correct if and only if Esther is unhappy. Why should the fact that Esther is not unhappy make that response incorrect, inappropriate, misplaced, inept, futile, or vain? It can only be if something hangs on the response's being correct—if its correctness matters somehow. And whatever hangs on the correctness of the response, or makes its correctness matter, must make it, as it were, matter *to* the response itself.

What does it mean to say that something hangs on the correctness of the response? It must mean that something of value, other than the response itself, is affected by the correctness of the response—by whether or not Esther is unhappy. And this other thing of value must, in a sense, be of value to the response. According to the evaluative theory, this other thing can only be of value to the response if the response is assessable as good or bad according to whether this other thing is good or bad.

But this requires that the response be assessable in terms of some orectic value. For the definition of alethic value provided by (AV) in the last section ensures, in effect, that alethic values are applicable only to responses or beliefs. To treat a response as good according to whether something *else* is good is, in effect, to insist that there must be some mention of value in the relevant condition of correctness for the response. And what that mentioned value applies to must be some state of affairs, since it is only something's being the case which could turn on whether or not Esther is unhappy. That means that the inevitably mentioned value must be what I called an *operator* value—one whose attribution can always be formulated in terms of an evaluative operator. If the condition of correctness of a response includes ineliminable mention of an operator value, the response is assessable with respect to an orectic value, according to (OV), the definition of orectic value given in the last section. So we have the first half of the holism of assessability: any response assessable in terms of an alethic value must also be assessable in terms of an orectic value.

Why must every response which is assessable in terms of an orectic value also be assessable in terms of an alethic value? A response assessable in terms of an orectic value counts as good or bad according to whether some state of affairs is good or bad. The question to ask is: why is it *that* state of affairs whose goodness or badness determines the goodness or badness of the response? It cannot just be the *goodness* or *badness* of the state of affairs which matters to the response, for then any other state of affairs of the same value as that one would be just as relevant. In that case, it must matter to the response whether the state of affairs possesses some feature other than just its goodness or badness. But, according to the evaluative theory, that it matters to the response whether the state of affairs possesses that other feature just means that the response is good or bad according to whether the state of affairs possesses that feature. But, since this other feature is precisely not a matter of the goodness or badness of the state of affairs, the relevant condition of assessment here cannot involve an ineliminable operator value. But that means that it cannot be a condition of assessment with respect to an orectic value. So the response must also be assessable with respect to some alethic value. And that gives us the second half of the thesis of the holism of assessability.

The thesis of the holism of assessability seems to me in any case to be plausible. These arguments simply serve to explain, within the framework of an evaluative theory, something whose truth we are already likely to accept. It will be the first half of the thesis which is most important to my immediate concerns: the claim that no response can be assessable with respect to an alethic value without also being assessable with respect to an orectic value.

11.4. Values and Evolution

We are now in a position to see why evolution cannot generate a theory of content; nor can it underwrite the ascription of genuine content to anything.

Consider the example I used in the last section. Some part of the visual system is taken to be responding in a way which is correct if and only if there is light of a certain wavelength at a particular location. According to the thesis of the holism of assessability, the response can only be assessable in that alethic way if it is also assessable in terms of an orectic value. We must be able to find something which counts for the system or organism as a good, which the correct detection of light may be held to promote. The response will then be assessable orectically as good or bad according to whether that good-for-the system is somehow good or bad.

Whatever the immediate goal of a system or organism may be which the detection of light might be held to further, if its status as a goal is underwritten by evolution, it can only be a good of any kind in so far as it promotes what evolutionary processes ultimately sustain: that is, I take it, the survival of genes. And promoting the survival of genes can only make something good in any way at all if the survival of genes is itself somehow good.

But the survival of genes is no kind of good. Absolutely speaking, it is neither good nor bad: in itself it is just evaluatively indifferent. Nor can we plausibly think that an organism really has as a goal the survival of its genes. We think fondly that an organism might have as its goal the survival of its species—though even this requires a peculiar kind of chauvinism to seem attractive. And evolution does not appear to allow anything even as bizarrely heroic as that to be the 'goal' of evolutionary processes.[6]

Furthermore, evolution has no need itself to think of what is sustained by evolutionary processes as a good. Not only are the processes themselves conceived of with no thought for notions of value; the role of the 'goal' or end of evolutionary processes in the theory makes the association of value with it extraordinary. We begin with the *explanandum*: the fact that there are such complex creatures as human beings whose parts and behaviour have such multifarious correspondences with features and events in the natural world. It is then shown that these features can be explained as resulting from the very long-term operation of certain naturalistically describable processes. The notion of the end or 'goal' of these processes is then defined as whatever it is that tends to be preserved or sustained in such processes. It is almost unthinkable that one could let one's conception of what *matters* be determined in such a way.

'*Almost* unthinkable', I said, and with good reason for the cautious formulation. Here is Dawkins in a famous passage:

They [the replicators] are in you and in me; they created us, body and mind; and *their preservation is the ultimate rationale for our existence.* They have come a long way, those replicators. Now they go by the name of genes, and we are their survival machines.[7]

---

[6] Thus, e.g., R. Dawkins, *The Selfish Gene* (2nd edn., Oxford: Oxford University Press, 1989).

[7] Ibid. 20.

The italicized phrase (the italics are mine) reveals a commitment to the value of the 'goal' of evolutionary processes, which is echoed in the phrase 'survival machines'. And this in a book one of whose principal purposes might seem to be to show that evolution is not guided by the kind of evaluative considerations which a misty romanticism might hope to read into it.

Anyone who thinks I am over-reading Dawkins here should recall the first paragraph of *The Selfish Gene*, which ends like this:

We no longer have to resort to superstition when faced with the deep problems: Is there a meaning to life? What are we for? What is man? After posing the last of these questions, the eminent zoologist G. G. Simpson put it thus: 'The point I want to make now is that all attempts to answer that question before 1859 are worthless and that we will be better off if we ignore them completely.'[8]

Note that Dawkins does *not* think that the answers to these questions are 'No', 'Nothing in particular', and 'No definition should be expected', respectively. He does not think the questions are somehow ill judged, misplaced, or based on false assumptions. He thinks that they can be taken straight, and answered straight, by evolution. The passage I quoted first gives his answers.

These two passages from Dawkins have attracted much criticism.[9] If what I said about the role of the notion of a 'goal' or end of evolutionary processes was right, they seem to deserve criticism. Moreover, saying that these passages misplace value in the world seems to capture exactly what looks so offensive about them. There seems no reason to defer to evolution for our assignment of any value, unless we are convinced by the scientism which we have independent reason to reject.

There appears to be no sense in which the survival of genes is a good. There can, therefore, be no sense in which anything which owes its evaluative status to its links with this evolutionary end is genuinely evaluative. The assessment of the behaviour of organs appears to be just arbitrary. It does not *seem* arbitrary, of course. But this, I take it, is just a result of a wishfully romantic conception of nature, combined with a certain systematicity in the arbitrariness. All we need is one once-and-for-all arbitrary assignment of value to whatever is counted as the end of evolutionary processes,

[8] R. Dawkins, *The Selfish Gene*, 1.
[9] See Dawkins's notes to the two passages: ibid. 261, 270–1.

and the relative evaluation of everything else is then fixed, determinately, and in a way which permits empirical testing. But the non-arbitrariness (in a non-technical sense) of the determined evaluations should not blind us to the arbitrariness of the initial assignment of value.

The absence of any real value from evolution seems to me quite fatal to evolutionary theories of content. This is not just from a point of view which is already committed to an evaluative conception of content. It is crucial to evolutionary theories of content themselves.[10] Such theories aim precisely to capture the notions of 'normativity' and correctness which Kripke was exploiting in his arguments agains dispositional theories of meaning;[11] they are concerned to allow room for error. The idea is that error will be explained as malfunction, and malfunction will be parasitic on function, and function will be determined by evolutionary role.

This immediately provides grounds for suspicion. We have here a chain of thought which links something which exploits value quite explicitly, at one end, with whatever the causal processes of evolution sustain, at the other. It requires the notion of function to incorporate value, but it hopes to ground that notion in something which is not evaluative.

Am I saying, then, that there are no biological functions? Is it not true that the function of the heart is to pump blood? To put it baldly: yes, I am saying that; and, no, it is not true that there is a function of the heart which is to pump blood. This insistence assumes that we are taking these words seriously and literally: that if something has a function, it can *malfunction*; it can go *wrong*; it can *fail*. Strictly and literally, there is no such thing as heart failure.

I think nothing of real value is lost by denying that there are literally biological functions. We can still talk of the characteristic operations of organs; we can still count on our hearts, for example, continuing to do what they do. And I am not denying that there would not now be hearts in people's chests if they had not pumped blood, and if the hearts in the chests of their ancestors had not pumped blood. But this fact on its own is not enough for a notion of function which licenses talk of malfunction and error.

In fact, any conceptualist should have been suspicious of an evolutionary theory of content from the beginning, since it seems to

---

[10] See, e.g., McGinn, *Mental Content*, 156.
[11] Kripke, *Wittgenstein on Rules and Private Language*, 37.

be a form of Platonism. We have the idea of causal structures of some kind ('representations') which are fitted or suited to the world as a result of adaptation. But as usual it is forgotten that the words of the theory and the mind of the theorist must themselves be on one side of this relationship. According to the theory, it must be an open question, to be settled by empirical investigation, whether the words of the theory actually mean anything, and the theorist actually thinks anything. But it can never be allowed to be such an open question. It must be already settled that any adverse experimental results will refute the theory, rather than show the theorist to be, as it were, empty-headed. If that is already settled, we seem to have no more than a pretence of an empirical theory; and yet an evolutionary theory of content needs it to be more than a pretence.

11.5. Thought and Morality

If we add the thesis of the holism of assessability to the general claim of an evaluative theory of content, we get a fairly striking result. Something can only count as a thinker, a concept-possessor, capable of getting things right or wrong in the way relevant for truth, if its responses are also assessable in terms of orectic values. That means that its responses are good or bad according to whether something in the world is good or bad. And that sounds as if to be a thinker one must also be *morally* assessable.

That conclusion seems quite reasonable to me, but it needs to be handled with some care, and it requires some revision of a popular conception of what morality involves.

Here is the case for saying that assessability in terms of orectic value is moral assessability. First, it is an assessment of behaviour (or states of mind); and this is the right topic at least: virtue is not about eye-colour. Secondly, according to the definition of *intrinsic* assessability, it is a kind of assessment of behaviour which licenses an assessment of the person whose behaviour it is. Just as a person with an incorrect belief is mistaken herself, so someone with a wicked desire is to that extent wicked herself. (So we are not talking about behaviour looking pretty, for example.) And, thirdly, we are talking about the kind of assessment which, if one wants to talk in terms of imperatives at all, issues in a categorical and not merely a hypothetical imperative. We are not talking about what is good (or useful) *if* one happens to want something or other; the question here is what one ought to want—or, more generally, what it is *good* to want.

But these are quite formal requirements: they do not single out a particular province of concerns as the special focus of morality. They do not restrict us to the kinds of thing which we might imagine a caricature preacher recommending or condemning, or which might form the topic of a television debate. Orectic assessment includes, for example, being appalled at someone's aesthetic insensitivity, or finding someone's sense of humour distasteful. If this is moral assessment, then morality is not just a matter of what might be required by the demands of society, for example; its concern is the more rounded and ultimately always more influential one which is focused in the question of what sort of person one should be.

A helpful intuitive way of thinking about what it is like to assess someone in this kind of way is to think of P. F. Strawson's 'reactive' attitudes.[12] Strawson takes gratitude and resentment as a nicely opposing pair. If one is grateful to a person, or resentful of what someone has done, one has an attitude in which the benefit or harm done is relevant, but not decisive: it is also crucial that the person to whom gratitude is felt or the grudge borne should have been the doer of what was done, and that what was done was done with a good or an ill will.

Here is a fuller list, from another Strawson:

feelings, more or less considered and complicated, of condemnation and approbation, of gratitude and resentment, of despite and scorn; certain feelings of admiration for people's achievements and creations; certain aspects of feelings of hatred, anger, love, affection, and so on; feelings of guilt and remorse, pride and shame with regard to oneself and one's doings.[13]

All of these show the crucial features that the person towards whom these attitudes are felt is the doer of what was done, and did what was done with good or ill will. That means, in the technical terminology of the evaluative theory of content, that all of the responses involved are intrinsically assessable with respect to

---

[12] P. F. Strawson, 'Freedom and Resentment', *Proceedings of the British Academy*, 48 (1962), 1–25.

[13] G. Strawson, *Freedom and Belief*, 85.

orectic values. It therefore follows that to be a thinker, a concept-possessor, is to be something towards which attitudes like these may properly be held.

I will not fight over the question whether to be subject to this kind of regard in general is to be morally assessable. Certainly some moral assessment is included in these attitudes: being orectically assessable at least *overlaps* with being morally assessable. My own preference is for an unrestrictive conception of the province of morality. This could allow, for example, that a distasteful joke or a sexist attitude might be immoral in itself, and not because someone was, or was even likely to be, upset or offended or harmed by it. This seems to me to do justice to our actual feelings. Someone who is appalled by the treatment of violence in a film, for example, does not seem to me very likely to be appalled at it *because* it has upset her, or because it may lead to violence in the real world. It seems to me that she is likely to be appalled—and might be rightly appalled—just because the treatment of violence shows a wrong attitude to violence (although she might have to press one of the other points if she wants legislation on the issue). It is unclear how this kind of point could be made proper sense of, without adopting an unrestrictive conception of morality.

What about small children and aliens? I take it that gradually more of the reactive attitudes become gradually more appropriate in the case of small children. What is required for concept-possession is that some of these attitudes should be appropriate. I take it that that is achieved quite early, although it is not a precise matter. It also seems to me intuitive to count small children as thinkers quite early (say by around six months), although again it is not a precise business. It might sound severe to say that concept-possession requires moral assessability, but once it is realized that this is only true if we adopt a broad conception of the concerns of morality, it seems not to do any very great violence to the way things look.

As for aliens, the issues are different. We have no right to assume that we can tell or even understand what matters to a creature from a distant planet. It would seem to follow that we could not, in those circumstances, tell what such a creature thought. That seems to me quite acceptable. It does not yet follow, of course, that they do not have thoughts, or even that we cannot tell that they have thoughts—provided that some kind of reactive attitudes to their behaviour can be appropriate, or can even be appropriately felt by us without our knowing exactly what matters to them. But it is anyway rather natural to think that we would find it hard to tell what an alien thought.

The general point, that, to count as having thoughts at all, one must in fact be morally assessable (on the generous conception of morality), follows from the two crucial claims of this chapter: that we should adopt an evaluative theory of orectic attitudes, and that the thesis of the holism of assessability is true. It also strikes me as natural: if one actually tries to think of a person who thinks, but is not an appropriate object of reactive attitudes, one ends up with a picture of an android, which soon becomes a mere machine, and then not a thinker at all.

The link between thought and morality provides us with a kind of transcendental argument for a form of moral realism—if orectic assessability is indeed a form of moral assessability. If we allow that broad conception of morality, it appears that certain moral distinctions must be as real, as thoroughly objective, as the distinction between non-evaluative truth and falsehood. Each kind of distinction requires the other kind: there seems no room for granting one an objectivity that the other does not possess.

This may seem surprising, but I think the surprise is created just by the fact that we can secure agreement on non-evaluative matters even between people who disagree over morality. This does not prevent it being true that anyone who thinks is necessarily committed on various moral issues, and committed to the objectivity of moral facts.

12

Understanding People

12.1. How it Looks and how it Is

The task of this chapter is to provide a conception of the kind of explanation which we get from knowledge of people's beliefs, desires, and other attitudes. This should meet the *explanation condition* ((C10) of 8.1). The conception must be both in tune with the evaluative theory of content, and consistent with the controversial demands of Chapter 8. The account must be non-causal, and must assimilate the 'mind–body problem' to a range of other central philosophical issues.

The first thing that needs to be done is to ground a philosophically unorthodox conception of the behaviour which we explain in terms of belief, desire, and the rest. This was, in effect, required by Chapter 8, and is certainly needed for the evaluative theory of content. After all, it has to be *essential* to each relevant response that it belongs to a type which includes both non-accidentally correct and incorrect responses. First, we should remind ourselves explicitly of the picture which makes this seem difficult. What now follows is a version of that picture.

We move about the world, negotiating objects which lie in our path, recording their presence. Some of the objects which we encounter move around. We watch them carefully. We get to be able to anticipate their movements, so that we can duck or step aside, or grab hold of them. Some of these objects we taste; we chew them if they taste all right; we swallow them. We get to be able to anticipate which objects taste nice, which are swallowed easily, which satisfy the wants which we discover in ourselves.

But among the objects around us, some are not so easy to predict. They bend over even when we feel no wind. Parts of them flap around and shake in ways that are quite unexpected. And the activity of these objects affects us hugely. Sometimes bits of them hook on to us. When they do that, sometimes it hurts, but sometimes it feels nice. Sometimes their appendages bring food and drink within grabbing range; sometimes they take them away. It seems at times as if our whole life depends upon the terrifyingly unpredictable behaviour of these things. It is vital to us to find some method, however *ad hoc*, of predicting what they do.

We frantically set about subjecting these things to experiments. We hit them, we scratch them, we stroke them, we dribble on them. We wave our arms at them. We make all kinds of noises, stamping our feet, slapping things, shouting, screaming, cooing, bubbling with our lips. What we notice is that, when we do something striking enough, the objects always make *some* kind of response. Changes in the environment, if they are sufficiently grand, almost always produce some visible effect in the movements of these things. So we decide, as a preliminary heuristic manœuvre, to classify the movements of the objects according to the kind of change in the environment which provokes them.

Unfortunately, the same type of change in the environment does not always seem to produce the same kind of response. Different objects seem to respond in different ways to the same environmental changes. Even the same object does not always seem to respond in the same way to the same kind of change. We try to see if we can discern similarities in the responses which we had not noticed, which might match the similarities we can see among the environmental changes. We make a little progress, but the differences are still too great for systematic prediction. So we try to see if there are similarities in the environment which we had not noticed, so that we can revise our classification of types of response. Again, we make a little progress, but we just cannot make the similarities in the behaviour match the similarities in the environment closely enough.

What are we to do? We are reluctant to abandon the classification of movements in terms of similarities in the environment, since it does seem that there is *some* correlation between movement and environmental change. So we decide to posit an extra factor, something which can vary independently of the environment, but which combines with the effects of the environment to produce particular types of response. We now cast about for some way of getting a line on this extra factor.

I shall stop the fable there, not least because I am not clear how we could produce even a cardboard version of desire, to match the cardboard version of belief which seems to have been constructed.

The fable is a caricature, of course. Even so, it is not without a certain sinister attraction; and some may even hope that an improved version of it can be developed which would not have the naïveties and infelicities of this one. Naturally, that is not a concern of mine. All I want of this fable is that it should have the crucial factors which must be shared by any improved version, and that it should have some intuitive appeal. The task will then be to resist the appeal by showing what is wrong with those crucial features.

What is central to the conception which guides the fable is that it is scientistic. As the subjects of the fable, we are given only those attitudes which it is imagined (however half-bakedly) could be underwritten by science. What we perceive is just what is imagined to be scientifically describable. What we want is just what is imagined to be conducive to our survival, and hence, in the long run, to the preservation of our genes. And our intellectual ambitions seem to be restricted to the efficient and reliable procurement of what we want and avoidance of what we fear. Our intellectual interests are, therefore, pictured as being aridly scientific—although the story could allow us to play around with other things, for relaxation, in the evenings. One feature of the story which makes the conception of intellectual enquiry so *aridly* scientific—obviously more arid than any scientist could live with— is that it allows no room for wondering whether we ought to want what we do want, unless perhaps we recognize that certain intermediate goals which we find ourselves with are not in fact conducive to the furtherance of our larger ends.

The picture is a chilling one, but it (or some variant of it) will find some adherents—not least because it appeals to the daredevil in us: could we find life livable if this was all there was? And certainly the conception of the mind which in the story we find ourselves developing is common enough: what is imagined is, in effect, functionalism growing out of behaviourism. We are moving towards the idea of a kind of state which is correlated, on the one hand, with a type of feature in the environment, and, on the other—in combination with other such states—with a type of feature of behaviour. And the predictive direction of the correlations makes it reasonable to describe the states as being defined in terms of causal role. In this picture, the correlation with a type of feature in the environment is what makes such a state have content: the content is specified by specifying the kind of environment with which the state is correlated.

Of immediate concern to us is the conception of behaviour which the fable involves. Behaviour is essentially the observable causal product of those processes which are set going by the environment. This description has two features which are both important. First, behaviour is by definition observational relative to the theory for predicting it. Secondly, the essential properties of the behaviour are just the scientifically describable properties. I imagined that as subjects of the fable we might feel driven to classify the behaviour according to similarities in the environment. But *what* we classify remains the same: just the peculiar range of flaps and wobbles with which our enquiring eye is confronted.

What we have in the story is obviously just a version of what I called the 'folk-psychology' myth in Chapter 8. There my concern was principally with the view that explanation in terms of belief and desire is causal, though inevitably I had to attack the conception of behaviour involved. Here my concern is principally with the conception of behaviour, although the causal view of the explanatory relation will soon look weak once that is questioned.

The immediate point of conflict between the scientistic fable and the evaluative theory of content is precisely in their differing conceptions of behaviour. The evaluative theory requires, in effect, that it is essential to each of the relevant responses that it is intrinsically assessable in the way it is.

The scientistic fable allows only scientifically describable properties to be essential to each response. Given the basic assumption of the evaluative theory, that value is not a scientific property, the two views conflict. So I need to undermine the fable's conception of behaviour.

In the fable, the conception of behaviour is determined by the incestuous pair of doctrines that there are only scientific facts, and that perception is a scientific process. (The pair are incestuous, since there is a good story which makes each the parent of the other.) I shall try to make it plausible that the conception of behaviour which the evaluative theory of content requires can only seem offensive from within some such fabulous setting. If that is the only real threat to the necessary conception of behaviour, the evaluative theory will seem quite safe.

I shall try to describe the way responses would look if they were intrinsically assessable with respect to alethic and orectic values. I shall try to make it plausible that the way these responses look is just the way they are. This should also have the advantage of giving some intuitive feel for what the abstract talk of assessability in terms of orectic and alethic values amounts to. And it will also confirm the evaluative theory of content in general.

I shall give three examples: two which show what is involved in intrinsic assessability with respect to the value T, and one which focuses on orectic values.

1 *The Missing Top Step.* You are sitting on a chair in an upstairs room. You have a clear view of the top of the staircase, and the last few steps leading to the top. You see someone walking slowly up the stairs. She is humming. She is also reading a paper. Each step is taken laboriously, because she is concentrating on her paper. She reaches the top of the stairs, and then takes one more step. She falls forward, bewildered. That last step of hers is intrinsically assessable with respect to the value T as good if and only if there is another stair there. There is not: she has a false belief.

2 *The Emperor's New Clothes.*[1] You are in a crowd in a conventional eighteenth-century fairy-tale town. The people in the crowd are roaring with laughter, shaking their heads, wiping their eyes, covering their faces. The emperor walks along a cleared path through their midst. He is wearing a spectacular periwig, a pair of shoes with ornate buckles, and nothing else at all. His face wears an expression of courtly benevolence. At each particularly shrieking splutter he turns towards its source, smiles, and raises his hand slightly, as if in blessing. Each of those gestures—indeed his demeanour throughout his progress through the crowd—is intrinsically assessable with respect to the value T as good if and only if he is being applauded. He is not: he has a false belief.

3 *The Benevolent Thug.* (This example is derived from a television advertisement for a newspaper; the view from each of the two perspectives was shown without comment.) You look along a street. There is scaffolding up the side of a building and over a pavement. You see a young man walking towards you, and an old man walking away from you. The young man looks like a thug. His expression suddenly turns wild. He lurches at the old man, knocking him to the ground. The action looks malicious, a piece of gratuitous violence. It appears to be intrinsically assessable with respect to some orectic value as good if and only if it is good to attack that old man.

[1] This is a variation of the original story, for which see, e.g., H. C. Andersen, *The Complete Andersen*, trans. J. Hersholt (New York: Heritage Press, 1942–8).

But the same sequence is also visible from another angle. If you had been there, you would have seen the young man look up towards the top of the scaffolding, where a large load was coming loose from a crane. You would have seen him start, look ahead to the old man, leap forward, and knock him just far enough away for the falling load to miss him. From this angle it would have been clear that the young man's act was intrinsically assessable as good if and only if it was good to save that old man's life.

These simple examples show how it looks when someone does something which is intrinsically assessable in the kinds of way which the evaluative theory of content exploits. There can be no doubt that the actions in question would just strike us as, in effect, intrinsically assessable in the ways mentioned. That is why it was possible to run the 'benevolent thug' sequence without comment in the television advertisement: it was obvious how the behaviour would be taken.

The examples also serve to situate the abstract terminology of the theory of content in the real world. False belief turns out to have a characteristic feel: it belongs with our sense of something being futile or pathetic, with a certain feeling of irony. It emerges as the very stuff of comedy—and of tragedy too, as Aristotle thought.[2] And the presence of a distinctive feel to false belief and ill will also explains how *acting* is even possible, and how people can be type-cast as innocents or villains.

The examples reinforce the evaluative theory of content in another respect. Once we understand the characteristic appearance of false belief, it is hard to resist the idea that truth is a value. On the truth of our beliefs hangs the question whether what we do is futile or whether we ourselves are pathetic. Who could fail to care about that?

Once we understand the way it looks when we find responses intrinsically assessable, why not allow that the way it looks is the way it is? Why not say that we can *directly perceive* the ineptness of the extra step, the pathetic nature of the emperor's misplaced confidence, and the unreflective heroism of the young man?[3] We can count something as *directly* perceived if its perception is not a

---

[2] Aristotle, *Poetics*, 1453^{a}9.

[3] For this kind of appeal to direct perception, see J. McDowell, 'On "The Reality of the Past" ', 136, and 'Criteria, Defeasibility, and Knowledge', *Proceedings of the British Academy*, 68 (1982), 455–79.

matter of inference from something which is more immediately perceived, and if its current perception is not merely the product of an unreflective habit based on a previous inference from something which is more immediately perceived.

The question whether we can directly perceive such things as the ineptness, inappropriateness, or courage of an action is important because it is hard to make sense of a thoroughgoing realism about thoughts and feelings in any other way—assuming, that is, that we are not to fall back upon a causal theory of the mind. If all we can strictly see is, for example, the bodily movement involved in an action, then—if we are not to appeal to special features of hidden causes of behaviour—it seems that we are forced to regard the rich appearance of such behaviour as strictly the result of our interpretation, of our construction or imposition.[4] And that seems either viciously circular or viciously regressive when we think about our own minds.

There is also a significant theoretical advantage in being able to say that we can directly perceive the way that behaviour should be assessed. It allows us to use the characteristic feel of these perceptions to complete various definitions in the theory of content. The crucial notions can be given an ostensive base, by appealing to the distinctive appearance of things to get someone to see what is involved, without attempting to define everything verbally. Anyone who can understand other people will in fact recognize these distinctive appearances, and will know how to apply the crucial notions in new cases, without explicitly deploying the concepts of content.

But we should be clear quite how rich our conception of perception must be if we are to accept this. The advantages are not to be bought cheaply. It might seem demanding enough just that we should accept that *value* can be perceived. But that is not the end of it. In effect, we have to be able to see *in the behaviour itself* most of what is normally thought to belong to the thoughts and feelings which may be cited to explain the behaviour. There are two particularly striking aspects to this.

First, the content of the belief which explains the behaviour can be visible in the behaviour itself. Thus, in the case of the missing last

---

[4] Thus Dennett in 'True Believers', in his *The Intentional Stance*. His view is not dissimilar from Davidson's; see, e.g., D. Davidson, 'Belief and the Basis of Meaning', in his *Inquiries into Truth and Interpretation*, 141–54.

stair, the woman took that extra step because she thought there was another stair. And what we seem to see, if we attend properly to the way it strikes us, is just that. In seeing the act as inept, we are seeing it as animated by that content. And this requires that we see the circumstances in which the act is performed as, in a sense, part of the act itself, intrinsic to its identity. The 'circumstances *in* which the act is performed', in the sense relevant here, are the circumstances *in response to which* the act is performed; and it is seen as essential to that act that it is a response to those circumstances, appropriate or inappropriate according to how things are in those circumstances. Otherwise, the act could not strike us as inept.

Secondly, we already have, visible in the act itself, the basis of the kind of counterfactual which we would normally associate with explanation in terms of belief. So, for example, we would normally accept something like this:

(1) She would not have done that if she had not believed that.

This seems to follow directly from what has just been said. It is essential to *this* act that it is appropriate or inappropriate as *these* circumstances dictate. So there would not have been *this* act if it had not been animated by *this* content.

Perhaps someone might think that a more generously construed counterfactual is actually warranted by explanation in terms of belief. Something like this might be suggested:

(2) She would not have done anything which even looked like that if she had not believed that.

Suppose she had done something which looked just like this, but in virtue of a different belief. In that case, what had appeared to be the circumstances relevant to the assessment of the behaviour would not in fact have been. That is, the appearances would have been deceptive. But that means that the case imagined is irrelevant to our present concerns: what we are talking about here is what is available in perception, assuming that things are as they appear.

Perhaps it is thought that yet another counterfactual is what matters—perhaps this one:

(3) She would not have taken that extra step, if she had not believed that.

There are two ways of taking that extra step. The step might be taken as part of a general situation, which includes the fact that the extra step is appropriate if and only if there is another stair. But on that reading, (3) adds nothing which was not in (1). Alternatively, the step might have been taken in different circumstances, subject to different conditions of appropriateness. But on that reading, we have no reason to believe (3). When we say that someone does something because she believes something, we are not at all committed to saying that she would not have done something which could be described by the same action verb, for example, if she had not had that belief.

This elaboration shows what the evaluative theory of content must assume which would be difficult to accept from within the scientistic fable. The scientistic fable always sees two things: a bodily movement of a certain kind, and the environment which surrounds or precedes it. The evaluative theory must insist that there is a single thing to be perceived which cannot be analysed down into the scientifically discernible pair. The single thing is just this: a response well suited or ill suited to its circumstances. What the evaluative theory needs is that there should really be that single thing, there to be perceived as a single thing.

Since the scientistic fable has itself been argued against and abandoned in the very adoption of the evaluative theory, the fact that the required conception of perception is objectionable from a scientistic perspective is no reason for the evaluative theory to be worried. Are there any other reasons for worrying about it?

Here is a simple thought: we cannot count as directly perceiving that a piece of behaviour is inept, for example, since we could so easily be wrong. That looks very simple: it seems to be a covert appeal to epistemological infallibilism. (Perception is a way of knowing; knowledge requires infallibility.) If it is, it should be dismissed without hesitation. It is not clear, however, what the force of 'so easily' is, although the phrase is naturally included in a formulation of the objection. The proper response would seem to be a reminder of how often and how easily we get it right. But perhaps there is a subtler thought lurking behind that simple front. It is a challenge. The evaluative theory of content needs to explain how error can be made sense of. And the challenge becomes more precise if the evaluative theory is to meet the demands of the form of conceptualism which was developed in Part I. If an action looks inept, but is not, there must be something which it would be to know that it is not, despite the look of things.

Here is how I might come to know that the apparently inept extra step was not in fact inept, because the condition for its appropriateness was not what it had seemed to be. It is essential to the notion of *intrinsic* assessability that the assessment of the behaviour warrants an assessment of the person whose behaviour it is: if the behaviour is good, then the person is to that extent good too (see 10.5). This can only be a mark of difference between intrinsic and merely non-arbitrary assessability if some constraint on assessment is hereby imposed. The obvious source of such a constraint is the fact that people have psychological histories.

It is, therefore, natural to insist that a supposed condition of appropriateness for a particular response can only be its true condition of appropriateness, if that response, with that condition, fits the psychological history, before and after the response, of the person whose behaviour it is. The requirement that this conception of the response should *fit* a person's history is not readily analysable, but some things can be said about it. It does not mean just *cohere with*, in the sense of being harmonious with; that is one way of fitting, but not the only way. A conception of a response can fit a person's history while being inconsistent with what we otherwise take them to believe, if the person has changed her mind, or if she is inconsistent. But changes of mind and inconsistencies of character themselves have their own distinctive appearances. If one had the whole relevant history before one, it seems to me that one could tell for sure whether or not someone had a particular belief, provided that it is in fact determinate that she does.

A few remarks about this are in order. First, it is, of course, assumed that one may take one's impressions of other responses at face value. But this is no different from the way in which one demonstrates that the appearance of a bend in a stick in water is an illusion. Secondly, it has to be all right not to say anything very specific about what coherence amounts to. Again, this is no different from the kind of thing one may appeal to in the stick-in-water kind of case. Thirdly, there is nothing disturbing about the idea that it might not actually be determinate whether someone has a given belief. This has nothing to do with Quine's thesis of the indeterminacy of translation.[5] It is not suggested that every case might be indeterminate. All that is being considered is the kind of

---

[5] W. V. Quine, *Word and Object* (Cambridge, Mass.: MIT Press, 1960), ch. II.

indeterminacy which is obvious to anyone who has tried ascribing beliefs to an author (Hume, say) on the basis of a text. (And it is not as if it would have helped to ask Hume what he meant; that might make him make up his mind, but there is no reason to suppose that he was any clearer than us about what he thought, at the level of interpretation at which real issues of indeterminacy arise.)

Finally, it is no part of the evaluative theory to insist that it must always actually be possible to tell for sure what someone thinks, even when it is determinate. This is because it is not essential to the evaluative theorist's conception of behaviour that it should be observable to a third party. That is another point of difference with the conception of behaviour provided by the scientistic fable. In the fable, the relevant behaviour is essentially observational relative to the theory embodied in talk of belief and desire. On the evaluative conception, in contrast, to observe the behaviour is, literally, to observe the belief; and unobserved behaviour will embody unobserved belief.

It looks, then, as if the challenge can be met, and in a natural way. It is natural because it makes legitimate such corrections of interpretation as, 'I know her: she wouldn't have meant it like that'.

There is another persistent worry about allowing so much to count as being directly perceived. Some will think that it is totally non-explanatory; worse, it might seem to *block* explanation. If we allow all *that* to be just directly perceived, what could need explanation?

This kind of worry needs careful treatment. We need to ask what it is legitimate to demand an explanation of, and what kind of explanation such a legitimate demand requires. My suspicion is that the worry only looks really worrying if we confuse distinct kinds of explanatory demand.

Here is a legitimate question: how could anything which has developed by evolution, from the kinds of beginnings which evolution imagines, have developed an ability to tell reliably, just by looking, whether or not some piece of behaviour is inept? We should note what has to be explained: an ability to spot ineptness just by looking. That, after all, is the ability we have. There are two kinds of strategy which might be employed to answer that question, which we might call *modest* and *contentious* respectively.

The modest strategy is not unambitious. The idea would be to build (or describe how to build) a succession of systems under the following constraints. The first system in the succession must be sufficiently simple to be unproblematically explicable in evolutionary terms. We would have to explain the movement from each system to its successor as the effect of evolutionary forces in an appropriate environment. We would have to explain any modification in any particular system as being the product of inherited tendencies and an appropriate environment. And the last system in the succession would have to be able to register unambiguously the presence of such properties as ineptness, or wickedness, or whatever, with pretty much the reliability of a mature human being. We might imagine that a light comes on when there is apparent ineptness, does not come on when there is no apparent ineptness, and flickers when it looks indeterminate. If we were able to describe each modification carefully enough, and to explain which modifications were really necessary, we might have an explanation, of a kind, of how something like us could reliably spot ineptness just by looking.

Suppose such a strategy were successful. There are several things to note about it. First, nothing in the engineering or the engineering history of the final system entitles us to say that the light coming on is *correct* if and only if the system really is presented with ineptness. That depends on *our* acknowledgement that there is such a thing as ineptness in the world, and upon *our* explanatory concerns in building the device: it depends upon the fact that the device is built to model what we already acknowledge to be *recognition* of ineptness.

Secondly, the existence and describability of a system of this kind would not mean that we had a *reduction* of ineptness or wickedness, or whatever. The system could only be built to match the judgements of a particular person or group of people, who might themselves be insensitive or morally defective. Even if a system were built whose light-flashings matched the judgements of the vast majority of human beings, this would not make the system authoritative on what was actually inept or wicked. The question whether it would be *right* to defer to its deliverances would not have been settled. (Suppose there was a *human being* whose judgements of value always coincided with the vast majority of human beings. It would not follow that her judgement should be accepted; we could not define rightness just as whatever she thought was right.)

Thirdly, nothing about the existence of such a system as the last in the imagined succession could determine whether ineptness or wickedness count as being directly perceivable. Suppose we say that the thing we have created counts as having a mind, as being a concept-possessor. It makes unreflective judgements of value on the basis of how things look. (It must, if it is to model *us*.) Does it count as directly perceiving value in behaviour? The issue remains exactly as it was before the project was considered.

It should be clear that, if our explanatory ambitions are confined to the modest strategy, the evaluative theory's insistence that we can directly perceive value in itself puts no block on explanation. It is true that it does not *provide* the explanation. But then, the evaluative theory is a *philosophical* theory, and the explanation sought here is not a philosophical one.

But what if we cannot build, or describe how to build, such a succession of systems as the modest strategy envisages? Then we cannot explain how it is that things like us can directly perceive value. But suppose we could *prove* these two things:

(i) That there could be no scientific description of a series of developments which led up to what would in effect be an ability to recognize value.

(ii) That if (i) were true and we could strictly *recognize* value, science would be incomplete.

What if we could prove that? Then we would have proved that science is necessarily incomplete. (Though I have no idea what a proof of (i) would look like.) We would not have proved that there is no such thing, in the real world, as recognition of value. This may sound dogmatic, but it amounts to no more than an insistence that it is not a matter for science to say what kinds of fact there are. And that is just to repeat the denial of scientism.

So much for the modest strategy. In comparison with this, it should be clear how unwarranted the demands of the contentious strategy are. The contentious strategy begins by recording the kinds of physical property which our sensory surfaces can be physically sensitive to, given their physical constitution. When the state of our sensory surfaces varies, the variation can be traced to variations in just those physical properties. Let us call the particular variation in external physical properties to which a particular variation in the state of our sensory surfaces can be traced the *information directly registered* in the variation of the state of our sensory surfaces. We then make a stipulation of the following form:

> (DP) A person can only *directly perceive* some state of the world if that state of the world can be deduced from the information directly registered in variations in the state of her sensory surfaces by means of an algorithm which meets a certain restrictive condition *R*.

The idea might be that perception, strictly so-called, is thought of as being localized, occurring in particular sense organs, and the restrictive condition *R* is supposed to prevent the use of algorithms which appeal to information of too distant an origin (too distant in either space or time). Or there might be some other motive for a particular condition *R*, reflecting some allegedly intuitive sense of what can be the content of perception ('strictly so-called').

The general spirit of the contentious strategy is surely familiar: it can be traced back to classical empiricism. The problem is obvious: no stipulation of the form of (DP) can be properly motivated. There may be good reason to classify information in terms of the kind of algorithm that is needed to deduce it from the state of sensory surfaces, but there is no reason, short of some kind of scientism, for supposing that such a classification corresponds to what can be directly perceived.

In fact, the contentious strategy seems inevitably scientistic. Provided we accept that the evaluative cannot be reduced to the non-evaluative, then no version of (DP), even if *R* is thought of quite generously, can permit values to be perceived. That would require physics to be authoritative over some values. And if value cannot be directly perceived, we will have some difficulty locating it, except by imposition, in the world which we can perceive.

The difference between the modest strategy and the contentious one can be interpreted as resting on a difference between two readings of this claim:

> (*) It must be scientifically explicable that we are so constituted that [we have the cognitive capacities we do].

The difference lies in the role of the bracketed phrase. For the modest strategy, we should take the phrase as *not* being governed by the operator 'it must be scientifically explicable that'; it functions merely to *identify* a way of being constituted. The contentious strategy, however, reads the phrase as being within the scope of the operator, and therefore demands at least a partial scientific explanation of what it is to have a cognitive capacity.

I have dealt with two sources of the objection that allowing us to count as directly perceiving value is non-explanatory. One makes a reasonable explanatory demand, which direct perception of value does not inhibit. The other makes an unreasonable demand. But both of these sources of objection assume that it is *scientific* explanation we want. There is another version of the objection which is worried by a loss of *philosophical* explanation.

It might be said: if we count ourselves as literally directly perceiving value, what limit can there be to the kind of thing which can be directly perceived? And if there is no limit, do we not count every truth as just 'barely' true—that is, not true *in virtue of* anything?[6] And does that not mean that there can be no philosophical explanations?

No, it does not. This objection assumes a foundationalist conception of philosophical explanation, according to which some things are forever 'problematic', and others are forever 'unproblematic'—the task being to explain the 'problematic' in terms of the 'unproblematic'. But this conception was rejected in 4.4 (see also 5.3). Nothing is problematic (or unproblematic) absolutely. We can engender a sense that a kind of concept or view is problematic by thinking of something else as unproblematic; but the positions can be reversed, so that what had previously seemed problematic is viewed as unproblematic, and what had seemed unproblematic is explained in its terms. This allows us to count all kinds of things as needing philosophical explanation, even if they are all to do with what can be directly perceived. So this final source of objection dries up too.

It seems that there are no good objections to the evaluative theory's claim that we can directly perceive the ineptness and wickedness of behaviour.

I have concentrated on what it looks like when someone else has a false belief, or a bad desire. The account insists that we need look no deeper than the *behaviour* to find the value in it. That might be thought to make our knowledge of other people's states of mind wholly different from the special intimacy we have with our own

---

[6] For this notion of the 'barely' true, see M. Dummett, 'What is a Theory of Meaning? (II)', in G. Evans and J. McDowell (eds.), *Truth and Meaning* (Oxford: Clarendon Press), 89.

thoughts, and therefore to leave us with a problem over our sense of our own minds. We need to explain how the account extends to our own case.

False belief shows itself as misplaced confidence. Belief in general will then have the character of confidence; what is believed is the condition which has to be met for that confidence not to be misplaced. It might be tempting to transform that into a description of the feel of our own beliefs as follows. Suppose that I believe that the evaluative theory of content is true. If I do, then I have a kind of confidence which is misplaced if the theory is false. Suppose I express that belief. I say confidently, 'The evaluative theory of content is true.' If I do that, I make a response which is intrinsically assessable with respect to the value T as good if and only if the evaluative theory is true. How does it feel? It feels like an expression of confidence with a consciousness of what would make that confidence misplaced.

That is what it is tempting to say. The interesting thing is that it does not seem quite right. If I say that I am conscious of what would make my confidence misplaced, I seem already to sense a threat to that confidence; and then it is no longer the confidence it seemed to be. If I behave with equal apparent confidence, while sensible of a threat to its legitimacy, confidence teeters over into mere bravado. True confidence seems inevitably unnoticed by the person who possesses it: the person simply acts and speaks. It will follow, if the general account of the characteristic appearance of belief is right, that one's own beliefs have no characteristic appearance to oneself. The special intimacy of one's own current beliefs consists in one's not noticing them.

But that consciousness of what would make one's confidence misplaced does play a role in revealing another way in which my beliefs are intimate or immediate to me. If someone challenges what I say, and I take the challenge to heart, I feel threatened. That sense of threat is the characteristic appearance of my *having been believing* something. The intimacy of what *I* have been believing to *me* consists in the fact that *my* taking a challenge to heart is a matter of *my* feeling threatened. The blush, the stammer, the general sense of disorientation, can only be a response to a claim's being challenged if the claim is one which I have been believing. When someone else's beliefs are challenged, the closest I can get to her discomfiture is sympathy.

This seems the precise counterpart, for one's own case, of the characteristic appearance of belief in the case of other people. Once again, it is entirely in tune with the evaluative theory. No one can think that feeling threatened is an evaluatively disengaged state of mind.

12.2. Liabilities

The definitions of the core cases of concept-possession characterized possession of a concept as a matter of being *liable* to respond in ways which would be appropriately intrinsically assessable (see 9.5). There would have been a corresponding definition of belief in terms of an appropriate liability, had it not been difficult to do that in extensional terms within the framework of level-one opacity. Ignoring problems of extensionality for the moment, let us now say that to believe that *p* is to be *liable* to make responses intrinsically assessable with respect to the value T as good if and only if *p*. The question is: what is a liability?

If there is as much in each response as I argued in the last section that there is, what role is left for the notion of liability to play? There seems almost nothing left for it to do, particularly in the light of the argument in 8.3, that explanation in terms of beliefs and desires is not directed towards prediction.

Almost nothing, but not quite nothing. The notion of liability was introduced in 9.1 for a particular and limited purpose. It is possible to have a concept without currently exercising it, and to have a belief without currently doing anything which might be explained in terms of that belief. The notion of liability was introduced just to create enough of a gap between belief, or concept-possession, and behaviour to make that possible. The word 'liable' was chosen deliberately, because of its roots both in vague dispositional talk ('Glass is liable to break if you drop it'), and in law ('You are liable for any damage that may be caused'). I shall now exploit both aspects of the word, though I shall lean more heavily on the legal associations.

I intend the dispositional aspect to remain extremely vague. 'She is liable to do it' is to be read as having roughly the predictive force of 'She might very well do it' or 'Don't be surprised if she does'. This will horrify a scientistically-minded philosopher, and not just because it is unspecific. What will seem disturbing is that this conception of a liability gives it almost *no* predictive force. That is exactly my intention.

We now need to explain why it should be possible to have a concept or a belief at a time when one is not exercising it or expressing it in behaviour. A causal theory of the mind has no problem with this. A cause can exist without its effect existing; this is particularly easy to imagine when the cause is only a contributory factor, rather than a total cause. The same goes for causal dispositions: they too can exist without actually having their characteristic effects. A causal theory takes beliefs and concepts to be causes of behaviour, or at least causal dispositions whose characteristic effects include behaviour. It was already committed to this: on a causal theory it is the causes of behaviour which make the behaviour significant—which license the description of it as intentional. So the causal theory can account quite naturally for the fact that we can have beliefs and concepts at times when they do not appear in behaviour.

What can the evaluative theory do to match this? We cannot count concepts or beliefs as causes of behaviour, since that would make talk of belief and desire directed towards prediction, which the arguments of 8.3 ruled out. And in any case that move would be *ad hoc*, since according to the evaluative theory it is not in virtue of its causes that behaviour is significant: the significance is intrinsic to the behaviour itself.

There is, however, an obvious enough explanation for the evaluative theory to appeal to. The fact that I have certain concepts and beliefs puts constraints on what the significance of my current behaviour is, even if my current behaviour does not itself manifest precisely those concepts and beliefs. This is connected with the point made in 12.1, that a conception of the significance of a particular response is in principle correctable in virtue of failing to fit the psychological history of the person whose response it is. If I have a belief now, there are constraints on what other beliefs I can have and be coherent, for example. And the fact that I have a particular concept shows something about the way I view things, which can inform someone's conception of my current behaviour. (If my values are all expressed in terms of the concepts of medieval chivalry, for example, someone should hesitate before attributing to me an attitude which only a hedonistic utilitarian could possess.)

This all suggests the following simple explanation of the fact that I can have beliefs and concepts even when I am not expressing or exercising them. If this were not possible, appeal to the psychological history of a person could put no constraint on, and provide no correction of, the interpretation of her current behaviour. And without that constraint, or that possibility of correction, we cannot make sense of an interpretation which seems to fit the appearances being wrong. And that would mean that there was no difference between seeming to think something or other and really thinking it. And that would mean that there was no such thing as really thinking anything.

In the light of that, this seems a reasonable definition of liability:

(L) s is liable at t to make responses which are intrinsically assessable in a certain way if and only if

it is already, and still, legitimate at t to assess reponses of s in that way.

What does 'already, and still' mean? I think it means different things, according to whether we are considering the legitimacy of assessing someone's behaviour in terms of a given concept, or in terms of a given belief.

If we are talking about *concept* liabilities, it can only be already and still legitimate to assess responses of s in terms of a given concept, if s has already acquired the concept, and has not undergone the kind of mental upheaval which would be involved in losing it.

What does that mean in terms which do not presuppose the concepts which a theory of content hopes to explain? In order for one to have acquired a concept, it must be possible at least to form a conception of what it would be for one to be incorrect or non-accidentally correct in those terms. Moreover, unlike with the case of computers, it is not enough merely that there be something which it *would* be for one to make a relevant non-accidentally correct response. It is surely required that one should *actually* have made a relevant non-accidentally correct response. The conditions for non-accidental correctness required that one's capacities must somehow be *adapted* to the subject-matter (to borrow the evolutionary metaphor). Unless some such condition has been met, it is hard to see how someone's thoughts could be said to be properly *about* a given topic, or how it could be just to assess them in its terms. And for a person's behaviour to be *intrinsically* assessable in a certain way, she must herself be responsible for the way in which her capacities are adapted to the subject-matter (see 10.5). And that does not seem intelligible unless she has actually made some relevant non-accidentally correct response.

What this means, given the link between the definition of non-accidental correctness and the analysis of knowledge, is that for *s* to have acquired the concept "*C*", *s* must have known that . . . *C* . . . , for some filling of the blanks.

So much for the 'already' part of the definition. What could make it *still* legitimate to assess someone in terms of a given concept? The natural suggestion is that to possess the concept "*C*" still, *s* must still know that . . . *C* . . . , for some filling of the blanks (although not necessarily the same filling as before). How can this be characterized without presupposing what a theory of content hopes to explain?

We might try to get at this by first characterizing in more detail what it is still to know something, using the concepts of content. If someone *still* knows something, she now does not need to realize it again, or be persuaded of it again. If one were to attempt to make her realize or persuade her, one might expect a characteristically impatient response. That impatience is a distinctive way in which someone responds to information she does not need. What we have here is the idea of a distinctive appearance of not realizing something for the first time.

We can use that idea to give a characterization of still knowing something. Let us say that *s* still knows that . . . *C* . . . , for some filling of the blanks, just in case two conditions are met. First, if she were now *forced* to respond in a way which is intrinsically assessable as good if and only if . . . *C* . . . , that response would not have the character of a realization (and if it seemed to have that character, then the whole response would not have been visible to us). And, secondly, that response would be non-accidentally correct, on that assessment. It should be noted that, although this characterization uses a subjunctive conditional, it does not have any evident predictive power. This is because it is not claimed that it is in any way *likely* that she will respond in a way which is intrinsically assessable as good if and only if . . . *C* . . . ; and there is no general conception of what it would take to *force* her to respond like that.

This is all suggestive for a parallel account of what is required for it to be already and still legitimate to assess someone in the way relevant to a particular *belief*. I propose that what is required is that the person should have done something intrinsically assessable in the way appropriate for that belief, and that she should not now need to draw that conclusion again, or need it to occur to her again. Each of those conditions seems to have a distinctive kind of appearance, so that one can say this: she still believes that p, just in case, if one were now to force her to respond in a way which is intrinsically assessable as good if and only if p, her response would not have the character of something occurring to her.

This seems to me to have the merit of showing our actual practice to be reasonable. Suppose Sheila asks me why Bob is singing to his goldfish. I say that it is because he thinks it will encourage the fish to breed. Sheila cannot believe that Bob thinks that. I can respond in various ways. First, I could describe Bob's behaviour in more detail, setting the singing in a larger context—which might include anxious peerings in the tank for eggs, or something like that—in the hope that I could display his singing as simply *part* of a pattern of behaviour which was manifestly an attempt to get his fish to breed.

But suppose that way of trying to justify my explanation does not work. In some cases, there might be nothing more I could do. Suppose, though, that I can do more here. If I try to do more, I am in effect discounting the evidence of the present behaviour. That is, I am trying to show that Bob has this belief even though he may not now be manifesting it. In the terms of the evaluative theory, I am trying to show that Bob is still liable to respond in appropriately assessable ways, even if it is true that he is not now responding like that.

What I might do is obvious. I might be able to tell Sheila that Bob told me the day before that this was the reason for his singing. There might then be a question whether he was joking, which I might hope to be able to settle with a fuller description of his demeanour at the time. If he was not joking, the question is whether he still believes it. We might ask him. Then we might hope to tell from his demeanour whether the point was occurring to him fresh.

Should we insist, as I have done, that one cannot have a belief unless one has actually made some response which is intrinsically assessable in the way appropriate for that belief? The insistence has the advantage of giving a pleasing symmetry to the attribution of liability. It *becomes* legitimate to assess someone's behaviour in a certain way when it first matters to something she does that things should be so, and it *ceases* to be legitimate to assess her behaviour in that way when it no longer matters to anything she does that things should be so. And the insistence does not seem implausible, when we remember that not all behaviour need be observed, and that what is meant by 'behaviour' can take such various forms: it can include everything from a momentary glance to one's general demeanour for months.

I have given an extremely thin account of the notion of liability. This is married to a conception of behaviour which is rich in itself, but no appeal has been made to anything *behind* the behaviour, or to any idea of a proper kind of causal basis for the behaviour. This might seem to make the general account of belief and concept-possession vulnerable, because it might seem not to be sufficiently realist about states of mind. The question which might be put to me is this: can I make sense of something whose behaviour is indistinguishable in appearance from that of a real thinking human being throughout its 'lifetime', but which nevertheless is not really a thinker, and has no concepts at all? The threat will be that, if I cannot, the evaluative theory is not much better than traditional philosophical behaviourism. A causal theory might hope to avoid the difficulty itself by insisting that there must be the right kind of causal basis for behaviour. That is, in effect, it will want some richer causal notion in place of my thinly defined notion of liability.

The question to focus on is this: why is the imagined thing not a concept-possessor? It will always turn out in the end to be because it is not really the doer of its deeds, is not itself responsible for what seems to be the success and failure of its behaviour. Perhaps the thing is really a kind of radio-controlled puppet, operated by aliens on another planet.[7] Or perhaps some aliens have been able to predict the events on earth in the thing's 'lifetime' with such precision that they have simply fixed the thing up to make plausible movements in every anticipated eventuality. It seems obvious that in these cases the evaluative theory would just say that the appearances are deceptive. Since the thing is not truly responsible for its behaviour, the behaviour is not in fact intrinsically assessable in the ways that it had seemed to be, and the thing is not a thinker.

---

[7] This example is due to C. Peacocke, *Sense and Content: Experience, Thought, and their Relations* (Oxford: Clarendon Press, 1983), 205.

The same tactic can be used for every imagined problem case of this kind. The moment the case has been specified in enough detail for it to be clear that the imagined thing is not a thinker, it has also been shown that the behaviour is not all that it appears to be. At the same time, the conceptualist demand—that there must be something which it would be to know that it is not a thinker—will also have been met: the description of the imagined case will tell us exactly what it would be to know that it is not a thinker.

Two features about this response might worry the objector here. First, how can I claim that what I would find out, in discovering that something which had seemed to be a human being is in fact a puppet controlled by aliens, is a fact about the *behaviour*, rather than its causes?

I do not need to accept that description. In the case of a real human being, all I need ever see is her behaviour. What I actually see, in normal circumstances, is no more than behaviour, but nothing less than its significance. But this requires that the circumstances to which the person responds when she acts must also count as, in a sense, a part of the behaviour. In the case of a radio-controlled puppet, it is unclear that we are entitled to this generously unified conception of behaviour. So we might want to say that, in this case, the discovery of the radio link is not just a discovery about its behaviour: it is a discovery about the causes of the behaviour. But this is because the behaviour which is really there has no intrinsic significance.

This fits well with one of the motives for refusing to find mentality or significance among the causes of behaviour in the case of real people. This motive derives from the argument in 8.6. I claimed there that the relevant kind of behaviour—behaviour which is apt for explanation by citing thoughts and feelings—is not caused at all. The reason was that no cause could be found for such behaviour which did not interfere with the fact that the *person* is responsible for it. Such behaviour is simply *done*. But there is no such difficulty with the behaviour of a radio-controlled puppet. The whole point of the example is that the thing is not responsible for what it does—not even in the most minimal sense of 'responsible'. So there can be no harm in talking about the causes of its behaviour. The point can be summarized like this. In normal circumstances, all one sees is the behaviour, and this is because the behaviour includes all one could need to see. But in the case of the

alien puppet or robot, the behaviour which is actually there is not the
behaviour I take to be there. To that extent, my mistake (if I trust the
appearances) *is* a mistake about behaviour. But, because I am
mistaken about the behaviour, I am to be corrected by being told
about the causes of the behaviour which is really there. In this sense, I
am mistaken through ignorance of the causes of the behaviour.

The second worry that might occur to someone, in the light of my
acceptance of the possibility of the radio-controlled puppet, relates
to the response I urged to eliminativism in 6.1. Might I not myself
turn out to be just such a radio-controlled puppet? And am I not
then forced myself to accept that I might have no thoughts? But I
said in 6.1 that this was not a possibility I could countenance.

I think I can say the same thing now. I could not rationally be
convinced that I am a radio-controlled puppet. What if someone
showed me film of peculiar beings on Mars, and showed me precise
correlations between their movements with a gadget and my own
movements? This could not rationally convince me. I might
question the film. I might question the relative timing of their
movements and mine. I might even think that all my movements
were being anticipated in some eerie way. But if I have any sense at
all, I will never accept that those beings are controlling me. It
remains true that, if they had been controlling me, then I would not
have been a thinker. We preserve the nicely realist possibility of
error. But, for that very reason, nothing can ever rationally
convince me that my movements are simply the product of someone
else's decision.

A causal theorist is likely to think that the extremely thin
conception of liability I have given throws away the last chance of
maintaining a robust possibility of serious error about other people.
I think that threat has been met. In any case, I cannot see how a
causal theory could do any better. The idea will be to explain beliefs
or concepts in terms of causal dispositions, or the causal base of
such dispositions. Then if the causal base is of the wrong kind, we
will be able to say that we do not have a thinker, even when we
have something whose behaviour is apparently indistinguishable
from that of a thinker. But what does it mean to suppose that the
causal base is of the wrong kind? Wrong kind for what? The wrong
kind to support the richly conceived kind of behaviour which is
essential for concept-possession. If that is all we can say, then a
causal theory has nothing more to offer than can already be

accommodated within the evaluative theory, and we have no need of a richer notion of liability than the one I have defined.

12.3. The Explanation of Behaviour

The princess kisses a frog. We wonder why. We are told that she believes that the frog is a prince. Her behaviour now becomes—well, not exactly unsurprising—but at least intelligible, given the special expectations concerning marriage and bodily transformation which prevail in fairy stories. In short, we have explained what she is up to.

So far I have given a definition of belief and concept-possession—in outline at least—in terms of intrinsically assessable responses and liability. I have argued that intrinsic assessability is perceptible, and that the notion of liability introduces no ulterior cause. But I have not explained what exactly is done by the report of a belief itself. What does it tell us, and how? In particular, what do the words in the 'that'-clause do?

It is clear enough what the shape of an account must be. When we ask why someone did something, what we have in mind is in a sense only part of the behaviour; it may only be part of the relevant movement. We are missing at least the circumstances which have to be suitable for the behaviour to count as appropriate or good. What we are told when we are supplied with the belief in virtue of which what was done was done is what those circumstances are; that is, what has to be the case for the behaviour not to be inept; that is, the condition under which it counts as good with respect to the value T. And that is the heart of the problem we need to address now: what does 'condition' mean here?

A thoroughly extensionalist conception will interpret that notion of condition extensionally, in terms just of the material biconditional. On such a view, what matters is getting the actual value, both alethic and orectic, of each response right. Any statement of the condition of assessment will do, provided that it is both truth-functionally adequate, and the product of a theory which is capable of yielding a truth-functionally adequate statement of the condition of assessment of every response. This would be something like a Davidsonian theory of interpretation resurrected within an evaluative theory of content.[8]

---

[8] See, e.g., Davidson, 'Belief and the Basis of Meaning', in his *Inquiries into Truth and Interpretation*.

Such a view will fairly clearly countenance the kind of indeterminacy known as 'the inscrutability of reference', and faces objections on that score.[9] But what I want to concentrate on is the simple point that this is an extraordinary conception of what we are concerned with when we say what people believe. In general, what we are provided with when we are told what someone believes is an understanding of her behaviour—indeed, an understanding of the person herself. What would a full extensionalist 'theory of interpretation' of a person provide? An ability to nod one's head when and only when the behaviour warranted it, and to shake one's head when and only when the behaviour warranted it. It may very well be that, in trying to acquire that ability, one is forced, out of one's way, as it were, to grasp something interesting about the person. That has to be the extensionalist's perverse hope, since an absolutely reliable nod-and-shake disposition, which seems to be the official goal of the theory, is on its own an absurd proxy for understanding.

What is wrong with the severely extensionalist approach is that it is instrumentalist, in very much the sense of 'instrumentalism' that is relevant to the philosophy of science. An instrumentalist philosophy of science counts predictive adequacy as sufficient for the truth of a scientific theory. What this seems to miss is an idea of scientific *understanding*, which requires of a theory at least that it should be predictively adequate for the right reason.

The parallel between an instrumentalist philosophy of science and an austerely extensionalist conception of understanding people is made all the closer if we think of an extensionalist conception as adopting something like a Davidsonian theory of interpretation of a person. In the Davidsonian tradition, a theory of interpretation is much like a scientific theory, and its aim is conceived of, more or less explicitly, as being to 'predict' the truth value of a person's attitudes.

We should expect to improve on the extensionalist conception by insisting that, in addition to correctly 'predicting' the value of a person's responses, we must assign value to the responses for the right reason. From the point of view of an evaluative theory, this will involve our determination of the value of the responses being

---

[9] For the way the indeterminacy emerges, see Davidson, 'The Inscrutability of Reference', in his *Inquiries into Truth and Interpretation*, 227–41.

grounded in the basis of those responses' counting as intrinsically assessable in the first place.

I argued in the last section that it can only be legitimate to assess someone's responses in the way appropriate to a given concept, if she has actually made some response which is *non-accidentally correct*, under the relevant mode of assessment. Otherwise, we would seem to be unjustly assessing her according to some standard which was not her own.

A response is only non-accidentally correct, according to the definition given in 10.3 (see also 10.2), if it is made in an *absolutely safe* condition. A condition is defined as absolutely safe only if whatever response is made in that condition is bound to be right. It was also required that it must be the case that the person would not have made any response in that condition if the condition had not been absolutely safe.

To make sense of this we need the idea of a *type* of absolutely safe condition. Two absolutely safe conditions, c_1 and c_2, count as being of the same type only if the fact that c_1 is of the same type as c_2 is explanatory of the person's making any response at all in c_1, when the response actually made in c_1 is non-accidentally correct. The very idea of a non-accidentally correct response requires that there must be associated with it a type of absolutely safe condition.

Given the argument in 10.6, that non-arbitrary assessability requires structure, any response which expresses or manifests one concept must express or manifest at least two. There will then have to be at least the possibility of at least two non-accidentally correct responses which might be made by the person, which are relevantly similar to any particular intrinsically assessable response, and whose conditions of assessment are different. Each will therefore have to be associated with a different type of absolutely safe condition, on the conception of a *type* of absolutely safe condition outlined in the last paragraph. So, for every intrinsically assessable response, there must be at least two types of associated absolutely safe condition, corresponding to the at least two concepts expressed in the response.

Now let us try to recapitulate these points. To provide *understanding* of people and their behaviour, we need not only to be in a position to get the value of their responses right: we need to be in a position to get it right for the right reason. Getting it right for the right reason seems to require that we understand the basis of the assessability of those responses. If we know the relevant types of absolutely safe condition associated with each response, we would seem to have precisely an understanding of the basis of the responses' counting as intrinsically assessable. So it seems natural to suggest that when we are told what someone believes, what we are told is precisely what the relevant associated types of absolutely safe condition are.

Let us now relate this back in a slightly different way to the austerely extensionalist conception we imagined. To the austere extensionalist, nothing matters ultimately beyond getting the value of the responses right. If this were all that mattered, then '*a* believes that . . .' could be regarded as an extensional sentence operator, for every *a*. If we hope to get the value of *every* response right, we will no doubt want to constrain substitution further, in the construction of a general theory of a person.[10] But these further constraints on substitution are no more than a theoretical device for generating correct assignments of value. As far as what matters about the person goes, an austere extensionalist should think that any two sentences with the same truth value will be equally good for expressing the same belief.

On the richer conception of understanding people's behaviour which I have been developing, this cannot be adequate. On this conception, what we should be providing, when we say what someone believes, is an understanding of the types of absolutely safe condition which are associated with the response we are explaining. And that means that two sentences will only be intersubstitutable within the context introduced by '*a* believes that . . .', for any *a*, if both sentences present to us the same types of absolutely safe condition.

That in turn has two consequences for our conception of words and their use, which I shall try to explain and vindicate in Chapter 13. First, words must somehow themselves be associated with types of absolutely safe condition. Secondly, that association must be exploitable in such a way as to prohibit certain intersubstitutions within particular linguistic contexts, like those introduced by propositional-attitude verbs. Although the explanation will be left until the next chapter, we have reason from within the evaluative

---

[10] This is the tactic of Davidson, in 'Truth and Meaning', in *Inquiries into Truth and Interpretation*.

theory of content for thinking these two things must be possible: otherwise we would be left with the absurdly austere extensionalist conception of understanding people.

Finally, we can reformulate these points in a way which should be legitimate if the evaluative theory is even roughly on course so far. Given the notion of intrinsic assessability, and the correspondence between the definition of non-accidental correctness and the analysis of knowledge provided in Chapter 10, a response which is intrinsically assessable with respect to the value T and is non-accidentally correct will be an expression of knowledge. A type of absolutely safe condition for such intrinsically assessable responses will therefore determine what has to hold for a certain type of thing to be known. It would seem, then, that concepts are distinguished by the different conditions which have to obtain for one to count as having knowledge expressible in their terms.

We end up with the following conception of the explanation of behaviour in terms of belief. What we provide when we cite a belief to explain someone's behaviour is an understanding of what would have to obtain for her behaviour to count as an expression of knowledge. The sense of 'condition' in the earlier talk of conditions of assessment is determined by that thought: two statements count as statements of the same condition only if the same requirements would have to be met to count as knowing what is described by both statements.

Does this count as *explaining* behaviour? I do not see why not. A request for explanation is normally expressed in a question like: 'Why did she do that?' It seems entirely in tune with our understanding of the word 'why' to hear this as asking something like this: 'What was the significance (or meaning) of what she did?' I explain the significance of what she did by explaining what was at stake in what she did, what she was risking, what was required for her behaviour to have value. That seems exactly what we take ourselves to be doing when we describe a person's attitudes— provided we do not feel forced to think of ourselves as participating even here in the project of reliably predicting the redistribution of matter and energy in space and time.

And we get out of it a conception of belief and conceptual content which meets significant requirements among those which were imposed in Part II. First, our view of content is thoroughly externalist. If what I do when I describe someone's belief is tell you what would have to obtain for her behaviour to count as an expression of knowledge, I can hardly divorce the content of the belief from the world to which it applies. There is simply no place here for content which is not world-involving. Indeed, the point is pushed home emphatically once we explicitly introduce the conceptualism of Part I. Conceptualism was characterized as holding that the nature of an object, property, or fact is determined by what it would be to have knowledge of it. If what I do when I describe someone's belief is tell you what would have to obtain for her behaviour to count as an expression of knowledge, I must have told you, according to conceptualism, what the world is which her thoughts concern.

Secondly, we have shown how a theory of content can be extensionalist at base without being austerely extensionalist through and through. Even to fix the actual world value of actual responses, enough has to be recognized to provide richly non-extensional constraints on the use of words in reports of propositional attitude.

Thirdly, it seems to me that, in these last three sections, our knowledge of other people's beliefs has been portrayed by the evaluative theory as having very much the kind of character we ordinarily take it to have. What it would be to know that someone is liable to respond in ways which are intrinsically assessable with respect to the value T seems just like what it would be to know that someone believes something. If that is right, the evaluative theory is able to meet the fundamental conceptualist condition on reductions, which was set by the thought that the nature of an object, property, or fact is determined by what it would be to have knowledge of it. (This was called the *knowledge-constraint constraint* (C2), in 6.2.) That is, the evaluative theory of content seems able to *meet* the fundamental condition of adequacy for reductions, as well as being able, in effect, to generate it.

12.4. Mind and Body, Self and World

In Chapter 8 I claimed that a good conception of the kind of explanation of behaviour which we provide by describing someone's thoughts and feelings should show that a proper response to what is known as 'the mind–body problem' is inextricably linked with a proper conception of the relation between a subject and the world, and with a proper response to what is known as 'the problem of free will'. I shall now try to show that the conception of the explanation of behaviour which has been developed in this chapter meets that requirement. This will also serve as a kind of broad-brush summarizing sketch of the larger features of the evaluative theory.

It is important to notice the modesty of the requirement. I shall not be trying to 'solve' the alleged problems. Indeed, I suspect that any description of the issues involved which presents them as problematic must be a misdescription. Nor will I try to present a conception of the underlying issues which prevents any redescription of them which recreates the problems. I shall just show how the evaluative theory presents the issues as interconnected, and I will attempt to make it plausible that the theory contains at least the seeds of a conception of the issues which neither renders them problematic, nor evades any genuine difficulties.

To think that there is a mind–body problem is to think that there is something which needs to be explained and is difficult to explain. What is felt to need explanation is the alleged fact that mind and body interact, or that the mental and the physical interact. The evaluative theory acknowledges no such interaction, and therefore no such problem. Better than that, it shows vividly that there *could* be no such interaction. How could something like *significance* interact with physical properties? This would require that significance itself be causally efficacious, and that it might be a physically measurable effect of physical changes.

So the evaluative theory holds that the issues are misdescribed if we find ourselves talking about interaction. What is needed is rather to understand what might be called the presence of minds in a world which also contains the objects, events, and processes describable by natural science, and by physics in particular. It is worth emphasizing that the task is to *understand* something. Although it is not generally sensible to contrast understanding with explanation, talk of explanation here is likely to be misleading. What would it be to *explain* the presence of minds in a world which also contains physically describable things? It is likely to sound as if what is wanted is either an explanation of minds as arising out of what is physically describable, or else an explanation of the existence of the world itself.

But to ask that we should explain the presence of minds as arising out of what is physically describable seems to be insisting on a form of scientism: it is as if we are asking for a *scientific* explanation of the generation of mentality. We may explain in scientific terms the presence of things which we think of as having minds; but that they have minds is not itself explicable in those terms. And to ask that we should explain the existence of the world is to insist, in effect, that we explain why there is something rather than nothing. In the sense relevant here, the world is not the universe: it is 'the totality of facts'. And nothing brought *that* into existence.

The task, then, is more safely described as being to understand the presence of minds in a world which also includes physical facts. That in turn is to be thought of as a matter of understanding the relation between mental facts and physical facts. The evaluative theory can be regarded as performing this task in two stages.

The first stage consists of subsuming the class of mental facts within the more general class of facts about value, and then characterizing the relation between value facts and facts of other kinds, including physical facts. Facts about value in general are supervenient upon, but not reducible to, non-evaluative facts: this seems to be required for it to be possible to make mistakes about value, and yet that it be value, particularly, which one is thereby mistaken about (see 9.4). And non-evaluative facts in general, I take it, supervene upon physical facts. I take this to be a stipulative condition on physics counting as the fundamental science.

In the first stage of the characterization of the relation between mental and physical, the evaluative theory takes the relevant mental facts (facts about content) to be facts about responses. The responses cannot be individuated in physical (or indeed value-neutral) terms, any more than the values which they have can be reduced to the non-evaluative. But there can be no response without some non-evaluative, and indeed physical, condition or other obtaining; and there can be no distinction between responses between which there is no physical difference. There can only be responses of the relevant kind in a world which includes what natural sciences can describe.

The second stage of the characterization of the relation between mental and physical facts consists in the evaluative theory's specification of the distinguishing mark of the relevant kind of value of responses. The value of a response, to be of the kind relevant to a theory of content, must be such as to license an assessment of the person whose response it is on the basis of the assessment of the response. (Someone with a true belief is herself right.)

This provides a check upon the assessment of responses. The assessment of any particular response must fit the whole history of assessable responses in the life of the person whose response it is. The notion of a person appears here as the focus of a certain conception of narrative unity. (One need not think that the kind of fit that is required need be more precisely specifiable than as the kind of fit that is required to make sense of the history as the story of a single person.) The evaluative theory need not be expected to try to define the concept of a person in non-evaluative terms. But, once again, there could not be a person without things being somehow or other among the facts describable by natural science. Indeed, the evaluative theory has no need of the notion of a person who has made no intrinsically assessable response. The person cannot be separated from her behaviour, and the behaviour cannot be separated from the facts described by natural science.

It should be clear how this characterization links the evaluative theory's conception of the issues underlying the appearance of a mind–body problem with those other large areas of philosophical dispute which I claimed needed to be connected with it. Let us consider, first, the question of the relation between the subject and the world which is the matter of her thoughts. On the evaluative theory, the world about which someone is concerned is defined as that whose condition determines the value of her responses. More precisely, its nature is determined by what would make her responses count as manifestations of knowledge. Crucially, though, the condition of the world which determines the value of a response is held to be intrinsic to the response itself: it just would not have been that response in a different situation. If it is also essential to the notion of a person, as the notion is used in the evaluative theory, that a person must have a history of intrinsically assessable responses, we will not be able to make sense, within the theory, of a person—a subject of responses and attitudes—who is dislocated from the world about which she thinks.

That is hardly a definitive treatment of the issue of the relation between a subject and the world. But it was only meant to be a beginning. It seems to me to be beginning in the right direction. The general orientation can be summarized by reference to Kant, whose spirit has been fluttering at our shoulder all along. The demand that, if a response is to be intrinsically assessable, its value must attach to the person whose response it is provides a kind of transcendental deduction—which is not altogether unKantian—of the concept of a person.[11] But the notion of a person which is thereby vindicated or located is not the notion of a noumenal self, or anything like that. For the person which is needed is a person who responds. The responses, and therefore the person too, are necessarily situated in the world which is responded to. And the responses, and therefore the person too, can only exist in virtue of the facts which natural science describes being somehow or other.

So we can see how the evaluative theory makes a beginning on the task of describing the relation between a subject and the world. Finally, I shall briefly describe how the theory can make a similar beginning on the apparent problem of free will. The evaluative theory is committed to people being responsible in a certain fairly clear sense of 'responsible'. It must be legitimate to assess people themselves on the basis of the value of their responses. I am in that sense answerable for what I do, a proper subject for the extensive range of what P. F. Strawson calls 'reactive' attitudes (see 11.5). The theory is, therefore, committed to people being free, in whatever sense of freedom is required to make sense of that particular type of responsibility. Not only that: it is claimed that there can only be thoughts, even—there can only be things capable of being true and false—if there is freedom in the sense which that sense of responsibility requires.

That means that we are going to be very unhappy indeed about arguments which purport to show that we cannot be free in the relevant sense. Indeed, we cannot rationally accept their conclusions. I shall now try to indicate the general style of response to those arguments which the evaluative theory suggests. There will obviously be details and technicalities which cannot be dealt with here.

We can distinguish between two very general kinds of argument for the claim that we are not truly responsible: those which rest on determinism, and those which do not. Let us begin with the latter kind.

Galen Strawson has presented an argument against the possibility of true responsibility which seems to capture the essential features of all those, very natural, arguments which do not rely on

---

[11] See Kant, *Critique of Pure Reason*, B131–5.

determinism. Here is a swift summary of it.[12] If we act freely, we do so when our actions are explained by our thoughts and feelings. When thoughts and feelings explain an action, they determine it. If therefore, we really act freely on our thoughts and feelings, we must be able to choose freely the things which determine what we do— namely, our thoughts and feelings. But we can only choose those thoughts and feelings freely, if our choices are themselves explained by (further) thoughts and feelings. But if the choices are explained by thoughts and feelings, they must be determined by them. We seem swiftly driven to conclude, with Strawson: 'True self-determination is logically impossible because it requires the actual completion of an infinite regress of choices and principles of choice.'[13]

This argument clearly rests on the assumption that our thoughts and feelings determine our behaviour in a certain strong sense of 'determine'. The sense of 'determine' needs to be strong enough to sustain something like this: once our thoughts and feelings are fixed, our behaviour is, as it were, out of our hands. This means that we, as agents, can only get in on the act if we can choose our thoughts and feelings. And that leads to the regress. What has happened is that we have been supplanted, as doers of our own deeds, by our own psychologies. I argued in 8.6 that any view which has this consequence has thereby eliminated the whole category of behaviour which is apt for explanation in terms of thoughts and feelings, and has therefore eliminated thoughts and feelings too.

Strawson anticipates this kind of objection, and contends that it misdescribes his position. Here is what he says:

It can be true both (i) that *a* and only *a* performed A, and (ii) that to cite *a*'s reasons is to give a true and full explanation of A—although (ii) entails (iii) that *a*'s reasons were fully determinative of A *in the present sense* [emphasis added]. For (iii) is entirely compatible with (i). To discern a tension between (i) and (iii) is to adopt a view of the nature of the agent/reasons relation that is completely untenable, whatever its initial attractions.[14]

The problem with this response centres round the phrase I have italicized: 'in the present sense'. The only present sense of 'fully

---

[12] See G. Strawson, *Freedom and Belief*, 28–9.
[13] Ibid. 29.
[14] Ibid. 39.

determinative' which Strawson is here entitled to is that sense, whatever it is, in which thoughts and feelings must be determinative of behaviour if they are to be cited in true explanations of behaviour. The position which he rightly says is 'completely untenable' is one which imagines that one can act independently of one's thoughts and feelings. But Strawson's remark is only a response to the objection to his argument if it follows from thoughts and feelings being fully determinative of behaviour in *that* sense that, once our thoughts and feelings are fixed, our behaviour is out of our hands. But, as I see it, that could only follow if our status as the doers of our deeds consists in our being supplanted, as the doers of our deeds, by our own psychologies. Which is absurd.

In this chapter we have developed a sense in which thoughts and feelings determine behaviour which does not have this conse-quence. They determine behaviour in the sense that they determine *what it is*. If we are prepared to risk flirting with the dangers of the traditional translations of Aristotle's conception of explanation, we might say that thoughts and feelings determine behaviour as *formal*, rather than *efficient*, causes.[15] To say that someone does something for *this* reason is to say that *this* is its significance—and that it has this significance is essential to its being this behaviour. And this has no tendency to take our behaviour out of our hands. For it was required for the behaviour to be assessable in the right way—for it to be significant for the right reason—that the assessment of the behaviour licenses a corresponding assessment of the person whose behaviour it is. That is, our thoughts and feelings can *only* be determinative of our behaviour in the way that the evaluative theory proposes if our behaviour really is in our hands.

Strawson's argument does not become worthless, however. It can survive as an argument against causal theories of the explanation of behaviour, and against conceptions of the person which dislocate the self from her own mind or her own behaviour. In that guise, it looks very much like the kind of argument presented in 8.6.

Let that stand as an indication of the evaluative theory's capacity to respond to those arguments against the possibility of true responsibility which do not depend on determinism.

Arguments against the possibility of true responsibility which depend on determinism tend to be more technical, and rest on

---

[15]   Aristotle, *Physics*, 194^{b}23–195^{a}3.

complications about modality which cannot be dealt with here. I shall just address a simple thought which I think these arguments all depend on. This is something on which the evaluative theory of content has something distinctive to say.

If any science is deterministic, it seems that physics will be. This may be because it is a regulative principle of physics that it must be deterministic. (Quantum mechanics seems to be deterministic at the right level of description, and chaos theory deals with processes which are deterministic, even if they are unpredictable.) However this may be, it is surely physical determinism which provides the most vivid threat to true responsibility, if anything does.

Why should physical determinism seem to threaten true responsibility? We are moved, I think, by this simple thought. The inexorability of physical processes—if determinism is true—appears to *constrain* our behaviour, preventing apparent options from being real options. If deterministic physics did not seem to constrain—if it left us capable of doing as we like—it is hard to see how determinism could seem to threaten our freedom.

This simple thought has not been examined closely enough. How *could* physical processes constrain our behaviour? We need to have the idea that physical processes are determined, fixed in reality, quite independently of mental facts, and that, once fixed, the nature of those physical processes determines everything else, including our behaviour. This seems to require these three things to be true:

(1) The physical facts might have been the same even if there had been no minds.
(2) The physical facts necessitate our behaviour.
(3) It is not true that our behaviour necessitates, or even contributes to the necessitation of, what physics describes.

'Necessitation' here is to be understood non-causally, along the lines of *making true*.

(1) seems obviously false if we take it literally: the supervenience of everything upon physics requires that, if the physical facts are the same, everything else must be the same. Curiously, however, it is a certain natural understanding of supervenience itself which makes one try to find some sense in which (1) is true. One is tempted to think that the supervened-upon facts are always more *basic* than those which supervene upon them—and that in a sense of 'basic' which is not simply captured by saying that there can be no

difference in the supervening without some difference in the supervened upon. It is as if, we are inclined to think, that upon which everything supervenes is just *reality*, the hard ground beneath every superstructure. Or, to revert to the Humean phrase, it is as if physics 'discovers objects as they stand in nature, without addition or diminution',[16] whereas everything else—and mentality in particular—is a kind of overlay which is spread upon the top. This would give us a sense—hard to grasp though it might be—in which (1) could be true. In any sense in which we can understand the supervening as *constructed* or *spread* or *projected* upon a base, or lower level, we can also understand that there might have been the base or lower level *without* the supervening level.

This is a perennially appealing picture. We have come across a version of it before (see 9.4). Its rejection is essential to an evaluative theory of content. This is because the evaluative supervenes upon the non-evaluative; if truth is then a value, we cannot allow the supervening to be somehow metaphysically derivative from the supervened upon. Its rejection is also essential to conceptualism, since it is a form of Platonism to suppose that any particular form of vocabulary gets us nearer to the real shape of the world than any other.

I suggested in 9.4 that this kind of conception of supervenience derives from a certain view of how the world has to be if it is to be a properly unified world. The picture depends on a foundationalist conception of unity: all the facts must be of the same kind. But an alternative conception of a unified world has been developed to meet the need: there can be facts of irreducibly different kinds, provided that each kind requires the other kinds. From this perspective the powerful and undeniable need for value facts— given an evaluative theory of content—actually vindicates the non-evaluative, rather than vice versa. And the same vindication can be supplied from supervening facts of any kind for what they supervene upon. Once the Humean spell has been broken, as it must be if we are to maintain an evaluative theory of content, the view that the supervening is somehow secondary to the supervened upon should no longer mesmerize us.

This puts us in a position to deal with (2) and (3). There is nothing offensive about (2) in itself: supervenience already requires

[16] Hume, *Enquiry Concerning the Principles of Morals*, ed. Selby-Bigge, 294.

it. (It should be noted, however, that supervenience does not require that there be any way of isolating just those particular physical facts which are particularly relevant to any particular piece of behaviour.) (2) is only threatening in conjunction with (3). Who would worry if physics 'constrained' our behaviour, if we could also 'constrain' physics in our action? Indeed, it would be odd to call this *constraint*. We only have a sense of constraint if we think that *both* (2) and (3) are true.

But *is* there any reason to believe (3)? If I raise my hand, do I not put demands on physics? Do I not force the physical facts to be a certain way? Certainly, no physical theory can be true whose prediction of the redistribution of matter and energy is falsified by my action. Why is this not a matter of my action necessitating that things be a certain way among the facts that physics can describe? We can safely think it is, provided that we can hold on to the thought that the physical facts are only the way they are because they explain the non-physical things which they do in fact explain.

Two things might seem to create difficulties for this response to the appearance of a threat from physical determinism. First, someone might think that the response requires attributing to me capacities which I do not in fact possess. Thus, it might be said, I am physically incapable of jumping to the moon just if I feel like it. Does not this kind of mundane fact show that I really am constrained by physics?

I do not think it does. If we call my inability to jump to the moon just if I feel like it a *physical* incapacity, we are in danger of equivocating over the sense of 'physical'. It is a physical incapacity only in the sense that it is not psychological incapacity: it is not that I am just too cowardly to be able to do it. There must be some restrictions on my physical capacities, in this sense, for me to be a person at all. I can only behave in the real world if there are non-psychological features of my behaviour. And there can only be non-psychological features of my behaviour if there are some things I just cannot do, for non-psychological reasons. But the property of not being able to jump to the moon just if I feel like it is not a property which is described in the language of physics. This incapacity is to be *explained* by physics: it does not take physics to vindicate its reality. Moreover, I could have had this incapacity even if the physical facts had been quite importantly different from what they are. If the incapacity is not itself a property to be described in the language of physics, my inability to breach it is not an inability created by the determinism of physics.

The other source of difficulty for the response to the appearance of a threat from physical determinism comes from a certain conception of the idea of a physical law. If it is determined by the laws of physics that the fundamental units of matter and energy will be distributed in a certain way here and now, and if their being so distributed is incompatible with my not raising my hand, say—then it might seem that I could only have acted otherwise by somehow changing the laws of physics. But that is impossible, it will be said: they can only be laws in virtue of not being able to be changed.[17]

I think this has things back to front. The laws of physics can only be laws if they are compatible with everything I actually do. If I could have done otherwise, then the laws of physics could have been otherwise. This will not be a matter of my *changing* the laws of physics: that would involve there being a physical process as a result of which the laws of physics ended up different; in which case the physical process would not be describable by the laws of physics; so it would not be a physical process.

The threat here seems to derive from thinking of the modality of the laws of physics—whatever that may be—as somehow the ultimate modality, determining everything which is possible in any other way. But this in turn seems to depend on just the scientistic form of Platonism which appeared to underlie (1). We resist it by reiterating that the physical facts are only the way they are because they explain the non-physical things they do. If we hold to that picture, we can see that physics can introduce no new modality. Nothing can be necessary or impossible in virtue of physics which was not already necessary or impossible. If I ever could have done otherwise, I still can. Physics can do no more than find a vocabulary in which it can actually *formulate* laws which are governed by whatever necessity was there anyway. It cannot find a modality which was not already present in the non-physical facts about things which physics must explain.

Going any further in the investigation of physical determinism would require an examination of the modality of physical laws, and a consideration of the idea of being able to do otherwise, which this

---

[17] This seems to lie behind P. van Inwagen's phrase 'render false', in his 'The Incompatibility of Free Will and Determinism', *Philosophical Studies*, 27 (1975), 185–99.

is not the place for. I shall conclude just by considering three propositions:

(4) True responsibility requires the ability to do otherwise.
(5) The ability to do otherwise requires that no physical law be strictly necessary.
(6) If no physical law is strictly necessary there are no physical laws.

These three propositions might seem to threaten the idea of true responsibility. They do not. Nothing can threaten the idea of true responsibility. The notion of true responsibility in play here is that notion of responsibility relative to which our behaviour is only explicable in terms of thoughts and feelings if we are responsible for it. To abandon this notion of responsibility is to abandon thoughts and feelings, concepts and theories, truth and falsehood. No one can rationally do that.

Those three propositions do certainly threaten something, though. They threaten physics. It is for the sake of physics that one of those three must be dropped. The boot, it seems to me, is on the other foot.

Let that be an initial indication of the distinctive orientation on the question of free will and determinism which the evaluative theory of content provides.

13

Word-Meaning and Opacity

13.1. What Needs to be Explained

This chapter will make a programmatic beginning on showing how an evaluative theory of content can meet these two constraints from 6.3:

(C5) A theory of content must generate the right substitution conditions for belief contexts.

(C6) A theory of content must explain what it is for words to be meaningful in the way they are.

There are two respects in which what this chapter provides will be merely programmatic. First, I shall attempt to show in outline how to get fine-grained intensionality only for the case of the kinds of expression covered by the definitions given in 9.5. Secondly, (C6) itself requires a complete philosophy of language: I shall just make some preliminary moves. Some constraints will be imposed implicitly on how language must be thought of if the evaluative theory of content is correct, but I shall not supply the complete philosophy of language which would ultimately be needed.

The question we need to address is what words have to be doing in belief contexts if they are to be subject to the kind of rich intensionality which plausibility and conceptualism both require; and therefore, correlatively, how it is that words can be subject to such constraints upon intersubstitution. A helpful focus is provided by Davidson's question, raised in connection with the related context of indirect speech: 'What are these familiar words doing here?'[1] The task is to understand how words can be constrained in the right way with respect to substitution *just in virtue of* properties they must anyway possess. We do not want to be bolting on extra properties in an *ad hoc* way, simply in order to achieve surface plausibility. For one thing, this would make it hard to see how belief reports could be understood in the way they can, by ordinary speakers of English (for example).

[1] D. Davidson, 'On Saying That', in his *Inquiries into Truth and Interpretation*, 94.

Davidson's question is often seen as a request for a semantic theory which shows that the behaviour of words in belief contexts is a function of (algorithmically deducible from) an initial assignment of semantic value, which is justified solely by their contribution to the semantic value of sentences which do *not* involve belief contexts. There is clearly something right about the motivation for this demand, but I think the insistence that the account of the function of words in belief contexts should be provided by a *semantic theory* is misplaced. I shall raise in 13.2 a general worry about the kind of approach to language which this seems to presuppose. But for now we should note just that it is unobvious that the use of words should always be so simply derivable from an initial semantic assignment—if it is not simply to be brushed aside as a merely pragmatic matter. The notorious intelligibility of such things as 'But me no buts' ought at least to make one pause before assuming that understanding should be modelled algorithmically.

I shall, therefore, confine myself to the more modest task of showing that fine-grained opacity within belief contexts can be secured by appealing to no more than might be required to understand the very same words *outside* belief contexts. And in talking about what might be required to understand those words outside belief contexts, I shall simply appeal to our sense, as people who understand English, of what obviously *is* required in certain situations. There might be a task here for a semantic theory to try to model that understanding, but for our purposes we do not actually need a semantic theory. All we need is the fact that we do understand words in the required way. That will be enough to answer Davidson's question: no miraculous new properties will need to be appealed to in order to explain the role of words in belief contexts.

The detailed claims about particular uses of particular kinds of expression will therefore rest on a direct appeal to what everyone who understands English can see. But something must be done in a general way to show that words already have at least the right *sort* of property to be capable of being subject to the relevant constraints. We need at least the outline of a theory of the nature of words even to get started here.

I shall try to provide a suitable outline of an account of the nature of words in 13.2. In 13.3 I shall address in a general way the question of what we are doing with words in belief contexts. The rest of the chapter will then be concerned with more detailed questions of intensionality for particular cases.

The chapter will inevitably leave an explanatory gap between the general account of what words are, which explains how they can be subject to the right *kind* of explanatory constraint, and the detailed suggestions about particular words, which rest on a direct appeal to the detailed understanding which ordinary speakers of English have. I think this gap presents no difficulty of principle, but it could only be bridged by a much more thorough philosophy of language than I can provide here.

13.2. Words

In 12.3 I offered a general account of the kind of explanation of behaviour we provide when we say what someone believes. The report of belief tells us the condition which has to be met for her confidence not to be misplaced, for her behaviour not to be inept or inappropriate. And the report of belief does not just provide us with a capacity to get the value of her behaviour right: it also reveals the basis of the assessment of the behaviour in relevantly similar non-accidentally correct responses. It can only do that if the words in the 'that'-clause of the belief report are associated with *types of absolutely safe condition* (in the sense of 10.2). They will then reveal the conditions which have to be met for the response we are explaining to count as an expression of knowledge. And that provides the fundamental constraint on substitution within belief contexts: two expressions will only be intersubstitutable within belief contexts if they are associated with the same type of absolutely safe condition, and therefore are equivalently revealing of the conditions which have to be met for the response in question to count as an expression of knowledge. What we need to do, then, is to explain how words *can* be associated with types of absolutely safe condition.

The general idea here is not at all new. Frege held that the condition which two expressions have to meet to be inter-substitutable within belief contexts is that they must have the same *sense*. Sameness or difference of sense he held to be determined by sameness or difference in the *mode of presentation* of the referent which is associated with the words.[2] The notion of a mode of presentation of something—of a way in which something is given—is essentially epistemological. I suggest that the notion of a *type of absolutely safe condition* provides an analysis of the notion of a mode of presentation. I shall accordingly use the notion of a mode of presentation to refer to the relevant epistemological mark of distinction between concepts, counting a mode of presentation just as a type of absolutely safe condition, on the assumption that the evaluative theory's analysis of knowledge is broadly right. That means that we can proceed with the rest of this chapter using the more familiar technical terminology of Fregean theories.

Under this redescription, the task we now face is the familiar one of making it intelligible that a word (either generally, or as it is used on a particular occasion) can be *associated with* a particular mode of presentation. The question to ask here is: why should it seem so difficult?

The problem is created by what we might call either the *chess-piece* or the *semanticist* conception of the nature of words—according to the character of our opponent. This kind of position is defined by its acceptance of the thesis of the *arbitrariness of the sign*: for any particular word, that very word could have meant something different. It is a contingent fact, on this view, that the word *red* applies to all and only red things. (It will also follow that it can only be known a posteriori: no knowledge of the nature of the word could allow one to infer its meaning a priori, since its meaning is not strictly part of the nature of the word.)

This conception of the nature of words is not quite as old as the hills, but only because the hills are very old indeed. It would be quicker to name those philosophers who have *not* held it than those who have. It is the conception which is Wittgenstein's concern in this famous paragraph:

Every sign *by itself* seems dead. *What* gives it life?—In use it is *alive*. Is life breathed into it there?—Or is the *use* its life?[3]

Anyone who thinks that the second sentence here asks a good question has already bought the ancient conception of the nature of words.

[2] Frege, 'On Sense and Meaning', in Frege, *Collected Papers on Mathematics, Logic, and Philosophy*, ed. B. McGuinness 158.
[3] L. Wittgenstein, *Philosophical Investigations*, trans. G. E. M. Anscombe (2nd edn., Oxford: Blackwell, 1958), i. 432.

If any particular word could have meant something else, how does it get to mean what it does? There seems no way in which it could have got its meaning except by having that meaning somehow *assigned* to it. Perhaps we do not need to think of the assignment as a deliberate act, ratified by explicit convention. But somehow a meaning will need to be *conferred* upon it which was not already intrinsic to it.

On an evaluative conception of content, conferring meaning upon something will be conferring some evaluative property on it. But it is hard to make sense of conferring a value upon something— whether it is done deliberately or not—if conferring value does not serve some other good, if the thing's having that value does not serve some *function*. It seems inevitable, then, that the thesis of the arbitrariness of the sign will involve some conception of the function of language.

It should come as no surprise to find that, as a matter of historical fact, those who have accepted the thesis of the arbitrariness of the sign have indeed supposed that language has a function. Their conception of the function of language has determined what they take to be assigned as the meaning of words. There are two broad traditions here. Here is Locke, representing one: 'The Comfort and Advantage of Society, not being to be had without Communication of Thoughts, it was necessary, that Man should find out some external sensible Signs, whereby those invisible *Ideas*, which his thoughts are made up of, might be made known to others.'[4] And he concludes accordingly: '*Words in their primary and immediate Signification, stand for nothing, but the* Ideas *in the mind of him that uses them.*'[5] Russell, representing the other tradition, says this: 'The essential business of language is to assert or deny facts.'[6] And he held that the meaning of a proper name is the object in the real world for which it stands.

The problems of these two views are familiar. Quite apart from the fact that it gives a very bizarre view of communication, Locke's view makes it hard to understand how words could be applied to *objects* at all (as he himself says). And Russell's view makes it impossible for there to be a finer-grained intensionality than factual

---

[4] J. Locke, *An Essay Concerning Human Understanding*, III. ii. 1; ed. P. Nidditch (Oxford: Clarendon Press, 1975), 405.

[5] Ibid. III. ii. 2; ed. Nidditch, 405.

[6] B. Russell, 'Introduction' to L. Wittgenstein, *Tractatus logico-philosophicus*, trans. D. Pears and B. McGuinness (London: Routledge and Kegan Paul, 1961), p. x.

equivalence; and so cannot account for belief reports being governed by the conditions on intersubstitution we all ordinarily believe in. (In the terminology of Chapter 3, it forces us into a 'facts-first' theory.) And this is quite apart from the oddity of Russell's conception when we think about the essential business of most of our activities when we speak.

But despite their faults, these two theories do at least provide clear and cohesive—if not coherent—conceptions of the function of language, if that is what we want. A Fregean theory, by contrast, will look very strange if we accept the thesis of the arbitrariness of the sign. We seem to need to assign to each expression not one thing—an idea, or a referent, or whatever—but two: the normal sense of the word and its normal referent. But this seems hard to motivate in terms of function, and it seems a puzzle that a particular kind of sense and a particular kind of referent should go together. It looks, from the point of view of the ancient conception of words, just an *ad hoc* manœuvre to deal with intensionality.

Things do not seem much better if we suppose that sense determines reference. Is the idea that we assign just the *sense* of each word, leaving the referent to fall out by implication? There is an intuitive difficulty with this, even if it is not easy to argue for precisely. Whatever is assigned as the meaning of an antecedently meaningless thing seems always to be taken as the referent: witness Locke apparently holding that words *refer* to the user's ideas. A Fregean theory would then seem, like Locke's, not to allow that words ordinarily refer to their ordinary referents. Alternatively, we might still insist on the need to assign explicitly both sense and reference; in which case we seem to be left with the appearance of an *ad hoc* device to deal with belief contexts. Words would seem to be being assigned a sense just as something for them to refer to in contexts of propositional attitude.

All this will make a Fregean theory look unattractive. I take it that it is this kind of appearance of oddity which makes Davidson say this:

Since Frege, philosophers have become hardened to the idea that content-sentences in talk about propositional attitudes may strangely refer to such entities as intensions, propositions, sentences, utterances, and inscriptions. What is strange is not the entities, which are all right in their place (if they have one), but the notion that ordinary words for planets, people, tables, and hippopotami in indirect discourse may give up these pedestrian references for the exotica. If we could recover our pre-Fregean semantic innocence, I think it would seem to us plainly incredible that the words 'The earth moves', uttered after the words 'Galileo said that', mean anything different, or refer to anything else, than is their wont when they come in other environments.[7]

This point seems to me entirely just, if we take 'refer' here to mean what it ordinarily does. And it seems to me that we will inevitably find ourselves taking the word 'refer' in that way, in describing the relation between a word and its sense when it is used in 'indirect' contexts, if we think of a word as having its sense because that sense has been *assigned* to it.

We have seen how a Fregean theory looks odd if we accept the thesis of the arbitrariness of the sign. I think that this is the only reason for thinking that a Fregean theory is odd. And I think the problem is not with the Fregean idea that words are associated with modes of presentation—or, on the evaluative theory, with types of condition of absolute safety—but with the thesis of the arbitrariness of the sign. So I shall argue briefly against that thesis and suggest an alternative conception of the nature of words. On that alternative conception, there is no serious problem for a Fregean theory.

The first thing to note about the thesis of the arbitrariness of the sign is that what is standardly used as the argument for it is no argument for it at all. Here is Locke again:

Thus we may conceive how *Words*, which were by Nature so well adapted to that purpose, come to be made use of by Men, as *the Signs of* their *Ideas*; not by any natural connexion, that there is between particular articulate Sounds and certain *Ideas*, for then there would be but one Language amongst all Men; but by a voluntary Imposition, whereby such a Word is made arbitrarily the Mark of such an *Idea*.[8]

Clearly, to think of words as just *sounds* is already to accept the arbitrariness of the sign. When that is stripped away, the argument is just this: the meaning of a word cannot be intrinsic to it, for otherwise it would be impossible for different words to mean the same thing. But that is just fallacious. The fact that *that* word could not have meant something different does not in the least prevent a different word from meaning what that word means.

---

[7] Davidson, 'On Saying That', *Inquiries into Truth and Interpretation* 108.
[8] Locke, *Essay*, III. ii. 1; ed. Nidditch, 405.

Secondly, we should be very suspicious of any theory which is inclined to treat words as just sounds, or just marks, because its motivation seems to be generally scientistic. It appears to be being assumed that the fundamental individuation of things is that which natural science might underwrite. Things so defined are assumed to be the proper object of our enquiry when we are investigating meaning; but it is hard to see any reason for this assumption other than the general assumption of scientism.

After those preliminary softening-up points, I shall now try to argue against the thesis of the arbitrariness of the sign. It is important to note first the generality of the thesis: all words are held to be so constituted that their meaning is not intrinsic to their nature. It will, therefore, be enough to refute the thesis, and to clear the way for an alternative conception of words, if we can show that we must think that at least some words have their meaning as intrinsic to them.

I will try to argue that one cannot make sense of the idea of word-meaning at all, unless one accepts the category of words which are essentially meaningful. Consider Tarski's famous sentence:

(1) 'Snow is white' is true if and only if snow is white.[9]

Tarski used this kind of schema to generate a condition which would make any predicate which met it count as a *truth* predicate—a predicate the conditions of whose application to sentences are *truth* conditions. Tarski's condition ('Convention T') was, in effect, that a predicate counts as a truth predicate if the condition for its application to any sentence can be stated by using a sentence which gives the *meaning* of that sentence. Thus, we might say, (1) is true because this is true:

(2) 'Snow is white' means that snow is white.

(I shall assume for present purposes that this is a grammatically decent way of stating the meaning of a sentence: we will ignore the apparent suggestion that a sentence determines the colour of snow.)

Now why is (2) true? Obviously because the quoted occurrence of 'Snow is white' means the same as the unquoted occurrence. But that means that what we are quoting is something which is already conceived of as having meaning. According to the thesis of the

[9] A. Tarski, 'The Semantic Conception of Truth', *Philosophical and Phenomenological Research*, 4 (1944), 405.

arbitrariness of the sign, this conception of the sentence must be a conception of it in terms of some properties which are inessential to it. The quoted use of 'Snow is white' now means something like this: the sentence which actually means that snow is white. So (2) is equivalent to this:

(3) The sentence which actually means that snow is white means that snow is white.

And (1) is equivalent to this:

(4) The sentence which actually means that snow is white is true if and only if snow is white.

Now here is the problem: how are we to understand the *first* use of 'means' in (3), and the use in (4)? What would count as a statement of the *meaning* of a sentence? The difficulty is not over finding an analysis of the notion of meaning here (though that might indeed be difficult). The problem is just to fix the *analysandum*. And the problem is acute: I cannot see any way of fixing the relevant notion of meaning which does not presuppose that sentences, the things which have meaning, are to be conceived of precisely *as* things which have meaning. The problem is often overlooked; it is too easily simply assumed that we have a clear idea of what word-meaning or sentence-meaning is. Certainly we do; but the question of what that clear idea rests on is forgotten.

Here are two ways of trying to fix the relevant notion of meaning. First, we might say that, on the relevant notion of meaning, a sentence can always be used to state its own meaning. This might run into trouble over indexicals, but, in any case, it requires one to think of a sentence as already having meaning. Alternatively, we might point to paradigmatic cases, like (2). But these cases only work as paradigms on the assumption that what is referred to by quotation already has meaning, and has the meaning it is naturally taken to have. (This second tactic, I take it, is in effect Tarski's own for the case of truth: statements like (1) are taken to be paradigmatic uses of 'true' as a predicate of sentences; and that in turn vindicates Convention T.)

Someone might hope to avoid the difficulty by using some formulation inspired by Tarski, like this:

(5) 'Snow is white' means-in-English that snow is white.

There are two ways in which we can understand this semantic predicate. On the first, it is defined in its application by a set of axioms and transformation rules within a semantic 'theory' (that is, *assignment*) for what might as well be regarded as a formal language. In that case, this question arises: why should we think that what is assigned as a result of applying those transformation rules to those axioms is *meaning*? (This, in effect, is the version for meaning of the problem for truth which Tarski's Convention T was designed to settle.) I cannot see any alternative to an appeal to examples—like (2), for instance. (And this is the version for meaning of the solution which Tarski provided for the problem over truth.)

Alternatively, one might understand the semantic predicate in (5) as a genuinely structured predicate, to understand which one must already know something about meaning. We might then suggest one of two reformulations of (5). The first represents it as saying just this:

(6) The English sentence 'Snow is white' means that snow is white.

But this again thinks of a sentence as something which means something. The second reformulation of (5), which takes the semantic predicate as genuinely structured, represents it as saying this:

(7) English-speakers would naturally take 'Snow is white' as meaning that snow is white.

But what is meant by the idea of taking a sentence *as* meaning that snow is white? We seem to need the idea that I can take the sentence 'snow is white', as it occurs unquoted in (7), as giving the meaning of a sentence, or as saying what a sentence means. But that brings in the notion we began with, which seems intelligible only by appeal to such paradigms as (2).

One could try various further alternatives, but the difficulty seems bound to recur. The problem is just this: we seem to have no fix on a notion of a word or a sentence meaning something which does not rest on a conception of words or sentences precisely *as* meaning something.

This is not quite enough on its own for the claim that one can only get a fix on the notion of a word or sentence meaning something, if one relies on a notion of a linguistic expression which is essentially meaningful; but it is nearly there. What we need to add is just that the sense of thinking of something *as* being thus and so, which is involved here, determines the identity of the things in question. And we surely have this here.

Our conception of what it is for a sentence to mean something seems to depend upon such paradigms as (2), or upon such statements as (2), considered as paradigms. To count (2) as a paradigm here requires that one read it in a certain way: it has to come out a priori. Failing to count it as true is a mark of failing to understand it in the required way. But (2) can only be a priori if the quoted and the unquoted occurrences of 'Snow is white' mean the same, and have to be understood as meaning the same for (2) to be understood.

But if that is true, what is thought to mean that snow is white must mean that snow is white, and not mean anything else. But that is enough to ensure that any inscriptions which look like my writing of 'Snow is white', or which sound like my sayings of it, but which mean either nothing, or not that, are not inscriptions or sayings of that very sentence. All that can count as an inscription of the sentence I refer to in (2), if (2) is taken as a paradigm case, is something which means the same. That is, I seem inevitably to be referring to an object—a sentence-type, if you like—whose meaning is essential to its identity.

The conclusion of this argument is that we can have no conception of a linguistic expression *meaning* something, in the sense of meaning we want, unless we allow ourselves a conception of linguistic expressions which are *essentially* meaningful, which, indeed, essentially mean what they do. Perhaps we can also make sense of linguistic expressions which do not essentially mean what they do. That is irrelevant. All that matters is that the thesis of the arbitrariness of the sign cannot be maintained in general.

This argument might seem implausibly abstract to be getting at the heart of what is wrong with the thesis of the arbitrariness of the sign. But I think that consideration of what the argument relies on shows that it is at least close to the point. The problem is that, in proposing the thesis, a theorist assumes that she has a clear notion of what word-meaning or sentence-meaning is. But the thesis itself would undermine the right to appeal to that clear notion. We have another version of the recurrent problem of a theory which saws off the branch on which it stands.

We have seen that the thesis of the arbitrariness of the sign seems scientistic; we have seen that it has difficulty in making sense of the position of the theorist herself. One might wonder whether the thesis is Platonistic, since it has these Platonistic-seeming features.

This is not the place to develop these points in detail here; a full response to Platonism about language would soon develop into a whole philosophy of language. But the charge of Platonism against the thesis of the arbitrariness of the sign does seem reasonable. The thesis appears to require that words be assigned meaning in fulfilment of some function of language. What would count as fulfilling that function has to be fixed independently of language for this to make sense. And to talk of function here, we must be able to imagine an inept assignment, one which did not get the words to fulfil the function which they are meant for. There is a standard, independent of language, to which language must conform.

It seems to follow from this that the thesis of the arbitrariness of the sign must take it to be an open question whether an assignment has worked. But given the function of an assignment, this means that it is an open question whether words are meaningful. And the same applies to all words at once. It has to be an open question whether any of our words actually work, whether our language has managed to be meaningful at all. But, in that case, the standard which words have to meet cannot be described in language—at least, we have no reason for thinking that what we take to be a description of the standard really is a description of that. The phrase 'things as they are in themselves' inevitably describes the way things are as the language portrays them. We then seem to have a problem for philosophy, which itself is a linguistic activity. We seem to have a philosophy which denies philosophy any right to think that what it is talking about is what it takes itself to be talking about.

This appears to be repeating the problems that were raised for Platonism in Part I. We can draw the link closer. If the thesis of the arbitrariness of the sign is committed, as I think it is, to the idea that language must conform to some standard which is fixed independently of it, we should ask whether that standard is fixed independently of the concepts of things which our words express. If it is, the thesis is directly Platonist, in the sense of Part I: we have the idea of the world being a certain way independently of our concepts, with our concepts having to live up to it. If it is not, then if language has to fit some independent standard, the standard is set by the concepts themselves. The concepts expressed by our words have to be fixed independently of the words themselves, and it becomes an open question whether our words really express the concepts they are meant to express.

It would follow from this that, if I use some such expression as 'the concept "red"', it must be an open question whether I have managed to refer to the right concept, or indeed to any concept at all. Someone could understand all about the use of the word *red* (dictated by the imagined assignment of meaning), and still not know what the concept "red" was, or even that there was such a concept. But it seems to me that we have no grip on the relevant notion of concept here. The only notion of concept which has been in play is one which takes concepts to be essentially what words may express. Our only conception of a concept is of something which we take ourselves to be expressing when we use words.

If the formulation of conceptualism in Part I was a suitable response to Platonism in relation to concepts, we might expect the denial of Platonism about language to look very similar. This was the denial of Platonism in relation to concepts:

(B) The nature of the objects, properties, and facts to which our concepts correspond is not fixed independently of the nature of the concepts which correspond to them.

The denial of Platonism about language ought then to look something like this:

(C) The nature of the things described by our words, and of the concepts expressed by our words, is not fixed independently of the nature of the words in question.

Am I prepared to accept that?

I see no reason not to. Clearly there is a threat that (C) will be read as an expression of an absurd idealism. The same threat was faced by (B), and dealt with in 1.3. I can see no reason not to adopt the same kind of response here. The solution is to see words, in the sense relevant to (C), as being timelessly existing things. A word is what everyone who uses the same word uses. We can think of it as an abstraction from all uses of it. There is a condition to be met by anyone who is to count as using that word in particular. The statement of the condition is an atemporal truth. The timeless existence of a word is a matter of there being an atemporally true condition which has to be met to count as using that word in particular.

The result of this seems to me to be exactly right. It is no longer a kind of accident that a use of that word is an expression of that concept, or part of a conversation about that object. And it seems to me to do no harm at all to think of words as abstract entities in this way. The temptation to think of words as concrete particular individuals is not readily distinguishable from the inclination to accept the thesis of the arbitrariness of the sign, and a scientistic conception of word-identity. (And we might note that the object to whose essential meaningfulness we are committed if we are to understand sentence-meaning at all is an abstract object, a sentence-type.)

These points need further development. For the moment I shall rest with the claim that the denial of the thesis of the arbitrariness of the sign is precisely in tune with the general conception of metaphysics which the evaluative theory of content was designed to conform to, and which it itself expresses.

Having cleared the ancient conception of the nature of words out of the way, we now need to replace it with an alternative which will enable words to play the roles in belief contexts which the evaluative theory requires them to. The natural suggestion, in the light of the criticisms of the thesis of the arbitrariness of the sign, is a simple one. Words are respects in which responses may resemble one another. More precisely, they are features of *evaluatively relevant* similarity between responses. An evaluatively relevant similarity between responses is one which licenses similar assessment of the responses in question.[10]

This suggestion seems to me to show nicely what is wrong with the thesis of the arbitrariness of the sign, and to get us in a position to explain opacity. If we think of *speech*, it is extremely natural to think of words as similarities between responses. We cannot think of the sounds we make when we utter particular words as things which we manœuvre around like chess-pieces. The sounds we make are precisely properties of our behaviour when we speak. Once words are written, of course, the temptation to think of words as concrete particular individuals increases. But it still seems natural to see the marks on a page as the residue of the behaviour of writing

---

[10] It should be clear that I am largely in sympathy with what D. Kaplan says in 'Words', *Aristotelian Society Supplementary Volume*, 64 (1990), 93–119. My proposal seems to fit words to behaviour more smoothly than Kaplan's (that words are a kind of continuant).

them, meaningful precisely in virtue of being reliable indicators of the character of the writing behaviour.

The suggestion also explains why it is so difficult to individuate words, as we naturally think of words, without appeal to meaning. As we naturally think of words, marks in the sand which just happen to look like type-face inscriptions of English words are not really words. Noises which just happen to sound like a friend's utterance of particular English words are not really words. German words are different from English words, even if they look or sound the same. And yet wildly different accents can all voice the same word, and wildly different handwritings can all inscribe it. The idea of individuating words without appeal to the kinds of fact which fix meaning seems doomed. This is only to be expected on the suggestion I have just made, since it involves the attempt to define in non-evaluative terms what counts as evaluatively relevant; and the basic assumption of the evaluative theory of content was that that is impossible.

Finally, we seem to get just what we want for an account of opacity. Words can only be evaluatively relevant if use of the same word licenses similar assessment of the behaviour of which that word is a feature. But it can only license similar assessment if use of the same word is correlated with something similar about the basis of the assessment of the behaviour in question. The basis of the assessment of the behaviour is the type of condition of absolute safety which would have to obtain for that behaviour to count as an expression of knowledge. So words must be associated with types of condition of absolute safety, or modes of presentation. How does a particular word get to be correlated with a particular type of condition of absolute safety, or mode of presentation? That type of condition of absolute safety, that mode of presentation, is simply defined as that which is associated with that word, with that similarity between responses.

Once the link with conditions of absolute safety is made, we have the materials for explaining both of the kinds of intensionality which a theory of content needs to explain. The very idea of a word is the idea of something which introduces a distinctive condition for knowledge. For the word *red*, say, to be meaningful, there must already be something which it would be to know that something is red. But that is enough to fix the nature of the property of redness, according to the knowledge constraint of 5.1. On the other hand, the word *red* might be associated with a particular way of knowing about that property: there is room for two words to be associated with different ways of knowing about the same thing. And that will be enough to allow that there can be informative redescriptions of the same fact, as was required for any interesting metaphysical theory (see Chapter 3).

Moreover, since a particular type of condition of absolute safety, a particular mode of presentation, must be associated with a word for it to be meaningful at all, there will be no mystery about a linguistic context (belief contexts, for example) within which words may only be intersubstituted if they are associated with the same mode of presentation. There is no *ad hoc* appeal to something which is introduced just for the sake of solving certain semantic puzzles. What we need to appeal to was always already there in the words themselves.

This means that there is no problem in principle with a Fregean approach to belief contexts. It is true that in a Fregean *semantic theory* sense will have to be *assigned* to words, in addition to their reference. But this is just the way that semantic theories work: they try to model by assignment what is there unassigned in natural language. Once we see that natural language is not meaningful in virtue of any assignment, and that words need sense in order to have reference, there can be no reason to restrict our assignments in semantic theories to what we can see a point in having been assigned to the words of natural language, and no reason to cavil at a semantic theory which assigns sense as well as reference.

This should be enough to make it plausible in principle that an evaluative theory of content has the materials for explaining intensionality. There are two kinds of issue which have not yet been addressed. First, there are the huge issues about the nature of language and the learning of language which have only been broached here. This is not the place to pursue those. Secondly, there is the question of how exactly I need to think that I am using words in belief contexts if they are to be subject to the restrictions which we think they are subject to. That question is what I shall turn to next.

13.3. Using Words to Report Beliefs

If we are to make sense of reports of belief, and of the fact that the words we use are subject to tight constraints on substitution, it is not enough just to say that words already have the right kind of property to be so constrained. We need also to be able to tell a plausible story about what we are doing with the words in belief contexts, which will explain how that property comes to be exploited.

Modern conceptions of propositional attitudes have been heavily influenced by Quine. Here is his influential account of what we are doing with words in contexts of propositional attitude:

in indirect quotation, we project ourselves into what, from his remarks and other indications, we imagine the speaker's state of mind to have been, and then say what, in our language, is natural and relevant for us in the state thus feigned . . . Correspondingly for the other propositional attitudes, for all of them can be thought of as involving something like quotation of one's imagined verbal response to an imagined situation.[11]

For Quine, the ascription of attitudes involves using an 'essentially dramatic idiom'.

This account is certainly wrong, since it delivers the wrong results for perspective-biased expressions. Where I would normally say,

(1) She believes that she is rather clever,

on the most natural reading of that report, Quine's account would have me say,

(2) She believes that I am rather clever,

which is quite another thing. It might be tempting just to make an exception for perspective-biased expressions, and try to patch up the account that way. But this would involve nothing less than abandoning the account. It is essential to the kind of dramatic role-playing which Quine imagines that one should speak from the perspective of the subject, that one should speak as if one were she.

This fault might seem to be a merely superficial difficulty, but we can see, from the perspective of the evaluative theory, that it actually strikes to the heart of the problem with Quine's conception. The problem is that the perspective one adopts when one plays the part of someone else is not a perspective from which she can be evaluated, from which her behaviour can be assessed. From within

---

[11] W. V. Quine, *Word and Object* (Cambridge, Mass.: MIT Press, 1960), 219; essentially the same view is held by S. Stich, *From Folk Psychology to Cognitive Science* (Cambridge, Mass.: MIT Press, 1983), 81–4.

the perspective of her belief, that belief cannot be questioned: the question whether she is right can only be raised from what we might call an interpretative distance.[12] Empathy may be a device one uses in order to reach an understanding of someone else, but empathy itself cannot constitute understanding. (This, incidentally, fits well with the account I gave of the phenomenology of our own current beliefs at the end of 12.1.)

This problem is reflected in the fact that Quine's conception of what we are doing when we report another's belief does not make us do what it was required that we do, by the account of the explanation of behaviour (see 12.3). There it was said that what I supply, when I tell you the belief in the light of which someone does something, is a description of the condition which has to obtain for her behaviour not to be inept. That is, I must tell you how the world she is thinking about must stand, if her confidence is not to be misplaced. But on the Quinean picture, there is a sense in which I am not describing a condition of the world at all: I am simply pretending to be her. Perhaps the pretence has *her* describing the world, but *I* am not here describing the world, or a condition which the world must meet for her to be right. (No more than an actor playing Hamlet speculates on whether he should commit suicide, when he utters the words 'To be, or not to be'.) For this reason, a report of belief in Quine's style would not locate the behaviour in the world, as I claimed that it must: it would simply produce more behaviour.

The simple conception of role-playing that Quine provides is therefore inadequate as a view of what we are doing with words when we report someone's belief. But the idea that there is something dramatic about belief reports does not seem altogether mistaken. After all, it is not all right for me just to describe the relevant facts in any way which I find convenient: that would collapse the distinction between factual equivalence and conceptual equivalence which is required for there to be informative redescriptions of the same facts (see Chapter 3). What we need is the idea that I describe the world, or a condition which the world must meet, from my perspective, from where I stand, but nevertheless in the way that the subject thinks of it. How can we make sense of that?

[12] Compare H.-G. Gadamer, *Truth and Method*, trans. W. Glen-Doepel (London: Sheed and Ward, 1975), 258–74; but Gadamer seems to think that the important kind of distance is temporal.

If I assert something, the words I use indicate how my behaviour should be assessed in virtue of the fact that a distinctive mode of presentation is associated with each word as I then use it. Someone understands my words, as I use them on that occasion, only if they know which modes of presentation are associated with them. Only then will she be in a position to give the right value to my response for the right reason. There is nothing difficult about telling which modes of presentation are associated with my words: they are simply the ones that have to be recognized by anyone who is to count as understanding what I say. (Some examples of the kind of thing which is involved here will be given in the next section.)

Suppose, then, that I assert (with a picture of Socrates before me):

(3) That ugly man is a philosopher.

To understand my behaviour, you need to know the modes of presentation associated with my words. Now suppose that I see someone else looking at a book of pictures of famous Greeks. She reacts to a picture of Socrates in a strangely ambivalent way. That response might be intrinsically assessable with respect to the value T as good if and only if that ugly man is a philosopher. Suppose it is. Suppose too that the basis of such an assessment of her reaction is in modes of presentation which are the same as those which you need to recognize as underlying my response in order to understand my assertion of (3). In that case, my assertion of (3) describes a condition which the world has to meet for her response to be appropriate, and does it in a way which reflects the basis of the assessability of *her* behaviour. In other words, my assertion describes a condition of the world, but it describes it just as she thinks of it.

This much would give us the right, in effect, to reports of the form '*a* believes truly that *p*', which imposed whatever degree of intensionality can be made sense of on the basis of the idea of modes of presentation. We are restricted to reports only of what are accepted as true beliefs by the fact that so far we have only admitted beliefs whose content the reporter is also prepared to assert. We get the full range of beliefs if we simply drop the dependence on assertion.

This leaves us with the following account. We can capture the content of someone's beliefs by describing the condition of the world which has to obtain for her behaviour not to be inept, and doing so in such a way that, if we had asserted it, our own behaviour would only have been intelligible in virtue of recognizing it as being associated with just the modes of presentation which form the basis of the assessability of *her* behaviour. Put simply, the point is just this: if I were to assert that sincerely, I would believe just what she believes.

Someone might think this is very like Davidson's 'paratactic' analysis of indirect speech.[13] And so indeed it is. It differs from that analysis, however, in not being a proposal about the 'logical form' of belief reports, and therefore not being committed on the question of whether the 'that' which precedes the expression of the content of the belief is a demonstrative. Davidson's resolutely externalist conception of the expression of content can be preserved without taking sides on questions about how belief reports are best modelled in a semantic theory.

This account is almost enough, but not quite. I am resolutely insisting that what I say someone believes, I say from my own perspective. That was necessary to make sense of the idea that we can evaluate someone's beliefs, and also of the thought that, in describing someone's beliefs, we locate her behaviour in the world. But that itself will inevitably mean that there is a limit to the sense in which I can say just what someone else believes. I cannot express in my own assertions points of view other than my own; so, in so far as what is distinctive of the modes of presentation which underlie someone else's behaviour depends upon her particular perspective, as it differs from mine or any other reporter's, no assertion of mine can itself be rooted in just those modes of presentation. All I can do in the way of saying just what she believes is to indicate which modes of presentation are involved: I cannot actually speak from within them. So if *she* says,

(4) I am rather clever,

the closest *I* can get is to say this:

(1) She believes that she is rather clever.

There is a sense in which this says just what she believes; and there is a sense in which it does not.

So much for the general account of what we are doing when we use words to say what someone believes. We begin with a conception of how words are associated with modes of presentation, in abstract outline at least. On the basis of this we have a

[13] Davidson, 'On Saying That', *Inquiries into Truth and Interpretation*.

conception of the modes of presentation which need to be
recognized to be associated with my words when I assert something
by anyone who is to count as understanding me. We can then make
sense of my assertion involving just the modes of presentation
which underlie the assessability of someone else's behaviour. In that
case, I can state, from my own perspective, the condition which the
world must meet for someone's behaviour not to be inept, and do it
in terms which reflect the basis of the assessability of her behaviour.
And that, according to the evaluative theory of content, just is to
say what she believes. The account also has the advantage that it
seems to capture what is right about Quine's thought about reports
of propositional attitude, without representing attitude reports as
simply play-acting.

There is a further question to be considered: is the same mode of
presentation always associated with the same word? The question
needs to be made a little more precise for it even to be interesting:
clearly, for example, different modes of presentation are associated
with different uses of *she*, or *that*. Let us assume that, in talking
about the same *word*, we are talking about a word with the same
reference, and whose reference is fixed semantically in the same
way: that is, in particular, we assume that it has already been
determined that the reference is fixed demonstratively, or anaphorically. Suppose, then, that we have a word with a certain reference,
whose reference is fixed either demonstratively, or anaphorically,
or whatever. Let us count a use of a word as a use of the same word
only if all of these features are the same. Can the same word in this
sense be associated with different modes of presentation?

What hangs on this is whether the opacity of belief contexts is
flexible, with different constraints upon substitution for the very
same words being imposed in different circumstances.[14] Some
might be happy to accept that there can be flexible opacity for the
case of demonstratives: there can be different 'demonstrative'
modes of presentation of the same thing. I shall try to make it
plausible in the next two sections that there can be flexible opacity
for almost any kind of expression. This will allow the intensionality
of belief reports to be as fine grained as anyone could want. The
downside—if it is a downside—is that very little explanation can
be provided by a semantic theory of attitude contexts. One can

[14] For this point, see M. Morris, 'The Varieties of Sense', *Philosophical Quarterly*, 38 (1988), 385–400.

always deal with the contexts in an abstract manner by assigning a sense to words, and insist on sameness of sense as the condition for intersubstitution within attitude contexts. But the sense of a word will vary from occasion to occasion, in a way which is hard to imagine being explicable in terms of a semantic theory.

A more austere, conservative position will insist on rigid opacity except where flexibility can be characterized in a way appropriate to a semantic theory. In general, the same mode of presentation will be associated with the same word. For the success of the evaluative theory of content in general it does not matter which option we choose. The evaluative theory allows us to see that words must be associated with modes of presentation if they are meaningful at all, and hence to see how we can use words to report beliefs, in a way which introduces an intensionality which is at least fine grained enough to allow for informative redescriptions of the very same facts. This much is true whether the opacity of belief contexts is flexible or rigid.

13.4. Opacity and Simple Singular Terms

I shall now turn to the task of explaining in some detail how we can make sense of flexible opacity, at least for the case of the kinds of expression which were covered by the definitions of 9.5. This section will deal with simple singular terms; the next section will be concerned with simple one-place predicates.

The definitions in 9.5 specified what is required to count as possessing a *level-one* concept of the relevant kinds. Talk of level-one concepts relies on a kind of minimal opacity. A singular-term position is subject to level-one opacity if co-referring simple singular terms can be intersubstituted there, *salva veritate*. There were two reasons for stating the definitions in terms of level-one opacity. This allowed me to present the definitions as (nearly) meeting the extensionality condition in a readily comprehensible way. And it allows me now to meet half-way those who are sceptical about finer-grained restrictions on the intersubstitution of singular terms, so that I can show how richer constraints can be generated.

But we should recall what I said at the time. Although level-one opacity makes it easily intelligible how the extensionality condition can be met, it is not strictly necessary for the purpose of meeting that condition. This will become clear, if it is not already, once I have explained how richer constraints on intersubstitution can be generated. But the fact that it is not strictly necessary for the extensionality condition that we suppose that some expressions really are subject to level-one opacity means that the evaluative theory itself does not need to take a stand on the way any particular expression is used.

To make sense of level-one opacity, we need to make sense of a peculiarly minimal mode of presentation. That is, in the terms of the evaluative theory: we need to make sense of a particularly broadly individuated *type* of condition of absolute safety. For singular terms, this might be expressed as the mode of presentation of the object in question *as the object it is*. That is, all that is required of the relevant mode of presentation is just that it be a mode of presentation of that object. To be a condition of absolute safety of the right *type*, all that is required is that it be a condition which will be absolutely safe for knowledge of that object. A singular term can have just this kind of mode of presentation—this sort of type of condition of absolute safety—associated with it, as it is used on some occasion, if it is enough to count as understanding the singular term, as it is then used, that one recognize which object is meant.

It is important to be clear here that there is no suggestion that one can have brute or bare knowledge of an object, a kind of access to an object which involves thinking of it in no way at all.[15] The point is rather that, for this kind of mode of presentation of an object, any way at all will do, provided that it is a way of thinking of the right object. What we need is an *unrestricted* kind of mode of presentation, not a bizarrely restricted one.

What we are concerned with here is the use of singular terms inside belief contexts. But it is a fundamental requirement on an account of words *inside* belief contexts that we do not appeal to features that they do not already have *outside* belief contexts. If we do not meet that requirement, we leave it a mystery how words really can be constrained in the appropriate way; the earlier sections of this chapter have been designed to put us in a position to meet that requirement. It follows that singular terms can only be

---

[15] Cf. M. Dummett, 'What is a Theory of Meaning?', in S. Guttenplan (ed.), *Mind and Language* (Oxford: Clarendon Press), 126.

subject to level-one opacity *inside* belief contexts, if they can be used with an appropriate sort of sense *outside* belief contexts. That means that the condition for understanding them outside belief contexts, in the particular kind of use in question, must ensure that they will be subject to level-one opacity within belief contexts. Let us call the general kind of sense which a singular term must have outside belief contexts, if it is to be subject to level-one opacity inside, L1 sense.

There are, in fact, two kinds of L1 sense. First is the obvious one: it should suffice for understanding a singular term, in a particular kind of use, just that one know which object is meant, without any more specific knowledge of the mode of presentation involved. Call this L1*A* sense. Secondly, a singular term may be used outside belief contexts in such a way that, although understanding of it *there* requires more specific knowledge of the mode of presentation involved, these more specific features cannot, or need not, be exploited in belief contexts. Call this L1*B* sense. Of course, for L1*B* sense one also needs to know which object is meant, in order to count as understanding the term; but even to know *that* one will need to know something more specific about the mode of presentation involved.

It is plausible to suggest that only a *simple* singular term (in the sense of 9.5) can have L1 sense. This is clear enough in the case of L1*A* sense. It never suffices for the understanding of a descriptive phrase that one should know which object is meant. And a term with L1*A* sense cannot be a semantically unstructured expression which is conceptually equivalent to some descriptive phrase. To say that it is conceptually equivalent to some descriptive phrase is just to say that in order to understand it one must understand it as expressing the concept which the descriptive phrase expresses. But the point is also plausible for L1*B* sense: it is hard to see why semantic complexity should be the kind of thing which can be ignored, left unexploited, in belief contexts.

It seems at least initially plausible to suppose that many ordinary proper names can be used with L1 sense. If they are, this will be in virtue of their being used with L1*A* sense: it will suffice for understanding them, in such uses, that one knows which objects are meant. This seems plausible, because it seems that we can often count as understanding someone's use of a name without knowing anything specific about how she thinks of the object in question.

If I then use a name with L1*A* sense within a belief context, that context will be subject only to level-one opacity, in that position at least. Such a use will license the intersubstitution of co-referring names, similarly used, within belief contexts. But it will not automatically legitimate the substitution of a description for a name, since descriptions cannot be used with L1 sense. So the use of a name in a belief context can count as genuinely opaque, even when co-referring names can be intersubstituted. And this use of proper names will not legitimate the replacement of a name so used by a co-referring name used with a *richer* sense (a kind of sense to be explained later in this section).

This is enough to explain many puzzles about substitutivity which concern names. The puzzles arise when we substitute a co-referring name—which shows that we are using both names with L1 sense—and then claim a contradiction—which requires that we are understanding the names as having a richer sense.

We should note that, although level-one opacity prevents *automatic* replacement of a name with L1 sense by a description, it does not rule out a description's being substitutable for the name in particular cases. But it also does not *require* that some description be so substitutable (a different one for each subject, perhaps), or that, in order to think about an object, a subject must have a concept expressible by means of a description which picks out that object uniquely. In order to be able to think about an object, one's behaviour must be associated with a type of absolutely safe condition which determines that object in particular as the object of one's thought; but it is not required that one know enough about the type of absolutely safe condition to be able to tell how it does this. (This is in line with the opposition to epistemological internalism expressed in 10.4.)

I want ultimately to be able to make room for flexible opacity. For the case of names, this will be a matter of allowing there to be two interpretations of these two descriptions of Kripke's Pierre:

(1) Pierre believes that London is pretty.
(2) Pierre does not believe that London is pretty.[16]

If there can be flexible opacity for names, there should be a reading of these two reports which makes them contradictory, and a reading which makes them consistent. If names can be used with L1

---

[16] Kripke, 'A Puzzle about Belief'.

sense, we can get at least a reading which makes them contradictory. If we read 'London' as having L1 sense here, then (1) will just
assert, and (2) will deny, that Pierre has a belief about London to
the effect that it is pretty.

A plausible case can also be made for saying that most indexical
expressions can be used with L1 sense. I shall divide uses of
indexicals into two classes: anaphoric and demonstrative. The
division should be taken as exhaustive, so that a use which is not
anaphoric is demonstrative. This is a slightly unnatural use of
'demonstrative' but it serves to make the points I need here.

I shall consider just the case of personal pronouns, since these
seem to exhibit the important features of the class of indexicals as a
whole. Two kinds of personal pronoun can be used *only*
demonstratively (in the sense of 'demonstrative' I have just
introduced): first-person and second-person pronouns. If I say 'I am
late', although it is not enough for *me* to use this sentence with
understanding that I know just which object is meant, I think that
that is enough for someone else to understand me. Similarly for uses
of *we*: mere recognition of the referents is not enough for the
referents themselves to understand such uses, but it is enough for
excluded observers. Again, if I say 'You are late', *you* need to know
more than just who is meant, but others do not.

But it is true, of course, that, in order to understand such
expressions, someone must understand how pronouns work, and
hence must be able to recognize them as involving rather special
sorts of modes of presentation. This is needed, in the case of these
expressions, in order just to know which object (person) is meant.
That means that if *I, we, and you* are to have L1 sense, they must
have it in virtue of having L1*B* sense. What is required, then, is that
the specific features of the modes of presentation involved should
be generally unexploitable within belief contexts. And that is surely
plausible. The features in question are perspectival, and perspective
is precisely something which is not shared by both subject and
reporter, except in the special case where subject and reporter are
the same.

There is in fact another way in which something of the specific
features of the relevant modes of presentation can be exploited, but
this will require some quite strong conversational presumptions. I
shall return to this later, and ignore it for now. Otherwise, where
subject and reporter are different, it seems that even demonstrative

personal pronouns can have L1 sense. That is quite natural anyway. Consider this:

(3)   She thinks that I am slim.

This is naturally read as being true equally in virtue of the subject's having read an unreliable report about me, or in virtue of the subject's having seen me in a bad light. No special mode of presentation—more specific than just a mode of presentation of me—is attributed to the subject by the use of 'I' here. This means that we should expect nothing to be lost, as far as the accuracy of the report of her attitude is concerned, if we allow such an indexical to be replaced, within a report of another's belief, by a co-referring name, provided that the name is used with L1 sense. Or again, nothing will have been lost if we allow a name used in a report with L1 sense to be replaced by a co-referring demonstrative indexical, provided the indexical too is used with L1 sense.

A pleasing consequence of this is that you can report the very same belief as I report in (3), by saying this to me:

(4)   She believes that you are slim.

Demonstrative uses of *he* and *she* follow exactly the same pattern. Anaphoric uses are more complicated. It is plausible to think that some anaphoric uses of indexicals can have L1 sense; but some certainly cannot. The first thing to note is that, to understand an anaphoric use of a word, one must understand both that it is anaphoric, and what it is anaphorically related to. An expression used anaphorically may be anaphorically related to some previously used expression, or—if we want to be very generous—to some other making evident of a circumstance or object. Let us call this, whatever it is, the *anaphoric source*. Clearly, then, what is needed to understand an anaphoric indexical will depend on the nature of the anaphoric source. If the anaphoric source is itself an expression used with L1 sense, then we should expect the anaphorically related indexical also to have L1 sense. This can carry over to anaphoric uses of indexicals within belief contexts too. Thus suppose we have this:

(5)   He is a nice man, but she believes that he is a crook.

Suppose the anaphoric source for the use of 'he' here is a use of the name 'Jones'; suppose too that the use of that name is a use with L1 sense. Then we ought to be able to move from (5) to this:

(6)   He is a nice man, but she believes that Jones is a crook,

provided that 'Jones' is used with L1 sense here too. This move looks odd as I have presented it, but this is just because of a natural stylistic presumption. The presumption can be cancelled, or outweighed, if we imagine that (5) is preceded by this short narrative:

(7) Jones is unfailingly kind to everyone, from shopkeepers to children; his friends rely on him; his only fault is a studied shabbiness of dress: he always wears a sinister-looking brown hat.

If (7) precedes (5), the switch to (6) will seem to be the result just of a familiar desire for stylistic variation. Nothing about the content of the subject's belief is lost in the move.

In general, then, whether an anaphoric indexical has L1 sense will depend upon whether it has an anaphoric source with L1 sense. But there is an apparent exception to this, in English at least. This is the case of anaphoric uses of indexicals within belief contexts whose anaphoric source is provided by the predication of belief itself. These are cases where the indexical is anaphorically connected to the identification of the subject of belief as the subject of belief, or the time of the belief, or to the location of the subject at the time of her belief. In these cases, we refuse to accept that the indexical may be used with L1 sense.

For the case of personal pronouns, an indexical in a belief context which has this kind of anaphoric source will always be understood as being associated with a first-person mode of presentation, or else will be supposed to be being used transparently—that is, as not genuinely within the belief context at all. A transparent reading will generally seem odd. (In fact, transparent readings are almost always unnatural anyway.) That is why there is only one natural reading of *this*, for example:

(8) She believes that she is rather clever,

where the second 'she' is anaphorically connected to the first.

It is not enough to count as understanding the second use of 'she' in (8) that one recognize who is meant, or even that one take its anaphoric source to be the first use of 'she'. One can only count as understanding that second use of 'she' if one recognizes that no other co-referring singular term can be substituted for it automatically, without losing something of the content of the belief reported.

This would be strange, and hard to understand, if this was a phenomenon which occurred only within belief contexts. It would seem that more has somehow got into the sense of a word as it is used in belief contexts than it can possess outside belief contexts. Fortunately, however, this kind of thing does not just occur within belief contexts. Consider this:

(9) Ethel felt her foot,

where 'her' is linked anaphorically with 'Ethel'. Now compare (9) with this:

(10) Ethel felt Ethel's foot.

I take it that, if (9) is true, then so is (10). But one would not count as understanding (9) if one took it to say no more than (10). To think that (9) says no more than (10) would be to think that it was merely incidental to the character of the action that the foot felt was the agent's.

It might be thought that there is some covert intentionality in (9) which is the cause of this; but I do not think this is right. We might compare (9) with this:

(11) The bridge collapsed under its own weight.

Something would be lost if we replaced (11) with this:

(12) The bridge collapsed under the (that same) bridge's weight.

(11) characterizes the collapse as being essentially, as one might say, a self-collapse; that is lost in (12).

There is a natural way of dealing with all of these cases, using the materials we already have to hand. The anaphoric source of the relevant indexicals is not just the pronoun, the name, or the noun phrase. It is the pronoun, the name, or the noun phrase *in its context*. It was the weight of the bridge, the bridge as the collapser, which caused the bridge's collapse. It was Ethel's foot, as the foot of the agent, which was felt. And it is she, as the believer of the belief, who is believed to be rather clever. If we think of the anaphoric source of these indexicals under a broader construal than we were perhaps initially inclined to, we can preserve the original suggestion: an anaphoric indexical has L1 sense if its source is a term with L1 sense, whether it occurs inside or outside belief contexts.

The suggestion is supported by consideration of the other indexicals whose particular mode of presentation is associated with the perspective of the belief itself. Consider this, for example:

(13) She thought that it was then too late,

where 'then' refers to the time of the belief. It seems to me that 'then' cannot be understood here, unless one recognizes the time it refers to precisely *as* the time of the belief.

This does not explain all that needs to be explained, of course. We need to understand why the anaphoric source of the second 'she' in (8) is *automatically* taken to be the first 'she' *in its context*, to be understood only by thinking of her *as* the believer of that belief—if that is indeed what happens. In the case of the bridge in (11), this seems to need explicit direction (made with the use of 'own'). But there might be various explanations of this difference. The point remains that, if we take a broad conception of the anaphoric source ot the relevant indexicals, there is no need to suppose that any magic is worked by belief contexts. The sense of an anaphoric indexical depends upon its anaphoric source. The anaphoric source of the second 'she' in (8) is not a singular term used with L1 sense, so we should not expect it to have L1 sense itself.

This leads directly on to consideration of simple singular terms which have a richer sense than can be accommodated by level-one opacity. Let us begin with anaphoric indexicals. Consider this:

(14) Ralph believes of the man in the brown hat that he is a spy.[17]

'He' is to be read as being used anaphorically. The anaphoric source is the description. A description cannot have L1 sense, so 'he' cannot have L1 sense either. This leaves us with just two readings of (14). The first takes 'he' as occurring transparently— not genuinely within the belief context. This is pretty unnatural. The second takes (14) to be reporting the very same belief which we might also report like this:

(15) Ralph believes that the man in the brown hat is a spy.

And that is surely the natural reading of (14) anyway. The elaborate 'believes of' locution does not succeed in ensuring that 'he' is read transparently.

But this does not mean that the phrase 'the man in the brown hat' expresses Ralph's concept of the man. The phrase could serve just to *identify*, for those of us who have read Quine's story, the

---

[17] This example records the debt which everyone discussing propositional attitudes owes to W. V. Quine, 'Quantifiers and Propositional Attitudes'.

particular kind of epistemological connection with the man which is in play here. This is a common use of descriptive phrases within belief contexts. Recall this:

(1) Pierre believes that London is pretty.

We might try to explain Pierre's otherwise surprising belief by saying this:

(16) Pierre believes that the city he heard of in his youth is pretty.

This is not naturally read as expressing Pierre's concept of London: it simply serves to identify the epistemological link between Pierre and the city which is at work.

We have now identified three kinds of opacity to which an anaphoric indexical can be subject. First, it can be subject to level-one opacity, if its anaphoric source is a term with L1 sense. Secondly, its anaphoric source may be a description. In that case there are two possibilities. The description may serve to express the subject's concept: it will then only be replaceable without loss by a conceptually equivalent description. Or else the description may serve just to identify the mode of presentation involved; and then it will be replaceable without loss by any description which identifies the same mode of presentation.

These points will be helpful for the consideration of proper names. Names seem to function anaphorically. What is distinctive about *proper* names, as opposed to indexicals, is just that they can preserve anaphora in the long term, being capable of sustaining connections through the course of a whole narrative, or with care, and a bit of luck, across large expanses of history. If proper names function anaphorically, they will have L1 sense only because in the course of their history they have come to be recognized as being associated with modes of presentation so various that there is almost nothing in the way of a common descriptive core, or distinctive set of associations, which has to be grasped by anyone who is to count as understanding them. It can then be true that there is no specific mode of presentation which is distinctively associated with a name.

Nevertheless, there are some uses of names in English which are naturally understood as connected with specific anaphoric sources. The famous pair, 'Hesperus' and 'Phosphorus', provide an obvious example. Consider the following two sentences, uttered in sequence:

(17)(i) Phosphorus appeared in the morning; Hesperus appeared in the evening.

(ii) One day it occurred to someone that Phosphorus and Hesperus might be the same thing.

No one is going to suggest that there is an opaque context in (17)(i). 'Hesperus' and 'Phosphorus' can be swapped there, or we can just use 'Phosphorus' in both name positions, without affecting the truth value of (17)(i). Nevertheless, we cannot do that without affecting the *sense* of the sentence. I think it is clear that, in order to understand (17)(i), we need to recognize each of these names as associated with a different, and quite specific, anaphoric source. That is, we need to recognize that each is associated with a different, and quite specific mode of presentation. The very choice of different names is properly understood as linking each name with a particular anaphoric source.

We seem to have here a use outside belief contexts of names with a sense richer than L1 sense. That same use is exploited inside the belief context in (17)(ii). Hearing (17)(ii) after (17)(i), we must link the use of 'Hesperus' there with its use in (17)(i), and the use of 'Phosphorus' there with *its* use in (17)(i). But if that is right, intersubstitution will make a difference to truth value in (17)(ii). If we had followed (17)(i) with *this*,

(17)(iii) One day it occurred to someone that Phosphorus and Phosphorus might be the same thing,

we would have attributed to the person in question an unintelligible realization. The proper anaphoric source for this use of 'Phosphorus' has been established or revealed in (17)(i): we have no room here for making sense of a difference in the modes of presentation associated with the two uses of the name.

Some people will think that this can only be made sense of if we suppose that the names are being used as disguised descriptions. But this is not at all obvious. (17)(i) and (17)(ii) might comprise all I know about the history of this astronomical discovery; that is still enough to mean that mere knowledge of which object is meant is not enough to understand those words as I use them in (17)(i). And if this minimal background is enough to give the names different senses in (17)(i), then so will it be in (17)(ii).

Perhaps I know a *little* more than this. Perhaps I know that Phosphorus is the planet which appears in a certain place in the morning, and that Hesperus is the planet which appears in a certain place in the evening. (This, apart from the identity, is just about all I do know, in fact.) So I can replace each of the uses of the names with the relevant descriptions. This hardly conforms to the requirements of a standard descriptional theory. These descriptions are certainly not uniquely identifying, unless we read them as incorporating some demonstrative; so no Russellian analysis is appropriate. And the descriptions need not express the concepts of the person who made the discovery: the ancients, I think, thought that Phosphorus/Hesperus was a star, not a planet. Rather, the descriptions serve to identify, in a way that is convenient to us, the relevant modes of presentation. There is thus no reason to think that the names are conceptually equivalent to any uniquely identifying Russellian description, in order to think that the sentences in (17) work as I have suggested.

Perhaps it will be said that at least the *subject* whose thought makes (17)(ii) true must have had a pair of descriptive concepts of the standard sort, if there is to be the block on substitution which I have claimed. Not so: he (I expect it was a he) might have known no more than is expressed in (17)(i). (Perhaps his ignorance liberated him from the preconceptions of his age.) Even if he knew more, there is no reason to think that this could be captured by a description appropriate for Russellian analysis. And even if it could be, it is quite irrelevant in any case. For it is not required for an understanding of (17)(ii), with the names being read as having rich sense in virtue of their anaphoric connections, that one should have any idea of the relevant subject's descriptive concepts, if he had any.

I have tried to show how different proper names for the same object can have different rich senses, by locating them explicitly in different conversational contexts. But once the point is made, it should be clear that explicit location in a context which indicates the anaphoric source of two names is unnecessary. Thus, suppose we are confronted with these two descriptions of someone:

(18) Myrna believes that Plum is something to do with the stage.
(19) Myrna does not believe that P. G. Wodehouse is anything to do with the stage.

The mere fact that there are two names here intuitively makes these two reports unproblematically consistent, even though Plum is in fact P. G. Wodehouse. This is naturally explicable on the account I have offered. The mere fact that there are two names (even if one is in a sense a part of the other) makes it possible and readily intelligible that there are distinct anaphoric sources with which they are connected. Appeal to each of those anaphoric sources can be expected to reveal the epistemological link between Myrna and the writer which supports each of the two reports. We do not need to know anything very precise at all about these presumed distinct anaphoric sources in order to understand that (18) and (19) are consistent.

Things are all fairly obvious, even without any explicit location of belief reports in a conversational context, or in a history of use of names, when we have distinct names to appeal to. But if we do introduce the background explicitly, it should be easy enough to see how different rich senses can be given to the *same* name. Consider this pair of sentences, to be understood as a sequence:

(20)(i) Phosphorus appeared in the morning; Phosphorus appeared in the evening.

(ii) One day it occurred to someone that Phosphorus and Phosphorus might be the same thing.

Whether or not 'Phosphorus' is used in different senses in (20)(i), it certainly is in (20)(ii), on the most natural reading. The two uses in (20)(ii) are connected anaphorically with the different uses in (20)(i). We make this explicit by careful inflection, as we often do for tricky cases of anaphora. And in case anyone should think that there is something special to belief contexts about these new rich senses, I can go on to say:

(20)(iii) And in fact Phosphorus is the same thing as Phosphorus.

No one, I think, can properly understand (20)(iii), as it is meant, without recognizing that 'Phosphorus' is used here with different rich senses.

This puts us in a position to pass the original test of flexible opacity. I wanted a sense in which the following two sentences might be consistent, in addition to a sense in which they might be taken to be inconsistent:

(1) Pierre believes that London is pretty.

(2) Pierre does not believe that London is pretty.

It should be easy enough. We simply need to preface them with something like this:

(21) London is the city whose beauty was described to Pierre in
      his youth; London is the city in a squalid quarter of which
      Pierre now lives.

If I follow that with (1) and (2), carefully inflecting my voice to
indicate the anaphoric connections, it ought to be easy enough to
understand them as consistent. And, in case anyone should think
that there is something peculiar to belief contexts about the rich
senses of 'London' which need to be appealed to here, I can also say
(to Pierre himself, for example):

(22) But London is London.

And clearly (22) cannot be understood as it is meant, just in virtue
of knowing which object is referred to.

When we see how little is needed to make (1) and (2) consistent,
it should be clear that we can individuate modes of presentation
almost indefinitely finely, and use the same name with richer and
richer sense.

We have a reading on which (1) and (2) are consistent, to
contrast with the reading provided by level-one opacity, on which
they are inconsistent. But there is obviously also a reading on which
they are inconsistent which does not rest on level-one opacity.
Imagine (1) and (2) prefaced just by this:

(21)(a) London is the city whose beauty was described to Pierre
         in his youth.

If that provides the sole linguistic background for (1) and (2), we
will take 'London' to be linked anaphorically with the same source
in both (1) and (2). And then the two reports will be inconsistent.

We have produced richer senses than L1 sense for anaphoric
indexicals, and for proper names. We can do the same for
demonstratively used indexicals too, though this can be done only
in special cases. There are two kinds of case. Consider first this
report:

(23) She believes that *he* is a spy.

I can make it clear from the way I say this that no more illuminating
expression of her concept of the person can be given than I provide
with 'he'. If I do, the demonstrative is used within the belief context
with something richer than L1 sense—by default as it were. I use
the demonstrative myself simply in order to indicate that *she* would
use a demonstrative to express her own thought. But I do not speak
from her perspective; this is not a piece of pretend quotation. I

simply say as little as I can about the person in order not to misrepresent the directness of her confrontation with him.

This is a slightly unnatural procedure, and needs quite strong conversational presumptions. I would normally just say something like this:

(24) She believes that the person she is staring at is a spy.

This will not seem to misrepresent her thoughts if we understand it properly. The phrase 'the person she is staring at' is not to be understood as expressing her concept of the man: it simply identifies the kind of epistemological link between her and the man which is in play.

The other cases in which demonstratives can have rich sense are those where the subject and the reporter of the belief are the same. Suppose I say:

(25) I believe that I am quite safe.

It will not in general be possible to replace the second 'I' with some co-referring simple singular term, while preserving truth. I will also have to *know* that the terms are co-referring. The same goes for 'you' in this:

(26) I believe that you are in danger.

Indeed, someone with an identical twin in a hall of mirrors might easily be referring to the same person with both 'I' and 'you' in (25) and (26).

This kind of rich sense for demonstrative indexicals within belief contexts is readily intelligible in terms of their use outside belief contexts. Demonstrative indexicals have L1 sense only in virtue of having L1B sense. That is, one can only recognize which object is meant by understanding that the object is thought of in a fairly specific sort of way, but the specific features of the way of thinking are not generally exploitable within belief contexts. The reason they are not exploitable is that they are perspectival features, and the perspectives of the subject of a belief and of its reporter are generally different. Inevitably, though, where the perspective of the subject is the perspective of the reporter, these specific features will matter.

So much, then, for our account of the constraints on substitution within belief contexts to which simple singular terms may be subject.

13.5. Opacity and Simple Predicates

The account of the constraints on the substitution of simple predicates (more precisely, simple one-place predicates) within belief contexts follows the pattern of the account which has just been provided for simple singular terms. I shall explain what would be involved in level-one opacity for simple predicates, and then try to motivate a similar ascent into richer and richer layers of sense. Because the account is so similar to that for simple singular terms, I shall confine myself to considering just one example of a simple predicate.

A belief context imposes level-one opacity with respect to a predicate position just in case it is possible to intersubstitute co-extensive simple predicates at that position. That can only be possible if simple predicates can be used outside belief contexts with a peculiarly minimal kind of sense, associated with a peculiarly minimal kind of mode of presentation, or a particularly broadly individuated sort of type of condition of absolute safety.

What we need is an extension of the notion of L1 sense. We could, once again, distinguish between L1*A* sense and L1*B* sense: a predicate including a tensed verb will have L1 sense only in virtue of having L1*B* sense. But I shall ignore this distinction here, effectively treating all verbs as tenseless. What we need for L1 sense for predicates is just that it should suffice for understanding a predicate that one know which objects the predicate is true of. This would require a predicate with L1 sense to be associated with a peculiar kind of mode of presentation of the property correspond-ing to the predicate, which one might express as a mode of presentation of the property as the property which is possessed by the objects it is actually possessed by.

This might seem to be an absurdly thin conception—too thin to count as a conception of a *property* at all. It should be remembered, however, that it is not being claimed that mere co-extensiveness is sufficient for property identity. The phrase 'the property which is possessed by the objects it is actually possessed by' does not provide an *analysis* of the notion of a property of any kind: the notion of property is presupposed. According to the version of conceptualism developed in Part I, one only has a property at all when one can make sense of there being something which it would be to have knowledge of it. As this idea was itself developed in the evaluative theory of content, we can say that there can only be a property whose instances are just among *those* objects if there is a condition of absolute safety in virtue of which one could correctly classify each object, and which one would only have been in because it is safe for that application. That imposes some quite severe restrictions on what can count as a property.

Consider a predicate 'x is F'. We have introduced the idea of a kind of epistemological condition, in virtue of which someone might classify—with absolute safety—all the objects which are actually F. But the notion of absolute safety itself has modal consequences. The kind of epistemological condition just mentioned would enable someone to classify correctly the objects which are actually F in *any* world in which they are F.

The conceptualist conception of a property is this: the property corresponding to any predicate is just the property of being classifiable absolutely safely in virtue of the kind of epistemological condition associated with that predicate. What is required for a predicate to have L1 sense is *this*: it must be possible to *identify* the kind of epistemological condition associated with the predicate, on the use in question, by means just of the actual world extension for which it is absolutely safe. But once the identification has been made, the kind of epistemological condition we have picked out will determine what the predicate applies to in any world.

I take it that it is never possible to identify the relevant epistemological condition in this way if the predicate is complex. To see what is involved in thinking that a *simple* predicate can be used with L1 sense, I shall focus on a particular example, the kind of example which is at the heart of a number of philosophical disputes. Let us suppose that 'x is red' is a simple predicate whose syntax is describable in terms of the categories of standard first-order predicate calculus. To get an idea of what might be involved in the claim that this predicate can be used with L1 sense, let us begin by imagining a rather unusual person, whom I shall call Finger. Finger has extremely sensitive fingers. She can tell by touch whether an object is one of those we call red. She can do the same for objects of different colours too. She is uncertain of how to classify objects just when we are uncertain whether to count them as precisely this colour or that. This is an ability which she has learnt in just the kind of way in which we have learnt to make colour judgements. That is, her judgements certainly count as judgements of knowledge of *something*. And not just any old something: she is reliable in the discernment of some property which at least has the same actual instances as redness.

Does Finger have the concept "red" in virtue of this ability? If she calls the things she classifies appropriately 'red'—that is, using a word which is indistinguishable in superficial appearance from ours—will her word 'red' mean *red*? If she has the concept "red", in any sense of 'concept', if her word 'red' means the same as ours, in any serious sense of 'means the same', then it is plausible to think that the predicate '*x* is red' can be used with L1 sense. For if we are prepared to count a mode of presentation as different from ours as Finger's is, as a mode of presentation of the right kind to be associated with that word, then it is hard to see any reason to cavil at any other different mode of presentation.

There are two difficulties in the way of this. The first is that the word *red* is so persistently associated for us with a visual mode of presentation, that it will be hard not to see that persistent background as, in effect, the anaphoric source for all current uses of *red*. In that case, someone will only normally be counted as understanding a use of *red*, as we now use it, if she associates it with that background of persistent association. That will mean that *red* will only be capable of being used inside belief contexts to express a concept with links to the visual in particular.

This is something that could change. If there were a lot of people like Finger, who used words superficially indistinguishable from our colour words, no doubt it would soon become unclear that a specifically visual mode of presentation is associated with the word. The word might then have changed its sense, but perhaps not its reference.

But that presumes that the second difficulty can be met. This is that it seems that redness is actually a specifically visual *property*.[18] As we normally use the word *red*, a visual mode of access is always ultimately authoritative about whether something is red. We might build an automatic redness detector, which did not work in anything much like the way that our eyes work; but its deliverances

[18] For this kind of view, though not associated with conceptualism, see G. McCulloch, 'Subjectivity and Colour Vision', *Aristotelian Society Supplementary Volume*, 61 (1987), 265–81.

are to be accepted, if they are, only in virtue of having been ratified by judgements made on the basis of sight.

There is nothing particularly surprising about the idea of a specifically visual property, from the point of view of the conceptualism developed in Part I. On that view, the nature of *every* kind of property is determined by what it would be to have knowledge of it—in effect, by what kinds of perspective count as authoritative about its presence. Colour properties—and indeed the so-called secondary qualities in general—are remarkable only in that a very specific kind of perspective counts as authoritative about them.

If redness is indeed a specifically visual property in this sense, the predicate '*x* is red' can only have L1 sense if there could be no one like Finger, and if no *other* kind of condition could count as being absolutely safe for the singling out of the red things in particular (apart from the kind of visual condition with which we are familiar). That is, '*x* is red' can only be used with L1 sense—if redness is a visual property—if there is no predicate co-extensive with it which does not itself rely for its authoritative application on just the kind of visual awareness which makes one authoritative about redness.

I suspect that in fact this condition might be met. It seems to me unlikely that any predicate constructible on the basis of knowledge of the physical facts in virtue of which red things are red will be co-extensive with '*x* is red' itself—whether we appeal to wavelength, intensity, shading, or whatever. We will expect such a scientific predicate not to be vague: it may admit of degrees, but I think it should not be vague. Where use of the word *red* might lead one to say (truly) of a particular object that it is simply indeterminate whether it is red, we will expect our colour-science predicate to apply to a certain particular degree, which is not the same thing.

If this is right, then we would expect that '*x* is red' can indeed be used with L1 sense, both outside belief contexts and inside. If, then, there are dialect colour words which match the extensions of the standard English ones, we ought to be able to make sense of intersubstituting them with their standard English counterparts inside belief contexts. As with simple singular terms used with L1 sense, this does not prevent belief contexts being genuinely opaque with respect to predicate positions which are subject to just level-one opacity. For we cannot intersubstitute *complex* co-extensive predicates there: it does not permit one to replace 'x is red' with 'x is red and, in the case of right-angled triangles, the square of the hypotenuse is equal to the sum of the squares of the other two sides', for example.

Suppose, then, that 'x is red' can indeed be used with L1 sense. Suppose that there is a dialect colour predicate which is co-extensive with it. Let us invent one: 'x is rudge'. It will then be possible to intersubstitute 'red' and 'rudge' within belief contexts, provided both words are used with L1 sense. But we can easily make sense of a richer sense for both words, if we are reasonably liberal in what we require of someone for her to count as understanding colour words. (Allowing blind people to count as understanding colour words—presumably in deference to those who can see—will be liberality enough.)

All we need is that it should be possible for two reports like these to be true of someone who understands both words:

(1) Elvira believes that my mother's car is red.
(2) Elvira does not believe that my mother's car is rudge.

These two reports can be unproblematically consistent, if 'red' and 'rudge' are each linked with different patterns of use, or different histories of use. It will be natural, of course, to explain the consistency of these two reports by means of two further descriptions of Elvira's state of mind, like these:

(3) Elvira believes that my mother's car is the colour called 'red'.
(4) Elvira does not believe that my mother's car is the colour called 'rudge'.

But the fact that the difference in the relevant modes of presentation depends on more-or-less explicit *linguistic* knowledge is special to the kind of case we are considering: it is not essential to the idea of linking particular uses of words with particular linguistic contexts. The reason that the difference here depends on explicitly linguistic knowledge is just that the general difference in history between a standard word and a dialect variation is simply a difference in the kind of language spoken in different places.

If that is right, we ought to be able to imagine indefinitely rich senses for predicates, as well as for singular terms. The procedure is the same as for singular terms, although the kinds of situation we have to imagine are a little more out of the way. Consider, then, the case of a strange sceptic who believes that things periodically change colour without her noticing.[19] (This is a coherent suggestion, given only a minimal conception of the objectivity of redness.) Suppose, in particular, that she thinks that things have changed colour overnight. Although it is not necessary, we might add that, for the sake of convenience in conversation with other people, she continues to use what appears to be the same word to describe the same things. She thinks, however, that what we count as the same predicate is really ambiguous.

I can characterize this sceptic's state of mind with respect to some particular red thing coherently, if not fully illuminatingly, with a pair of sentences of a sort which is familiar from the discussion of singular terms:

(5)(i) This is red today; this was red yesterday;
(ii) The sceptic believes that this is red, but not red.

(5)(i) shows that I am endorsing common sense. In (5)(ii) the two uses of 'red' are linked back to the two uses in (5)(i). And to show that there is nothing special to belief contexts about this very rich sense, I can say (perhaps to the sceptic herself):

(5)(iii) But if this is red, it is red.

No one can understand (5)(iii) as it is meant, without recognizing that the two uses of 'red' are associated with different, very specific, modes of presentation.

If this is right, this kind of example suggests that we should be able to make sense of very flexible conditions of substitution for almost any kind of expression.

13.6. Opacity and the Evaluative Theory of Content

There are two concluding points to be made about the evaluative theory and opacity, in the light of the treatment of simple singular terms and predicates which I have suggested.

First, we can see now how we might define concept-possession without explicitly relying on the idea of level-one opacity. Here is the original definition from 9.5:

(S) A subject *s* has the level-one concept "*a*" at a time *t* if and only if

---

[19] I used this example in 'The Varieties of Sense'.

s is liable at *t* to make responses each of which would be an *r* such that, for some '*E*', *r* is intrinsically assessable with respect to the value T as: good if and only if *Ea*.

It should now be clear that we could have written *this* instead:

(S*) A subject *s* has the concept "*a*" at a time *t* if and only if

s is liable at *t* to make responses each of which would be an *r* such that, for some '*E*', *r* is, *in a way appropriate for that use of* '*a*', intrinsically assessable with respect to the value T as: good if and only if *Ea*.

This definition meets the extensionality requirement just as well as (S) does. But it would have been a little much to swallow in one gulp.

The second point that emerges from the discussion of the use of simple singular terms and predicates in belief contexts is quite how little help a semantic theory is likely to be in explaining opacity. If we are to account for simple expressions' having any kind of sense richer than L1 sense without appeal to something like a descriptional theory of names, it seems we need to appeal to something like the history of expressions, which is itself something like an appeal to anaphoric connections. But if we can do that at all, it seems we can set up local linguistic contexts almost at will, and use them to generate richer and richer senses of terms. But this does not appear to be the sort of thing that anything even in the general spirit of a semantic theory could explain.

We can put this formally as an argument, as follows:

(1) There are co-referring names which are not automatically intersubstitutable within belief contexts.
(2) That is only intelligible if either (*a*) a descriptional theory of names is true, or (*b*) names get their senses in virtue of anaphoric connections.
(3) No descriptional theory of names is true.
(4) If names get their senses in virtue of anaphoric connections, the opacity of belief contexts depends on factors which cannot be explained by a semantic theory.

so:

(5) The opacity of belief contexts depends on factors which cannot be explained by a semantic theory.

The advantage of setting this out as formally as this is that it shows clearly what has not been decisively established. In particular, I have not decisively established (2). But we should remember that certain alternative accounts of belief contexts (Quine's quotational account, for example) have been ruled out before we even begin on this argument. (2) certainly looks very plausible.

Consideration of what gets brought in with appeals to anaphoric connections—at least if they are of the right kind to explain 'Hesperus' and 'Phosphorus', and other similar examples—seems to make (4) irresistible. I take it that others have sufficiently dealt with (3).

It all seems to hang on (1). But denying (1) seems only to be capable of motivation by an antecedent commitment to the fundamental explanatoriness of semantic theories. And that motivation should already have become suspect, given the arguments of 13.2. I conclude that the argument is indeed good, and that we have, in belief contexts, a case of something which a semantic theory ought to be able to explain—if it is to be properly explanatory at all—which it cannot explain.

I considered in 9.3 a suggestion which would make this unsurprising, if content is indeed shot through with value. The suggestion was that it is in virtue of the temptation to try to construct non-evaluative rules for the evaluative that such things as the liar paradox seem genuinely problematic. If the suggestion was right, the same point might be felt to apply here. It is no surprise, the argument would go, that semantic theories cannot explain the function of words in every context; for they attempt to provide mechanical rules for the determination of a question of value.

I am not sure about this, just as I am not sure about the original suggestion. However that may be, though, it does seem that there is nothing in the kind of resources I have appealed to in order to explain the opacity of belief contexts which is out of tune with an evaluative theory.

On the other hand, it should be clear that there is much that needs to be explained. The suggestion that words are assessment-relevant similarities in behaviour at least makes it intelligible, given the rest of the evaluative theory of content, that words can *have* something like Fregean sense. But there is a huge gap, to be filled in by a decent philosophy of language, between *that* and the kind of detailed operation of anaphora which was exploited in the account of opacity.

This should reveal the extent to which what is offered here, in the way of a theory of content, is incomplete. In Part II, I set ten constraints upon any theory of content. All but two have been met, I think—at least in outline. The two which have not are the two I mentioned at the beginning of this chapter:

(C5) A theory of content must generate the right substitution conditions for belief contexts.

(C6) A theory of content must explain what it is for words to be meaningful in the way they are.

It is the lack of substantial detail in response to (C6) which makes the theory incomplete with respect to (C5).

Since I have found myself in this chapter working away from a traditionally analytical conception of language, it seems appropriate to refer here to another tradition:

Before I read Stendhal, I know what a rogue is. Thus I can understand what he means when he says that Rossi the revenue man is a rogue. But when Rossi the rogue begins to live, it is no longer he who is a rogue: it is a rogue who is the revenue man Rossi. I have access to Stendhal's outlook through the commonplace words he uses. But in his hands, these words are given a new twist. The cross references multiply. More and more arrows point in the direction of a thought I have never encountered before and perhaps never would have met without Stendhal. At the same time, the contexts in which Stendhal uses common words reveal even more majestically the new meaning with which he endows them.

What we need is a philosophy of language which can make sense of *that*. A whole new can of worms.

[20] M. Merleau-Ponty, *The Prose of the World*, trans. J. O'Neill (Evanston: Northwestern University Press, 1973), 12.

Bibliography

BACH, K., 'Actions are not Events', *Mind*, 89, (1980), 114–20.

BARWISE, J., and PERRY, J., *Situations and Attitudes* (Cambridge, Mass.: MIT Press, 1983).

BLACKBURN, S., *Spreading the Word* (Oxford: Clarendon Press, 1984).

BRINK, D., *Moral Realism and the Foundations of Ethics* (Cambridge: Cambridge University Press, 1989).

BURGE, T., 'Belief *De Re*', *Journal of Philosophy*, 74 (1977), 338–62.

BURNYEAT, M., 'Wittgenstein and Augustine *De Magistro*', *Aristotelian Society Supplementary Volume*, 61 (1987), 1–24.

CHURCHLAND, P., 'Eliminative Materialism and the Propositional Attitudes', *Journal of Philosophy*, 78 (1981), 67–90.

—— 'Folk Psychology and the Explanation of Human Behaviour', *Aristotelian Society Supplementary Volume*, 62 (1988), 209–21.

DAVIDSON, D., *Essays on Actions and Events* (Oxford: Clarendon Press, 1980).

—— *Inquiries into Truth and Interpretation* (Oxford: Clarendon Press, 1984).

DAWKINS, R., *The Selfish Gene* (2nd edn., Oxford: Oxford University Press, 1989).

DENNETT, D., *The Intentional Stance* (Cambridge, Mass.: MIT Press, 1987).

DESCARTES, R., *Philosophical Writings*, ii. *Meditations on First Philosophy*, trans. J. Cottingham, R. Stoothoff, and D. Murdoch (Cambridge: Cambridge University Press, 1985).

DUMMETT, M., 'What is a Theory of Meaning?', in S. Guttenplan (ed.), *Mind and Language* (Oxford: Clarendon Press, 1975), 97–138.

—— 'What is a Theory of Meaning? (II)', in G. Evans and J. McDowell (eds.), *Truth and Meaning* (Oxford, Clarendon Press, 1976), 67–137.

—— *Elements of Intuitionism* (Oxford, Clarendon Press, 1977).

EVANS, G., 'Pronouns, Quantifiers and Relative Clauses,' *Canadian Journal of Philosophy*, 7 (1977), 467–536.

—— *The Varieties of Reference*, ed. J. McDowell (Oxford: Clarendon Press, 1982).

FIELD, H., 'Tarski's Theory of Truth', *Journal of Philosophy* 69 (1972), 347–75.

FODOR, J., 'Methodological Solipsism Considered as a Research Strategy in Cognitive Psychology', *Behavioral and Brain Sciences*, 3 (1980), 63–110.

—— *Psychosemantics* (Cambridge, Mass.: MIT Press, 1987).

—— *A Theory of Content* (Cambridge, Mass.: MIT Press, 1990).

FORBES, G., *The Metaphysics of Modality* (Oxford: Clarendon Press, 1985).

FREGE, G., *Collected Papers on Mathematics, Logic, and Philosophy*, ed. B. McGuinness (Oxford: Blackwell, 1984).

GADAMER, H.-G., *Truth and Method*, trans. W. Glen-Doepel (London: Sheed and Ward, 1975).

GETTIER, E., 'Is Justified True Belief Knowledge?', *Analysis*, 23 (1963), 121–3.

HAACK, S., *Philosophy of Logics* (Cambridge: Cambridge University Press, 1978).

HARMAN, G., 'Inference to the Best Explanation', *Philosophical Review*, 74 (1965), 88–95.

HEAL, J., 'The Disinterested Search for Truth', *Proceedings of the Aristotelian Society*, 88 (1987–8), 97–108.

HUME, D., *A Treatise of Human Nature* (1739), ed. L. Selby-Bigge, 3rd edn., rev. P. Nidditch (Oxford: Clarendon Press, 1978).

—— *Enquiries concerning Human Understanding and the Principles of Morals* (1748, 1751), ed. L. Selby-Bigge, 3rd edn., rev. P. Nidditch (Oxford: Clarendon Press, 1975).

KANT, I., *Critique of Pure Reason*, trans. N. Kemp Smith (London: Macmillan, 1929).

KAPLAN, D., 'Words', *Aristotelian Society Supplementary Volume*, 64 (1990), 93–119.

KRIPKE, S., 'A Puzzle about Belief', in A. Margalit (ed.), *Meaning and Use* (Dordrecht: Reidel, 1979), 239–83.

—— *Wittgenstein on Rules and Private Language* (Oxford: Blackwell, 1982).

LEIBNIZ, G., 'Explanation of the New System of the Communication of Substances, in Reply to what is said about it in the "Journal" of 12 Sept. 1695', in Leibniz, *Philosophical Writings*, ed. G. H. R. Parkinson (London: Dent, 1973), 125–32.

LEWIS, D., *Counterfactuals* (Oxford: Blackwell, 1973).

LOCKE, J., *An Essay Concerning Human Understanding*, ed. P. Nidditch (Oxford: Clarendon Press, 1975).

LOVIBOND, S., *Realism and Imagination in Ethics* (Oxford: Blackwell, 1983).

McCULLOCH, G., 'Subjectivity and Colour Vision', *Aristotelian Society Supplementary Volume*, 61 (1987), 265–81.

—— *The Game of the Name* (Oxford: Clarendon Press, 1989).

McDOWELL, J., 'On the Sense and Reference of a Proper Name', *Mind*, 86 (1977), 159–85.

—— 'On "The Reality of the Past" ', in C. Hookway and P. Pettit (eds.), *Action and Interpretation* (Cambridge: Cambridge University Press, 1978), 127–44.

—— 'Criteria, Defeasibility, and Knowledge', *Proceedings of the British Academy*, 68 (1982), 455–79.

—— '*De Re* Senses', *Philosophical Quarterly*, 34 (1984), 283–94.

—— 'Functionalism and Anomalous Monism', in E. LePore and B.

McLaughlin (eds.), *Actions and Events: Perspectives on the Philosophy of Donald Davidson* (Oxford: Blackwell, 1985), 387–98.

McGinn, C., 'The Structure of Content', in A. Woodfield (ed.), *Thought and Object* (Oxford: Clarendon Press, 1982), 207–58.

—— *Mental Content* (Oxford: Blackwell, 1989).

Mackie, J., *Ethics: Inventing Right and Wrong* (Harmondsworth: Penguin, 1977).

—— *Hume's Moral Theory* (London: Routledge and Kegan Paul, 1980).

Merleau-Ponty, M., *The Prose of the World*, trans. J. O'Neill (Evanston: Northwestern University Press, 1973).

Morris, M., 'The Varieties of Sense', *Philosophical Quarterly*, 38 (1988), 385–400.

—— 'Why there are no Mental Representations', *Minds and Machines*, 1 (1991), 1–30.

Papineau, D., *Reality and Representation* (Oxford: Blackwell, 1988).

Peacocke, C., *Sense and Content: Experience, Thought, and their Relations* (Oxford: Clarendon Press, 1983).

—— *Thoughts: An Essay on Content* (Oxford: Blackwell, 1986).

Pears, D., *The False Prison*, vol. ii (Oxford: Clarendon Press, 1988).

Platts, M., *Ways of Meaning* (London: Routledge and Kegan Paul, 1979).

Putnam, H., 'Reflexive Reflections', *Erkenntnis*, 22 (1985), 143–53.

—— 'The Meaning of "Meaning"', in his *Mind, Language and Reality* (Cambridge: Cambridge University Press, 1975), 215–71.

Quine, W. V., 'Two Dogmas of Empiricism', in his *From a Logical Point of View* (New York: Harper and Row, 1953).

—— 'Quantifiers and Propositional Attitudes' (1956), in his *The Ways of Paradox and Other Essays* (Cambridge, Mass.: Harvard University Press, 1966; 2nd edn. 1976).

—— *Word and Object* (Cambridge, Mass.: MIT Press, 1960).

—— 'Epistemology Naturalized', in his *Ontological Relativity and Other Essays* (New York: Columbia University Press, 1969), 69–90.

—— 'Goodman's *Ways of Worldmaking*' (1978), in his *Theories and Things* (Cambridge, Mass.: Harvard University Press, 1981), 96–9.

Russell, B., 'Introduction' to L. Wittgenstein, *Tractatus logico-philosophicus*, trans. D. Pears and B. McGuinness (London: Routledge and Kegan Paul, 1961), pp. ix–xxii.

Ryle, G., *The Concept of Mind* (London: Hutchinson, 1949).

Salmon, N., *Frege's Puzzle* (Cambridge, Mass.: MIT Press, 1986).

Schiffer, S., 'Ceteris Paribus Laws', *Mind*, 100 (1991), 1–17.

Segal, G., 'The Return of the Individual', *Mind*, 98 (1989), 39–57.

Stich, S., *From Folk Psychology to Cognitive Science* (Cambridge, Mass.: MIT Press, 1983).

Strawson, G., *Freedom and Belief* (Oxford: Clarendon Press, 1986).

Strawson, P. F., *Individuals* (London: Methuen, 1959).

—— 'Freedom and Resentment', *Proceedings of the British Academy*, 48 (1962), 1–25.

TARSKI, A., 'The Semantic Conception of Truth', *Philosophical and Phenomenological Research*, 4 (1944), 341–75.

TAYLOR, C., *The Explanation of Behaviour* (London: Routledge and Kegan Paul, 1964).

VAN INWAGEN, P., 'The Incompatibility of Free Will and Determinism', *Philosophical Studies*, 27 (1975), 185–99.

WIGGINS, D., *Sameness and Substance* (Oxford: Blackwell, 1980).

—— 'On Singling out an Object Determinately', in P. Pettit and J. McDowell (eds.), *Subject, Thought, and Context* (Oxford: Clarendon Press, 1986), 169–80.

WITTGENSTEIN, L., *Tractatus logico-philosophicus* (1922), trans. D. Pears and B. McGuinness (London: Routledge and Kegan Paul, 1961).

—— *Culture and Value*, trans. P. Winch (Oxford: Blackwell, 1980).

—— — *Philosophical Investigations*, trans. G. E. M. Anscombe (2nd edn., Oxford: Blackwell, 1958).

—— *On Certainty*, trans. D. Paul and G. E. M. Anscombe (Oxford: Blackwell, 1969).

WRIGHT, C., 'Strict Finitism', *Synthèse*, 51 (1982).

Index